"Dear Susan, my husband is a busy physician who never has time to read anything but medical journals. Every night he brings home a briefcase full of paperwork. Typically when I read aloud to him from an interesting book, he listens politely for two minutes and then goes back to his work. I began reading aloud to him about your dream house. After a page or two, I asked, "Isn't this interesting?" He said, "Yes, please keep reading." And he listened while I read twenty more pages. This is a first in our relationship!"

> — *Elyse Furlong, Health Educator*

"These ten skills have taken my team way past the gimmicks of "say this and do that" to being really interested in customers and supportive of each other. The shift has been amazing—from cutthroat and separate to cooperative and powerful. Thank you."

> — *Walt Smith, Sales Manager*

"This book puts many, until now, separate pieces together again—training, management, leadership, parenting and personal growth. Making sense of them all."

> — *Fran Ford, Vice President, Wall Street Bank*

"I feel like I'm sitting right there talking to Susan. Her stories make me laugh, cry and dream. I've never been so deeply touched by a book."

> — *Pam Watkins, College Student and Mother*

"Susan Collins has become a bedtime friend. This doesn't just feel like I'm reading a book—it feels like I know her. I look forward to spending time with her each night. She makes me feel her successes can also be mine."

> — *Marta Smith, Mary Kay Cosmetics Consultant*

"My God, I must have stopped dreaming when I started to work. This book woke me up. Now I am remembering the things I told myself I'd do. And I will."

> — *Michael Lubranecki, Twenty-Year Post Office Employee*

More praise from readers

"Susan Collins' ten success skills offer a user-friendly framework for living, no matter what your age. Her style is warm, inviting and evocative. As she tells her story, you realize it's your story and your children's story too."
— *The Reverends Hal and Sonya Milton, Unity Church, Knoxville*

"I wish all of our parents would read Susan Collins' book. It's in sync with what we are trying to do in the classroom, letting children be creative thinkers and explorers."
— *Stephanie Oshinsky, Preschool Director, Temple Judea, Miami*

"I have twenty-one years in the department and have taken the lieutenant test eight times and not scored high enough to be promoted. I decided read your book before attempting it again. I practiced your success sk and last month I took the exam and placed tenth out of 275 firem Before your book I felt this couldn't be done."
— *Vernon Oster, Fire Department, Miami, FL*

"Reading your book was as effortless as sitting on a couch and eati bag of potato chips. I just couldn't stop. I found myself sharing conc like success filing, with all my friends. They now are reading it. wonderful and important book."
— *Phyllis Marcus, Poet*

OUR CHILDREN ARE WATCHING

TEN SKILLS FOR LEADING THE NEXT GENERATION TO SUCCESS

SUSAN COLLINS

An essential handbook for parents, teachers, managers and those governing

BARRYTOWN, LTD.

Published by Barrytown, Ltd., Barrytown, New York, 12507.

Cover and text design by Risa K. Mina.

Library of Congress Cataloging-in-Publication Data
Collins, Susan.
   Our children are watching : ten skills for leading the next generation to success / Susan Collins.
      p. cm.
   Includes bibliographical references and index.
   ISBN 1-886449-03-1
   1. Success—Psychological aspects. 2. Leadership. I. Title.
BF637.S8C546   1995
158'.4—dc20   95-12103
                                         CIP

Manufactured in the United States of America.

Contents

Part Three: Leadership
Our success multiplies each time we lead someone else
to success

Foreword

This book goes to the very heart of leadership—the guiding and nurturing of each and every child on the planet. If a child is created, he or she needs to be led.

If we are parents, we must see ourselves as leaders of the highest calling, above corporate or career life, above civic responsibilities. Even if we are not parents, we are summoned to assist in leading each individual to the fullness of his or her potential, lest they become societal wards without hope or direction.

Through the generous outpouring of her soul, Susan Collins takes us deep into the realm of silent joys and sorrows, drawing us into humanness shared. The reader need simply savor the textures and tastes of her stories. The reading of these narratives will bring enlightenment. The study and application of these skills can result in powerful and lasting transformation.

Ms. Collins shares her wealth of experience, her drive to discover, her broad intellect and range of talents, and an unswerving faith in the power of humankind.

Settle back and enjoy, resting easy in the knowledge that your own internal "child" will be quite pleased and tickled that you took the time.

John A. Shearer
Chief Executive Officer
The Leadership Trust

Acknowledgments

The road to success is a zigzag, first pointing this way and then that. If we start with high intention, then magic and coincidence will guide us there despite our lack of knowledge about what lies ahead. The zigzagging path that led to *Our Children Are Watching* is a story worth telling. For thirty years I have been a speaker, talking across the country to large groups and small ones—executives and management teams, sales and production teams, teachers and parents, city and county employees, even the UN.

My strength is my stories. I can make a story so poignant that the room drops to absolute silence in a moment. My loyal seminar fans, tape-listeners, corporate clients, educators and innovators have begged me for years to write down my stories. But I never had time. Then when Hurricane Andrew rearranged our lives here in South Florida, postponing indefinitely the training projects I had scheduled, I decided to use the opportunity Mother Nature provided to tell my stories once again, this time in print.

But despite abounding confidence as a speaker, I was scared to death of writing. Ten years before I had submitted writing samples to become the next "Dear Abby" and the feedback I got was that I was a marvelous speaker, but I wasn't a writer. It was true of course, but I hated hearing it, and whenever my confidence would sag I would hear those fearful old words again, "But you aren't a writer." I had to make a choice—I could believe them, or I could use them to goad me on to become a writer.

It would be a challenging project and I would need a good coach. One day after aerobics, I laid my manuscript down on a bench in the locker room and a woman standing nearby asked about my book. Introducing herself to me, Bonnie Weisberg said she was a great networker and quickly scribbled down the name of a editor if I needed one. That editor has been my coach and way-shower ever since. Thank you Teresa Lee Baker for being the voice I could listen to until I learned to hear my own writing voice. With your help I am now as comfortable speaking in print as I am with my beloved microphone.

Many people served as guides along the way, reading chapters as I created them, hounds sniffing out the scent of what I wanted to say and leading me to it. They sat in my living room reading comfortably for hours, letting me look over their shoulders and ask questions whenever they hesitated. I gratefully used their feedback, even when it was uncomfortable, even when I couldn't figure out what to do with it for days.

My friend Charlie Stuart was my loyal early supporter, reading slight variations of the same beginning pages over and over. My lawyer-friends kept my thinking straight. Carolina Echarte reordered and reorganized, cutting and pasting pages, sensitive to the feelings her changes brought up in me. Bernie Kessler read and reread, challenging tiny phrases and asking lawyer-like questions I needed to find answers to.

My best friend Sharon Huff was my computer advisor and consultant, a phone call or a lunch away when I needed to know how to Select All or how to retrieve something I'd thrown in my computer Trash accidentally. She nurtured the love affair between me and my Mac. And my three Bernies held my hand whenever I needed a daddy or a brother, a grandfather or dear friend.

As always, my daughters lined up with my dream. Cathy called daily, knowing when she asked her usual question, "What are you doing today?" she'd get my usual answer, "Working on the book." Margaret knew she could always find me in the back room with my beloved Mac 5 a.m. to midnight six days a week.

Late one afternoon when my spirits were waning, my sister Fran called to tell me how five years earlier, when confused and discouraged with corporate America, she happened to notice my tape series on her shelf. Popping the first tape in her recorder, I was immediately there with her. My stories had gotten her through, and knowing that helped me get through too. Thanks for the phones calls and faxes and the thousands of incantations of "Book, book, book."

Harriet Beinfield, my dear friend and author of the best-selling book, *Between Heaven and Earth*, was a model and inspiration, turning my thinking upside down, then standing me back up straight again disoriented and dazzled but seeing my direction more clearly. I could hear Hari's voice chanting "richer words" in my head.

My duet-piano partner from twenty years ago, Jane Tamaccio, became my partner in polishing words and phrases much the same way we polished notes and phrases while preparing for concerts.

And somewhere along that long journey, deep inside I became a writer.

In a world that is changing as rapidly as this one, we need to think differently about leadership. Leading is not done by those few in high places, but by parents and teachers and managers and those governing—all working together to create the world that we want. We are now entrusted with the future of our planet. We must come together to create an effective team here on Earth.

Part One

INTRODUCTION

We are the leaders
whether we realize it or not

Actions speak louder than words

What messages are we sending?

Yes, our children are watching us at home and at work. We are the ones who are teaching them about success. We are the ones responsible for building their confidence and enthusiasm, their hope and tenacity. We can teach them to succeed in two ways—we can tell them how to do it or we can do it ourselves.

My grandmother always said, "Actions speak louder than words, my dear." And she was right. Researchers studying the components of communication—words, voice and body—concluded words are only 7 percent of our communication. What we do with our voice is 38 percent. What we do with our bodies, the energy we project is 55 percent.[1] So 38 plus 55, means 93 percent of our communication is not the words we use. We can tell someone we're thrilled, but if they hear our voice sounding flat, if they sense our bodies are rigid, our words will be contradicted. We may tell our children they can have what they want in life, but the way we live our lives may shout it's not true.

By being successful ourselves, we lead others to success—our children, our students, our employees and fellow citizens. The most precious contribution we can make here on Earth is to create the lives we want to be living, communicating in all ways, to everyone around us, that success is really possible.

Our children are learning to live their lives by watching the way we live ours—stopping where we stop, frightened by our fears, held back by our limits. Our children are learning to succeed by example—recording and replaying the messages we give them.

What messages have we been sending about success until now? Have we been able to complete our own dreams? Are we enjoying our homes and our jobs? Our families and friends? Are we living healthy, balanced lives? How has what we've been doing been affecting our children? How do they feel about the long work hours we're putting in? Or the struggle we have to go through to find time for them? Or the frustration we express over not getting enough done?

The voice of a storyteller

Who is this book for and what is it about?

Throughout history, storytellers have strung wisdom and information together so it could be passed from person to person. I am a storyteller. Through my stories I teach success and leadership skills in public seminars, schools and universities, major corporations, city and county governments. These stories are written to be read silently to yourself or out loud to others.

We are the ones who are leading the next generation to success—or failure. We are the parents and teachers, the managers and the ones working in government. This book is for us.

As our children grow up, the baton of their leadership is passed from one leader to another. Each one expects the preceding leader to have done their part of the job. Teachers expect parents to have taught life skills, confidence and discipline. Managers expect teachers to have taught academic skills, information and cooperation. Governments expect parents, teachers and managers to have produced successful citizens.

But what happens when the baton of leadership gets dropped along the way? What happens to the children who needed skillful leadership and never got it? How can they as adults pass on what they were never taught? How can they begin to learn the skills they will need?

We must develop the skills that will allow us to pass the baton of leadership smoothly from one team member to the other—from parent to teacher, from teacher to manager, from manager to those governing—the way experienced runners hand over a baton in a relay.

We can no longer afford to let success and leadership develop accidentally. *Our Children Are Watching* presents ten skills for leaders, whether they have been well led or not. Each chapter of this book presents a different success skill. Each skill builds on the skills that come before it. Each skill is illustrated by stories that tell how and when to use it.

The Pathfinder

In Richmond, Virginia where I grew up, there is a long boulevard with central grassy spaces punctuated by statues. Whenever my family drove down Monument Avenue we passed by Stonewall Jackson, Robert E. Lee and Jeb Stuart. I loved the stories my parents would tell me about long journeys on horseback, cold brutal winters, dwindling supplies, battles won and lost.

My favorite hero wasn't seated on horseback. He was Matthew Fontaine Maury, "the pathfinder of the seas," a man who spent his life tracing the winds and currents of our oceans. He was portrayed sitting astride the Earth, one long finger pointing to the seas. His Explanatory Instructions to Mariners *issued in 1848 allowed sailors to save ten to fifteen days on long journeys.*

As a young girl I used to sit on the grass in front of his coppery statue imagining we were talking. What sort of man would have had such a dream? How had he kept going when the way became difficult, when he was doubted and scoffed when no one agreed he should have taken on this task?

I never heard these answers from my hero. But knowing what he had done inspired me to trace, not the paths of the seas, but the paths of success, the ways of getting from wanting to having, from dreaming to experiencing, from being afraid to feeling confident. This book is about the long and miraculous journey from ideas to realities. How we create things. How we improve things. How we guide others to use what we discover. And this book is about how we lead others to dream dreams and create realities far surpassing even our wildest imaginings.

My own story

Navigating the rough waters of my life

How far have we come on the journey to our dreams? Have we run aground on fears and uncertainties? Have we become entangled in rents, mortgages and credit cards? Have we stopped dreaming about the experiences that really matter to us?

Like life, this book is emotional. I will lead by example, peering into the farthest corners and crevices of my memory to remind you of experiences long forgotten, places in your life where you decided to stop, feelings you vowed you'd never feel again. Why would you choose to join me on such a journey? Because along the way, you will recover the power you gave up, making it available for what you want to do now.

This book will assist you in reclaiming parts of yourself you may have lost—things you decided, or someone else decided, just weren't for you. Old unexperienced pain and sorrow will rise to the surface, bursting open like a bubble releasing the pure energy trapped there inside you. This book will assist you in reconnecting with your power so that you can make your own life the ultimate high adventure.

Personal power is generated by an inner emotional battery, charged by our positive and negative poles, the experiences we liked and the experiences we didn't. But over the years we have been taught not to talk about our negatives, to deny that they mattered. So then with only our positive-pole connected, with our negative pole left unattached, we have not had the power we needed to do what we wanted.

I've had many challenging experiences in my life, but those experiences have become the very reasons for my success. I had a wonderful life as a young child, walking beside the stroller on the way to the store, standing on a milk crate rolling crusts for lemon meringue pies, helping Mom make damson-plum preserves, black-eyed peas and homemade rolls. When I was young, my mother was the perfect mother, nurturing and supportive, protective and always there for me. In the evening my family took long walks to the playground or the Old Soldiers' Home, wandering together slowly, stopping to look at leaves or play hide-and-seek.

I loved learning. Curious about everything, I even knew the names of the weeds in my area. I had my own library with Dewey decimal numbers. I kept a scrapbook of famous paintings, gave concerts on the piano, played violin in an orchestra, collected seeds and unusual pods, shells and rocks, beehives and driftwood, old tools and cleverly made new ones. My two sisters and I lived a wonderful life.

But when we were old enough to say no to her, strong enough to say yes to what we wanted instead, my mother sank back into the pain she felt as a teenager during the Depression, when her father lost his millinery and she found her favorite brother dead in his room.

She began covering up her pain with a carefully hidden bottle of bourbon. I learned the sound of that certain cabinet door opening and closing, the look of blankness and fatigue that would be my mother shortly afterward. As time went on she left us more and more. Nobody knew what to do about her drinking, mostly because we never discussed it. That was the nature of the society we lived in, proper and polite but secretive and in denial.

As a teenager, my childhood disappeared. I had to take over for my mother. I still needed her mothering, but I realized she was gone—even though she still lived in the house with us. My younger sisters needed me to mother them. It took a long time to understand my loss. I wrote. I read. I thought. I knew I couldn't live like my mother did. But I couldn't live like my father did either. And I didn't fit in any better with my peers, giggling and dating, concerned about appearances and which party they'd go to this weekend, while I was worrying about what I would cook, whether I had to go shopping, and when we would visit my mom who was having electroshock therapy and couldn't even remember my name. When she finally came home, I had to go to the store to whisper in her ear the names of people she should know.

My dad was in terrible pain, but the way he dealt with pain was to be busy in business. A brilliant lawyer and accountant, a successful businessman and politician, he was a man of action but few words. He enjoyed the challenge of buying failing businesses and reorganizing them until they were profitable. I loved to go to his stores and factories, sliding down conveyor belts in huge cardboard boxes while he checked the sales tickets for the day. For years I had heard him repeat his dream over and over—"I want to make enough money to be able to afford to be a professor." In the years when he taught, he was happy and fulfilled, a wonderful teacher and a prolific storyteller, though most of his stories poked fun at us.

I went away to Smith College, exploring broad systems of thinking—sociology, psychology, philosophy and history—reading and writing voraciously. I had just made Phi Beta Kappa when I got a call from my father. My grandmother had died and my mother was in an institution. I had to go home to take care of my sisters.

I transferred to the University of Richmond where Dad was a professor, and childhood memories flooded back to me. When we were little, he would take us "out to college" to let us run around the track and jump over hurdles. Then, clutching bags of stale bread we had brought from home, we headed for the lake to feed hungry ducks and geese, shuffling noisily through piles of fall leaves obscuring bricked walkways all across campus.

When I started out my life, I saw everything as separate. Houses were on lots. Fences defined the boundary between home and the world. Schools were large stone-and-brick buildings each on its own block, surrounded by paved playgrounds and grassy athletic fields. Businesses and factories were far away and separate—a long drive to get there, and a long time to get back home. The government was also separate, the capitol was a place we would drive downtown to see. Parents were responsible for home, teachers for school, managers for work, officials for government. One had very little to say to the other, except when someone got in trouble.

As I've experienced more life, I've come to see things as connected instead of seeing them as separate. As I have traveled around the world, I've seen that people are more alike than they're different, despite external differences in clothing and cultures. They feel the same feelings, they want the same things, they have the same issues with success and with leaders. I have come to see teaching as an extension of parenting, managing as an extension of teaching, and governing as the extension of all these.

After graduating from college. I went to interview for a supervisory position with the telephone company. They asked me to role-play a conversation with a customer. The customer couldn't pay his whole bill on time and asked if he could pay it over time. But the world of my childhood was the only world I knew. In that world, people had to do things on time and follow rules exactly. Exceptions were impossible. So I said to my customer, "You have to get your payment in on time. There's nothing I can do." And I was shocked when, with all my credentials and honors and having said what I was sure was the right thing, they weren't interested in hiring me.

That job rejection deeply affected me. For the first time I could see my life from the outside. I saw fences surrounding me, separating me from other people and other choices. I had learned about life from my parents and teachers, from the bosses I knew, from their attitudes about what was possible and impossible, what could be changed and what couldn't. I was rigid in my thinking, brought up in a world of rights, wrongs, and impossibles, a world in which rules were unbendable. Things couldn't be changed just by asking. Fortunately I could see that my world wasn't working, and I was beginning to feel prodded, painfully pushed and shoved.

Finishing my schooling, I began my education. I was frustrated with the field of psychology as I knew it, sick of neuroses and psychoses and the varieties of disorders outlined in my textbooks and lived out in my life. My training experiences in state hospitals and VA's convinced me that I didn't want to do any more of that.

Fortunately I began my career as a research psychologist at the National Institute of Mental Health. It was a wonderful place for someone who loved to learn. I could read and research and conference every week with the finest in my field. While I was there, I took part in a research project on creativity. In the study, we were given a problem and told the reasons it couldn't be solved. A patient had a tumor that was inoperable. A laser beam powerful enough to destroy the tumor would destroy intervening tissue as well. They asked us how we would save this patient's life. After many false starts, a thought came to mind. We could enter with two or more laser beams, each one less powerful but able to destroy the tumor at the point where they met. It seemed unusual and unconventional to me, but when I presented my idea, they said researchers were already exploring that solution. This experience gave me my direction. Success and creativity would be what I'd study.

I married then and focused on family. My husband was a psychologist, a captain in the Army, so we moved wherever the Army wanted to move us. My twelve-year marriage was a re-creation of my family—brilliant, exacting, demanding and cold. I was in pain for years with one operation after the other—gall stones and kidney stones, bilateral inguinal hernias, headaches and sinus problems, one unusual neuralgia or the other. Finally a friend sent me to a doctor who sat me right down and laid it out plain and simple: "Mrs. Collins, whatever you're doing in your life is not working. Either you change, or it will continue to hurt you—it could even kill you." I was shocked, but I knew he was right. After years of counseling and trying, I decided to let go of my marriage.

I was the very first person I knew who got divorced. My kids didn't even know what the word divorce meant. We tried to explain it to them. But after listening for a few minutes, they asked if they could go back upstairs to watch TV. I knew what it meant even if they didn't. I wept at their naiveté. I cried about my future. Their father would live in this house, the house I'd just spent two and a half years fixing up, and we'd move someplace else. Everything I had ever dreamed of had just been erased. I couldn't see anything ahead. The future was blank.

Headaches and pain pulled me out of my past, straining and stressing and moving me forward. I'm glad my body wouldn't let me stay stuck forever, thankful for the part of me that wanted to move beyond dependence to independence. I couldn't be a good girl any more. I had to break the rules of my childhood to recover my health and happiness. After months of grieving, I finally headed forward. The ending of the life I had always thought I would live created the beginning of the life I wanted to live. My dreams for my two daughters continued leading me forward.

A single mother, I went off to work. I had to go on to whatever was next. I taught graphic arts, the gifted program and futuristics in the Pennsylvania public schools. I always thought I would be home like my mother was. I never imagined working full time and leaving my children, but suddenly I had to imagine it. I remember tying a house key around my older daughter's neck so she could let them both in after school. She used to complain to me, "Why can't you be a chocolate-chip-cookie mommy like all the other mommies?" Those moms were home all day baking cookies to have waiting warm on a plate for their kids after school.

The teenager in me grew up with my daughters. I learned things I hadn't had a chance to learn as a teenager—hair styling and makeup, putting together outfits, talking for hours on the phone. As a teenager the simple comforts of family life—like sitting around a kitchen table enjoying a conversation or hanging out in my bedroom with friends—had not been available to me. My comforts and best friends were reading and learning. I loved the mysterious process of moving from being afraid of something to becoming really good at it.

I was happy, a single woman choosing and exploring, establishing new relationships that were loving and sharing. My creativity flowered. From my earliest oil painting of pink flowers as a child, I journeyed on to become an interior designer, landscaper and photographer. My explorations with clay elephants in the first grade led me to open my own gallery, to become a potter and weaver producing primitive stoneware pots and elaborate wall hangings for hospitals, schools, and synagogues. From piano recitals as a child I went on to perform with quartets and orchestras, to play piano duets, an amateur among professionals. I had to overcome the terror of our concerts being recorded, or the ultimate heart-pounding distraction of our page-turner knocking the music down on our laps. From early days of baking fruitcakes with my grandmother, I went on to become a master cook specializing in vegetarian fare, crusty breads and hearty thick soups, and doing cooking shows on TV. My dad would be amazed at the cabinets I've built after my slow start at hammering, striking the nails of my fingers instead of the nails he had driven part way in a board for me. From early speeches at graduation, I went on to do thirty-minute interviews on CNN and three-day seminars for executives and leaders.

My desire to understand success and my interest in overcoming fears led me to master things I would have shied away from otherwise. I did what I later told participants in my seminars to do. I made a list of things I was afraid of doing, things I avoided like the plague. That dreaded list—which made my heart race and hesitate just to read it—and my commitment to overcome my fears, eventually led me on to develop advanced skills in mountain climbing, scuba diving and spelunking, and most fearful of all for me, ballroom dancing and aerobics. No one who sees me now would ever guess I had been afraid to move and dance, but I was. Mind things were easy for me, but body things were difficult. I was never picked to dance at cotillion. I even failed posture pictures in college, unable to stand up straight for an X ray of my spine. I was so painfully shy as a young girl that I was afraid to walk across a crowded room or answer a telephone if I didn't know who was calling.

Then suddenly my life changed drastically. The school system cut back and I was laid off. I went to work in business, wearing a suit, high heels and stockings, away from home long days in corporate America. There were no more leisurely summers together, or late afternoons cooking dinner with the kids, no more holidays we all had off together.

But the layoff pushed me relentlessly on toward my mission. I began working in sales and moved into sales training. Then I worked in management and moved into management training. I began exploring the route to success. I interviewed successful people. I studied. I learned and I taught. My desire to be a model for my daughters kept me going when I thought about stopping. I remembered what it felt like to have a mother who stopped. I remembered how much I had wanted her to talk to me, to listen and support me in getting what I wanted. Then I knew I had to keep going.

My favorite successes have been the successes with my children. I am most proud and excited about what we've accomplished together. One morning I had a call from an executive with The Upjohn Company who asked me to speak at their regional sales conference. We chatted for a few minutes about agenda and details, then he said that he had something special to tell me. "Your daughter Margaret will be honored as our top sales rep at this conference. When we told her about her award, we asked what the secret of her success was. She said that her secret was her mother. And she told us about the success skills you have discovered. Whatever you taught Margaret, we would like you to teach the rest of our team. There's just one last thing. We don't want them to know you're her mother until it's over. We want them to hear you for the professional you are." I was honored and gladly agreed.

I flew into Washington early that morning. Arriving at the hotel, I mingled with participants, not stopping when I passed my daughter in the hallway, not responding to her comments any differently than to others, not looking up when she stood beside me in the lunch line. At the end of the day, the participants were excited about what they had learned. I was standing in a knot of question-askers and hand-shakers when concluding remarks began. "Our award-winner Margaret Collins has an announcement to make." She stood up. And all she said was, "That's my mom." There was surprise and then a cry went up, "No fair Margaret. No wonder you're the best!"

The *Technology of Success* seminars introduced me to thousands of people, opening my way into families, schools, businesses, and governments. The pain and disruption I had experienced in my life had led me to discover the route to success. Perhaps you are a parent wanting to guide your child to success or a teacher wanting to help your students succeed. Maybe you are a manager developing a team or you are a part of a government struggling to do more for people. Or perhaps you, like me, have a dream, something you really want to create and contribute.

I am delighted to be able to share what has brought health and happiness to me and my family. Please use these ten skills and share them with others, so together we can lead the next generation to success.

Part Two

TEN SKILLS FOR SUCCEEDING AND LEADING

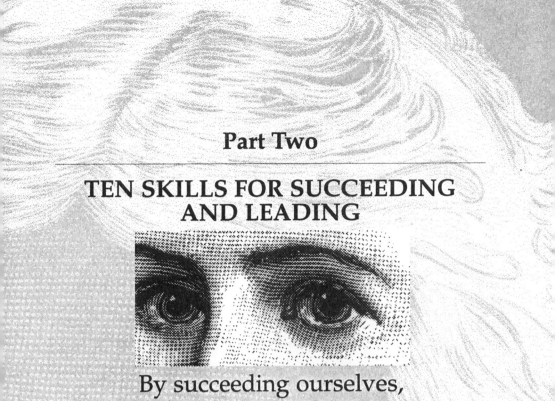

By succeeding ourselves,
we lead the next generation to success

Overview

A glimpse at the Big Picture of Success

We are entering the Age of Creativity and Leadership

More-better-faster is the mantra of our time. Work hours keep getting longer and longer. Jobs take us farther and farther from home, consuming more time and energy just to get there and back. Life is fast and furious. Our roadways are jammed with drivers rushing and pushing. Annoyance, fatigue and aggression keep mounting. Both parents work to make financial ends meet. Single parents try to do the job of two. Remarried parents struggle to combine families. Even with the assistance of baby-sitters and housekeepers, take-outs and microwaves, personal trainers and time-management systems, we can't get it all done.

Here we are still striving for success, that elusive experience that seems to lurk somewhere up ahead of us. When we do more, when we do better, then we'll feel satisfied. We'll know we're successful. But how much longer will it take? How much more must we do? We're frustrated and exhausted from the accelerating pace, from the endless technological advances and ever-expanding information base. Our energy is running low.

We learned about success from our parents and grandparents. They seemed to succeed with plenty of time to spare—time in the mornings to have breakfast and read the paper, time over lunch to chat with friends or neighbors, time in the evening to do the dishes together and play with the kids. They were loyal and obedient. Their jobs were secure. But their ways of succeeding don't work for us now.

Cities have become hostile territories harboring the dissatisfied and disillusioned, the disenfranchised and drugged. The satisfying sense of compatibility and safety we used to feel in our towns has been replaced by a terrifying separation and alienation. Our media reports epidemic rapes, robberies and murders. Children raised on violence kill peers and parents. Parents pushed past sanity shoot bosses and co-workers. According to CNN, homicide is the number-three cause of death in the work place in the United States. Murder by husbands and lovers is a prime cause of death among women.

What does all this have to do with success? It has everything to do with it. But to see that connection, we have to climb up high enough to catch a glimpse of the Big Picture. Success has three phases. In the first phase we succeed by following a leader, doing what we're told to do obediently and loyally. In the second phase we succeed by outperforming peers, doing more and more, better and faster, struggling to improve grades, scores and graphs. In the third phase we move beyond our past, beyond the rules and limits learned along the way, finally discovering our own power to create what we want.

No matter what we learn, no matter what age, we start off in first, over-coming fears and inertia, succeeding at following a leader's instructions, learning to perform our new skill safely and correctly. When we can do that, we are given our independence—our right to ride a bike around the block on our own, our permit to drive a car on the roadways alone, our license to begin practicing financial planning, law or medicine.

Shifting into second, the meaning of success changes. Trying no longer counts, we have to produce. Like rats on a wheel, we run faster and faster, producing and competing until we're experienced and efficient, until we're stressed and exhausted, putting more effort in but getting less satisfaction out, pressed harder and harder against the wall of creation until we finally break through, inventing a new way.

Moving beyond right and wrong, beyond more-better-faster, beyond pleasing others, success shifts a third time. Knowing what doesn't work drives us to discover what will work instead. In the third phase we communicate to find the expertise and assistance we need—wherever it is. Outcome-oriented and experienced, we begin to create new ways of doing things. "What do I want?" and "What do you want?" become our guiding questions. And for the first time we move from a vertical world scrambling up toward the top—to a horizontal world standing side by side as a team.

The shift from competition to leadership should be natural. Having learned to ride our bike, we teach a younger sibling. Having raised our own child, we help a friend or neighbor. Having learned to do our job, we gladly teach another everything we know. Or do we?

No, the process of success has become distorted, skewed by the disproportionate rewards given for competition, inflated by the pressures of housing and credit cards. We're like drivers only using second gear to get where they're going—jerking to start, grinding on the highways, but failing to shift to third because they're paid more to compete.

But staying stuck in second is producing a crisis for our children. The Baby Boom Generation, the largest generation in history, has finally come of age. We are the leaders now—the parents, the teachers, the managers, the ones governing. Together we face an historic dilemma. The rate of change in our world is accelerating so rapidly that the information we teach our children now will be long out of date by the time they will need it. This is the Information Age, the Age of Commerce and Industry. Our children won't have to know it all, they won't have to do it all, but they will have to dream it all.

We are entering the Age of Creativity and Leadership. Our children will need to invent products, develop systems and design ways of living we can't even imagine yet. But their success will depend on our leadership. If we continue to reward blind obedience, if we continue to bonus and promote cutthroat competition while ignoring and even punishing their creativity and leadership, then our children will not develop the skills they will need to succeed in their world.

Ironically, at this time when we most need creative leaders, when life and circumstances are changing faster than ever, the least-led generation in history has stepped up to lead—the generation whose parents had a 50 percent divorce rate, the generation that had both parents out working, the generation most frequently parented by day care and TV. This could spell disaster. Or, this could be exactly the opportunity we need to open ourselves up to new ways of leading.

There are three phases of leadership that mirror the three phases of success. As leaders, we must be able to teach those who follow us how and when to shift, sensing from our own experience when a phase-shift is needed. We are their "automatic transmission," shifting for them until they learn to shift for themselves.

When those we lead are in the first phase, we are responsible for everything they do. We must stay there beside them, constantly inputting and praising. But then when they can perform the skill safely and correctly, we need to begin backing off, giving them room to explore and decide, while we remain nearby to assist them. But when they are competent, when they begin to blaze their own trails, when they can create effective methods of their own, we need to cheer them on to wherever their dreams take them, relinquishing control unless they invite us to assume it. Or unless safety is threatened.

Leaders are like gardeners—tending success like a plant, providing a tiny fence or a sunny protective greenhouse, deciding on the right moment to lift that plant from its pot and set it out on its own. We watch that fast-growing seedling bending and twisting, overshadowing other seedlings as it reaches higher and farther and deeper. We continue to weed and prune until that plant produces a flower, until that flower creates seeds, until those seeds become realities—new products and services, new systems and technologies, new ways of living happy, healthy lives here on Earth. The completion of our dreams is the fruit of our success. The completion of our children's dreams is the fruit of our leadership. As leaders we are not only responsible for harvesting our own success but for cultivating the success of the next generation.

But we didn't start our lives as leaders. We started as followers. Our leaders were in charge. They decided right and wrong for us. They decided good and bad for us. They decided what we should and shouldn't do. Sometimes their sense of what was right for us was accurate, but many times it was distorted by the circumstances of their own lives. By the things they couldn't handle, by the things their leaders never taught them.

The First Success Skill

SUCCESS FILING

When our success file is full, we feel successful

L
ike the fruits of a tree—apple, pear or papaya—the fruits of success are often seeded, worked, tilled and weeded but then never picked. The satisfaction of the fruit goes untasted and unsavored.

I planted three eight-inch papaya seedlings outside my kitchen door, watering them each day throughout their first summer, weeding and tilling them as they grew to three feet, eight feet and then ten, eagerly anticipating cutting open that luscious ripe fruit, scooping out round black seeds from the center, slicing it into bite-sized pieces, lifting it to eager lips tasting and chewing and swallowing with pleasure.

But the fruit was so long in coming, that I gradually forgot about my trees, not even noticing when their first clusters of flowers bloomed. Not watching the fruits as they swelled and ripened from green to yellow to orange. Sad to say, most of my papaya have fallen to the ground unnoticed and unenjoyed.

Success is like that too. We work and work, making calls, attending meetings, putting in long hours, sustaining our efforts but rarely enjoying the fruits they should bring us. Even top performers aren't feeling satisfied, despite doing more and more, better and faster. In my *Technology of Success* seminars across the country, thousands of people said they felt successful every once in a while, when they did something Herculean, overcame incredible odds, or turned in nothing short of a miraculous performance. But they lived the rest of their lives in the valleys between those lofty peaks.

Millions of us have bought books about success. We've read them and applied them, even gotten results. But something was still missing. This book will fill in the missing pieces. After reading this chapter you will be able to define success clearly and practically. You'll know how to feel satisfied each day, recognizing successes you never knew you had, raising your confidence and enthusiasm for the future. You'll learn to lead others to feel successful too—your children, your students, your employees— giving you not only satisfaction but fulfillment.

Success can be elusive. Most people strive for a success that keeps moving out in front of them like the proverbial carrot dangling in front of their noses. I'll be successful when... But then the next goal is even larger, and we grind along hoping we'll be successful some day. But when?

How successful have you been so far?

When you look at your life, what do you see? Do you see all the times you've succeeded, or do you overlook most of them saying they were nothing?

What successes do you feel you've had up until now? Can you recall 10 of them? 20? 100? 200? 500? Or is it difficult to remember any successes at all? Most people who begin my seminars can recall 10 to 15 successes. They include such things as being chosen for a team, getting a part in a play, making the honor roll, graduating from high school, being accepted to college, buying their first car, meeting and marrying, having their first child, buying their first home, and receiving honors, awards, and bonuses. How many successes can you recall?

A few people in each seminar honestly feel they have never been successful. Whatever your number of successes is, this is your starting point. You will be able to add hundreds more to that number as we explore success in more detail.

What is success?

We spend our lives chasing it, but what exactly is it? How do we know when we've achieved it? I asked these crucial questions over and over. Participants in my seminars said that they felt successful when others told them they were. When they received awards, bonuses, or raises. When they were able to do things they hadn't done before, things they had seen others do. They felt successful when they overcame obstacles, things they weren't sure they had the time, money or skill to do, things that seemed very difficult. When they competed and won, beating existing records, producing more than others. They felt successful when they developed new methods, new systems and technologies. They felt successful when they were able to make what they wished for come true.

As they shared their stories, I heard certain elements mentioned again and again—frustration, struggle, effort, hard work, long hours, competition, opposition, scarcity, and deadlines. It's interesting to note that a deadline was a real line prisoners were forced to stand on while they waited to be shot during the French Revolution. Some things haven't changed. We still feel the same way about dealing with deadlines. Success, as my participants were defining it, didn't feel attractive.

One corporate head told me he had reached his career goals—he was a community leader, a marathon runner and a publicly acclaimed gardener. He had raised three healthy children and built a beautiful home—but recently divorced, he felt like a complete failure. Together we analyzed what success meant to him. "Success," he finally said, "was doing everything perfectly all the time."

Since then I've met many other people who were defining success as perfection, and they too were living with unnecessary disappointment and frustration. Their definition of success made its achievement impossible. Over the years I've joked with my perfectionistic audiences, telling them that Earth is a correctional institution. We're here to correct and correct and correct—correcting what we do, correcting what we want.

Success is completion

After hearing thousands of success stories, I offer you this simple definition. Success is completion. Success is being able to complete what we set out to do— each individual action, each specific step, each desired experience whether a big project or a very small errand.

Success is completion—completion of getting up and exercising, completion of eating a good breakfast, completion of having food in the house, completion of catching up on washing, completion of assignments, completion of phone calls we said we would make, completion of a bill that we have pending in Congress.

The word satisfaction comes from the Latin *satis*, enough, and *factere*, to do. Satisfaction means to do enough. Satisfaction doesn't always come when we finish things. Lots of people finish lots and lots of things but never feel satisfied, never feel they've done enough. Satisfaction only comes when we complete things.

Completion requires us to acknowledge that we did what we set out to do. Completion gives us power, putting an engine on our lives and a rudder we can steer. Instead of feeling like we're driftwood, pushed about by winds and tides. Each thing we complete adds to our power. My father used to tell me, "If you want something done, ask a busy man."

Satis-FAC-tion: Finishing + Acknowledging = Completion

We all know the satisfaction of checking completed items off our errand list. As we're checking we're acknowledging, "I said I would, and I did. That item's complete."

When we begin delegating tasks to others, whether those others are our friends, employees or children, we realize how important completion and acknowledgment are to us. Someone may have finished what we asked them to do, but if they didn't let us know they had, then we are worrying and wondering, feeling upset and annoyed because we don't have the satisfaction of knowing that completion.

Success means different things to different people. It's not just a home, two kids and two cars, a certain sum of money, or the right title. Success is as unique as the individuals who dream it up. Success may be returning a phone call we've put off for months. Success may be finding the right wallpaper for our room. Success may be reuniting with a relative we haven't seen in years. Success may be opening all our mail. Success may be catching up on filing. Success may be buying new tires. Success may be digging up a dead shrub in the yard. Success may be finding a sitter for

Saturday night. Success may be going to buy groceries. Success may be passing a licensing exam. Success may be finding a job. Success may be getting married. Success may be getting a divorce.

Completions release energy

When we invest money in a stock, our money is tied up until the transaction is complete—until that stock is sold. When we invest energy in a plan, our energy is tied up until that action is finished and also acknowledged. Each time we complete a plan, its accumulated energy is released blasting us into an even larger orbit of action.

"I wanted to, I could and I did." "I wanted to, I could and I did" is the propulsion system we use to keep our lives moving. Completions energize and propel us on to our next dream, next solution or opportunity. We know we're complete when we begin asking, "What's next?" Then we know that our energy has been released and is available to reinvest.

Incompletions make it hard for us to get out of bed. Our minds are filled up with all the things we have to do, so filled in fact that we can't manage to do any of them. In the computer world they call it "thrashing," when they've loaded so much data in a computer that until something is filed and saved, until space is made available, there is not enough capacity to produce the result.

Failure is incompletion

If we think back over the times we feel we've failed, they were the times we started things but never finished them. We didn't ask for assistance, or we asked and didn't get it. They were the times we failed to do whatever it took. The times we finished a task but never stopped to acknowledge we had, denying ourselves the feelings of success and satisfaction we had earned.

Failure is not a good reason to give up a dream—unless the truth is we no longer want it. Failure is a signal that we need to relook at our methods. Is this the best way to do this, or would other ways work better? We need to explore various methods until we find the ones that work.

Sometimes we fear failure so much we decide to stop dreaming, figuring if we don't dream and plan, we won't be disappointed. But when we stop planning, we also stop doing. When we stop doing, we also stop completing. When we stop completing, we no longer feel satisfied.

Why do we need to file our successes?

We each operate the most sophisticated computer in the world—our mind and body. We write programs and develop methods to complete them, exploring various methods until we find the ones that work for us. Each of our computers has its own operating capacity. When we complete a program, a plan or a dream, we have to file, save and label it to make that capacity available for use again. Filing our successes makes them accessible whenever we need them.

Why would we need to access our successes? When we decide whether we want to do something or not, we search through our success file to see if we've succeeded at anything similar. The word confidence comes from the Latin *confidere*, to have faith in. Seeing completions in our past lets us imagine completions in our future. Success in our past gives us faith in our future.

To be successful, we have to be able to take on the unknown—a new baby, a new class, a new management assignment, a new position in government—the challenges, the dilemmas, the problems we don't know we'll have to face when we start. To feel confident, we have to feel we'll be able to do whatever it takes.

But we've done our filing haphazardly until now, doing it sometimes but forgetting to do it at other times, filing some completions but not filing others. We've left millions of successes unfiled and long forgotten, focusing on our incompletions instead, on what we haven't been able to do or on what we haven't done well. Yes, we can success file in our minds, but we can multiply the value by writing our successes down. It's a good idea to start a success file, collecting and organizing your successes in a notebook or a folder, or storing them in your computer.

When we success file our own lives, the successes other people point out to us become merely welcome additions. We don't need their acknowledgment to feel satisfied and confident. We fill our own success file each and every day in the process of doing what we need to do and want to do, no longer needing to wait for someone else to notice us. We still like to receive praise but we don't need to have it.

We simply stop for a few minutes at the end of each day, reviewing and acknowledging the many things we've done—what we did when we got up, what we did during the day, what we did in the evening. We remember the actions we took, the problems we solved, the changes we made, the thousands of things we were able to complete that day— emptying the trash, feeding the dog, eating a good breakfast, quizzing our child's spelling, driving the kids to school, returning eighteen phone calls, turning a report in on time, having lunch with a friend, picking up dry cleaning, deciding on the location for the management conference—and on and on until we fall into bed.

We pat ourselves on the back, acknowledging the reality of what we could do. This process of reviewing, acknowledging and saving successes for future use is what I call success filing.

When our success file is full, we feel success-full

We need to take time each day to taste and savor the fruits of our success. We're successful every day, whether the last day of a project or any day in the middle. A completed project is a series of many, many successes.

The dream of completion is like the string in a necklace, holding our successes together one after the other—each action we've taken, each call we've made, each meeting we've attended, each task we've delegated and followed through to completion. We're successful every day, whether the last day of a project or any day in the middle. When our success file is full, we have the confidence we need to take on the unknown.

But when our success file is low, we feel dependent on others, lacking the confidence and enthusiasm we need to do what we plan. If we don't know that success is completion, if we aren't skilled in success filing, then we'll continue to live lives of burnout and breakdown—needing motivational tapes, overindulging in shopping, hoping to feel better, going on vacations just to keep going. But until we begin storing our own successes in our success file, the minute we turn the tape off, the minute we deboard the plane, the minute the alarm wakes us on Monday morning, we're up against the same pressures, working harder and harder to do better and better, but it's never enough. And we just can't understand what's the matter with life.

In the beginning of our lives our parents praised and applauded our first word, our first step, our first ride on a bike. We relished the sweet pleasure of their praise and rewards—their hugs and kisses, their cookies and lollipops. Most leaders do a good job of acknowledging early success-es—our first day on the job, our first attempts at managing, the baby steps we take in any new skill. But as we become more skillful, they may push us out on our own before we know how to success file, before we feel self-confident and ready to do it alone.

Many of us today share the fear of a power failure shutting our computer down and wiping out our work. Some of us use auto-save programs that save work automatically every few minutes. Without success filing each day, we suffer the same losses. The satisfaction of what we've done has been wiped out each night as we shut ourselves down to sleep. In the human computer however memories may be forgotten but not lost. You can learn how to retrieve your lost successes, jogging your memory to recapture lost confidence, satisfaction and fulfillment—filing your successes past and present. It's a good idea to file at regular intervals during the day, stopping for a moment to save and savor what we've accomplished.

I was fortunate to have a wise aunt who began giving me diaries for my birthday when I was six. Bound in soft leather, they each locked with a key. I loved saving memories, treasured moments and special occasions there. And I've kept a diary each year ever since allowing me to walk over to my shelf at any moment, select the proper year, reopen and rediscover the specific details of my life—the parts I had filed and saved, the parts that otherwise would have been long since forgotten.

Success is completion—and also deletion

We also create success when we delete from our lives whatever's not working—a relationship that brings us more pain than joy, a method we've been using for years, a familiar way of thinking. Success is completion and also deletion. Deletion successes are just as important as completion successes although most of us never realize it.

But letting go of what we have can be a challenging process bringing up old fears and insecurities. Letting go of friends and partners, familiar jobs and homes will create the space for new people and situations—the space for our dreams. Eliminating what we don't want allows us to use that same space to do what we do want. We need to be willing to change when our body signals us that something is wrong. When we're bored or we're angry for long periods of time. When we're frequently sick or having lots of accidents. Our inner computer sends us alert messages. "Attention programmer, do you still want this outcome? Are you going to complete it, or do you want to delete it? Are you using the best method? Or would another one work better?"Deletion success requires us to reexamine what we want, looking from up high, detached from our feelings, seeing our lives as though we were standing outside of them. Asking ourselves why we started doing this in the first place. Looking at the methods we have used up until now. Looking at other methods that might give us completion. But letting go can be a challenging process, bringing up old fears and insecurities.

Whatever we want and get also brings all the other things that come along with it. If we smoke all the cigarettes we want, we also get all the health problems that come along with it. If we eat all the desserts we want, then we also get all the weight problems that come along with it.

Deletion gives us flexibility and choice

Deletion successes give us the flexibility we need to stay healthy. The difference between a live body and a dead one is movement and change—completing and deleting, breathing in and breathing out, eating and eliminating, working and resting. We know someone's dead when they're rigid and hard. We feel like we're dying when we're doing the same things over and over, no longer choosing and no longer enjoying them. We need to stop doing things that don't work—giving up the smoking that has caused our hacking cough, letting go of the job that's given us an ulcer—moving past the false security of simply having someone or something.

Many people can't delete things, even things they don't want. They're afraid they'll have nothing, fearing there's a scarcity, avoiding the space between what was—and what will be. But if only we have the courage and creativity to dream into it, that space can become the space of creation.

The word decide comes from the Latin, *decidere,* to cut away from. We have to decide what we want in our lives, cutting away what we don't want. Life is a process of wanting and getting and deciding. And then wanting and getting and deciding again. We are continually pruning our methods and outcomes, learning to use time and energy more and more fruitfully.

Knowing what we don't want is the first step to discovering what we do want instead

Letting go doesn't always mean leaving. Letting go may mean rechoosing and recommitting. A young woman never felt "in love" with her husband, but she had chosen to marry him because it seemed to be the right thing. Three young children later, she was depressed and disappointed. Searching for someone new, she found another relationship and became deeply involved. That is, until her marriage was threatened, until she was about to lose her children.

Then she began acknowledging the positive qualities her husband had, acknowledging successes she had never stopped to notice, savoring and tasting what she was just about to lose. Suddenly her marriage mattered. And she chose to go back to him and work on their problems.

The barnacle story

The importance of deletion was driven home powerfully one morning at the beach. I was walking along the ocean enjoying a rosy sunrise when I stumbled over a light bulb washed ashore by the tide. Looking closely, I saw it had become home to a whole colony of barnacles. When it was out at sea, it had been a perfect home, with plenty of food and water all around it. Hundreds of baby barnacles had attached themselves to it, cementing their bodies permanently in place.

But I was worried about those barnacles now, high and dry on the beach with no food and no water and the hot sun climbing higher. That light bulb wasn't a perfect home any more. I tossed them out to sea as far as I could and continued to walk, enjoying the warm breeze and the lapping sound of the sea. When my time was half up, I turned around and headed back. There was the light bulb. The wind and the tide had brought it back to shore again, but this time I could see that the barnacles were dying. I was sad as I left them there—cemented to their fate.

All afternoon I thought of the times I'd attached myself to relationships, to habits, to jobs I couldn't let go of until I felt I was dying. Why do we attach ourselves to people and methods? It's really quite simple. If we go back in our success file to our earliest successes, they were the successes we had while depending on others—our parents and caretakers who fed us and held us and helped us survive. They did everything we couldn't do. They knew everything we didn't know. And we were dependent on them to file our successes, to build up our confidence, to figure out our lives for us. So now in moments when our confidence is low, we long for those confident and competent caretakers to take charge of our lives—at least temporarily.

It's difficult to delete people or things when our confidence is low, when we don't believe that we can be successful ourselves. But when we put our confidence in others, then we're afraid they will leave us, taking our confidence and certainty with them. It's essential for our health and happiness to build self-confidence, to build faith in ourselves.

Adding completions and deletions to your success file

Let's take a few minutes to add successes to your file. Now that you understand that success is completion—and also deletion, what other successes come to mind?

What else were you able to complete as a child or a teenager? What else did you complete last year or last month? What did you complete yesterday or so far today? What have you completed in relationships and career?

And what have you deleted? What habits have you given up? What relationships have you let go of, trusting in your ability to create what you want? And what did you create instead? What job changes have you made? When have you moved or shifted your direction? What have you let go of that made your life healthier and happier? That made dreams come true?

The Proof of the Pudding experiment

My grandmother always told me, "The proof of the pudding is in the eating." She said that the recipe could sound good, and everybody could exclaim over it, but the proof of its goodness was in eating it yourself.

I had been teaching about success for fifteen years around the world, teaching about the science of wishing and dreaming. And I was using my success skills to create exciting experiences like sailing to rain forests and black volcanic islands. I rode narrow-gauge trains around mountains in India, climbing slopes so slowly that children could run beside us selling their wares. I visited markets filled with exotic clothing and jewelry. I was introduced to fascinating people who invited me to teach and provided cars and drivers who took me wherever I wanted to go.

I had arrived at the point in my life and my career where I had everything I had ever thought I wanted. I was traveling and speaking, living in a condominium on the twentieth floor, overlooking turquoise waters stretching to the horizon, a glamorous life, safe and secure, concierge and elevators. My friends loved my home, gasping when they entered, stepping off the elevator and "coming into heaven"—white, bright, clear, mirrored walls and columns reflecting the bay wherever you looked.

But I felt disconnected living up that high. As a child I had felt more connected to Mother Earth than to my own mother. I had my own garden at four, my own tree I pruned regularly, my own plants I took care of. Other kids went out to play with friends. I went out to play with plants, birds and spiders, interested in how many locust shells were left on the trees, why locusts sang sometimes but not others. Why they climbed from their shells leaving them there for me to put in my pocket. I would wake up in the night longing for lush plants, for gardens to tend, for waterfalls and streams, for ponds of huge fish swimming silently among lily pads.

I had talked over and over to people who wished and dreamed but couldn't let go of what they had—to make space for what they wanted. I wanted to see if I could do that, so I decided to sell my home and all its contents to give myself the chance to use that same money to create the life my heart longed for.

Did I really have the courage and faith to let my home go? Did I really believe I could create what I wanted? Or was this all nonsense, and should I leave well enough alone? A buyer came along who wanted my home and its contents. It was sold, I let it all go.

For months I wandered with only two duffel bags, searching for my home while staying with friends and family. I began dreaming my new dream in more and more detail, remembering the things I had loved in my life, the details of houses I had known, the details of possessions left behind, my grandmother's kitchen, my parents' tools and utensils. I longed to have those familiar things around me again.

One day I passed an ugly, low-sprawling house with a sale sign. Boxy, naked, with nothing growing around it. How about that house? But my realtor said I would hate it, it was horrible inside. Suddenly something awoke in me. My heart picked up, my breath came faster. I don't know how I knew, but that was my house. I insisted on seeing it. When she let me in, I didn't see what was there. I was seeing my dream. I was seeing that house sprawling around a shimmering pond with lush tropical plants, bananas and heliconias. I walked around seeing, though nothing I was seeing was there in that cold, dark, lifeless house.

I was out walking one morning soon after moving into that huge empty house, reviewing the rules of the game I was playing. I was creating a much more lush and spacious home, using the money from the sale of the home I no longer wanted. But the purchase and the renovations would use up all that money. How would I be able to furnish this house?

Just at that moment I found my first treasure, a wonderful trunk that had traveled around the world, stuck full of stickers from the places it had been. Why would anyone throw this treasure away? Then I remembered something my grandmother used to say, "One man's trash is another man's treasure." Now I knew how I would furnish my home—from the street, from the discards, from the stray treasures put out on Tuesdays and Fridays, from garage sales and estate sales on Saturdays and Sundays. I had discovered my strategy—everything for nothing or next to nothing.

I looked forward to those special days as eagerly as the Little Prince had looked forward to Thursdays when the hunters always danced.[2] I would find treasures on those days. And I did. And soon friends got engaged in my game. They'd call me with the location of a palm tree they'd sighted or a huge pile of ferns they knew I wanted for my jungle.

Each month I made a long list of wants. Each day when I walked with my dog, he'd sniff and I'd sniff until we found what we wanted, discarded and waiting to be hauled to my house. And my home is now filled with antiques and quaint pieces—old trunks, Oriental rugs, lidded footstools that hold darning, statues and carvings, gold-leafed family portraits, old wire bird cages. Each thing that I found was like an old friend coming home. A cowhide chair I had wanted when I was in design school. A star-shaped light like the one I had twenty years ago. Old wooden snow skis, an oak tripod, an abandoned enlarger, a kiln like the one I had in Philadelphia. A coffee mill an eighty-year-old Swedish woman used her whole life. A blue Sunbeam mixer like the one my mother used to make mashed potatoes with. Old tools that my grandmother had, stuff that my parents had—soft, worn and familiar. I was home and attracting more and more of it— magically, amazingly, all the things from my memory and some that were even better. I was falling in love with everything in my life, integrating it all in who I had become.

Now my house has a Japanese garden, waterfalls, streams and huge colorful fish. A very large lop-eared bunny has the run of my property sleeping outside my window at night. Stray animals find their way here and settle in and stay. It's peaceful and quiet. Spiders hang carefully articulated webs over streams, stringing them onto waterfalls. Orchids and bananas and crotons grow everywhere. Each and every plant was found on the street, cuttings discarded because they had gotten too big for where they were.

I met a friend whose fish had spawned suddenly, producing thousands of tiny transparent fry he called "wish fish." There was no way to predict what they'd look like, but he knew they were koi. The rest would be revealed in a matter of time. I put some in my pond watching as they grew, as their colors came in. Studying books about koi, I discovered my "wish fish" were beginning to come true—kohaku, sankes, tanchos—the traditional patterns of red, black, and white were slowly emerging. Today they are thirty inches long, living pieces of art I treasure every day.

One day I got a call from a carpenter I knew. I had told him about my strategy for furnishing the house—everything for nothing or next to nothing. He had taken out a kitchen and was on the way to the dump with it when he thought about me. Did I want another kitchen that looked like a real good one, complete with all appliances? Of course I did, forget the dump and bring it all here. And that was my ultimate find—a white German designer kitchen and appliances by Miele, the finest in the world, and they'd never been used.

My grandmother's "proof of the pudding" had worked. I had tasted this delicious success for myself. I knew I could delete whatever I didn't want so I could complete what I dreamed of instead.

When our success file is full, we feel success-full.

The Second Success Skill

SHIFTING GEARS

What we mean by success
keeps changing

Whe I learned to drive, we had to take the driving test using a stick-shift car. Shifting was a crucial skill, and the Division of Motor Vehicles required us to demonstrate that we could shift gears correctly before they would issue us a license.

Different gears allow us to perform different functions. First gear is for starting. Second is for accelerating. Third, fourth or higher gears let us maintain our speed while using less power. But today many of us drive cars that have automatic transmissions, making us unaware of which gear we are in—unless something goes wrong.

Success, too, has gear-like phases. At first we succeed by following our leaders' instructions. Accelerating into second, we succeed by improving our performance. Then, shifting into third, we succeed by inventing our own methods for achieving the same result. Success may elude us when we are shifting phases automatically, when we don't know which one we need to be in.

We shift gears many times on the roadways each day—starting at lights, gaining momentum, cruising along the highway or stopping to pay a toll. On the road to success, we shift many times too—whenever we're learning to do something new. Whenever we're working to produce and compete. Whenever we're creating our own ways of thinking and doing things and leading others to use them.

No matter what we learn, no matter what age, we start to succeed in first, following a leader, learning to perform the new skill safely and correctly. Then we are given our independence—our permit to drive the car on our own.

Shifting into second, we succeed by competing. Trying no longer counts, our leaders now expect us to produce. Like rats on a wheel, we run faster and faster. Stressed and exhausted from putting in more effort but getting less out, we find ourselves pressed harder and harder against the wall of creation—until we finally break through, inventing a new way.

In the third phase, we succeed through creativity and leadership. Skillful and experienced, we finally begin to create the life we really want. We don't have to do it all by ourselves any more. We don't have to prove we're right or we're better. We communicate to find the expertise and assistance we need—wherever it is. "What do I want?" and "What do you want?" become our guiding questions. And for the first time, we shift from a vertical world scrambling up toward the top—to a horizontal world standing side-by-side as a team.

First-phase success: **Succeeding at following**
Second-phase success: **Succeeding at competing**
Third-phase success: **Succeeding at creating**
and leading

What we mean by success changes. And what we have to do to succeed keeps changing too. What works in first won't work in second, what works in second won't work in third. Success has often eluded us because we were shifting phases automatically, unaware of which phase we needed to be in.

Yes, success is completion and deletion, but the completion and deletion of what? What do we have to complete in each phase? What does each phase require us to delete? What kind of acknowledgments are available in each phase? What happens when we shift phases too soon or too late, or we fail to shift at all? How do we know when something is wrong? Learning to shift success phases appropriately will answer these questions.

Starting in first: Dependent and needy

Whenever we begin something new, we have to make the long journey in imagination from impossible to possible. And what do we think is impossible? What we think is impossible are all the things we've tried to do and failed, all the things our leaders have rewarded us for avoiding, and all the things we've never done before—everything new, everything different, everything exciting. Yes, all the things we haven't done before are filed in our failure file.

Whenever we begin something, we have to initiate a new inner dialogue. Accessing our success file, we begin talking to ourselves: "I've succeeded at this, and this and even this. I've seen others do that. Now I think I can do that too." This vital change of mind may be quite simple, just the next step in a succession of successes. Or it may be quite challenging, the next step in a succession of failures, forcing us to confront old fears and disappointments, old pains and frustrations.

The first phase is a scary phase. We know we don't know. And we're dependent on our leaders to simplify the skill for us, to break it down into easy, digestible pieces, to create the black-and-white rules we need as beginners—the rights and wrongs, goods and bads, always and nevers, have tos and musts.

Following these rules will hopefully keep us safe until we can gain the experience we need to decide "right" for ourselves, until we build the self-confidence we need to perform the skill independently. In the first phase we're successful when we can perform the new skill safely and correctly according to our leaders' standards.

First-phase driving

On my sixteenth birthday, my dad asked me to drive with him to the university where he taught. Once on campus, he pulled his car into the huge stadium parking lot, stopped and got out. With a smile on his face, he held out his keys and ceremoniously commanded me to slide in behind the wheel. Everything felt different over there in the driver's seat. I was excited and nervous as I turned the key in the ignition. Following his directions, I shifted into first and eased out the clutch ever so slowly, lurching and jerking, steering and accelerating and asking a million questions:

"When should I shift?" "Can I make it between those cars?" "When should I begin my turn?" I needed his constant input—and his constant reassurance.

Then he said it was time for me to practice driving on the highway. Fear clutched my chest as I began merging among fast-moving cars. Feeling pushed and panicked, I accelerated for the first time to a breathtaking 55. I stopped to pay tolls and climbed high-suspension bridges, distracted by water far below us. Then I drove the car home in bumper-to-bumper traffic, stopping on hills, fearful of rolling back into the car behind us. And when I didn't slow down quickly enough, Dad—trying to not yell—slammed down imaginary brakes on the passenger side.

First-phase scuba diving

Thirty years later I was back in the first phase again. Having passed the classroom tests and run-throughs in the pool, I was aboard a boat on the way to a reef, plowing through rough seas for forty-five minutes until someone shouted, "We're there." Looking around nervously, I discovered "there" was nowhere. There was nothing but open seas. The reef lay invisible, thirty feet below us. My heart raced, my stomach lurched. This was the moment I had been preparing myself for.

Putting on my gear I began obsequiously following my instructor around, asking questions I knew the answers to but asking them anyway. "Does the valve open this way or that way?" "Is my tank really full?" "Did I do that part right?"

When it was finally my turn, I maneuvered my heavily garbed spaceman-like body down the deck to the stern, and holding my mask, at the count of four I jumped in, weighted to descend despite inner panic holding me up. My mind was a blur, racing to get hold of my fears. Then clearing, equalizing and finding inner balance, I headed down to where my instructor was waiting to test us.

First phase on a computer

But learning to use my computer was even harder. Facing a deadline on my first book, *The Me Book*, I decided to buy a Mac to speed up the editing. But instead it slowed it down. I couldn't use that computer until

I stopped to learn how, unable to communicate with it, confused by error messages like, "Warning: Are you sure you want to remove the application?" No, I wasn't sure, afraid every time that warning box appeared or I saw the little bomb that came up with a system error. Pulling out the manual, I searched through the index, wishing I had an instructor there to tell me what to do and when to do it. Without a leader's constant input and praise I was making the same mistakes over and over. Old childhood fears and inadequacies resurfaced and I had to face them alone in order to finish my book.

The building of self-confidence is essential to the first phase

As our leaders are teaching us how to perform our new skill, they must simultaneously be teaching us how to success file that new skill. In the first phase, they are responsible for doing our filing for us, pointing out things we've completed and deleted and making sure we notice them. "Yes, that's good." "Yes, that's right." "Ah, that's just what I wanted." To succeed in the first phase, we have to keep going despite feeling scared and nervous, dependent and needy. These feelings offer a clue that we're in the first phase of success.

But as we learn to recognize our own successes, our leaders begin shifting the responsibility for success filing over to us, asking questions instead of giving us answers: "So what are the successes you've had today? What did you complete? What did you delete?" "What do you feel good about?" "What are you proud of?" And as they listen attentively to the successes we mention, they also point out the successes we failed to notice.

Our first-phase leaders are responsible for making sure that our success file is full every day, building the self-confidence we need to shift into second and perform independently. They may point out our successes in person or spell them out in print, using tests, grades and evaluations to assess our understanding of the basics.

Leaders act as our "automatic transmission," shifting success phases for us until we can learn to shift for ourselves. But busy parents and teachers often decide how much time and energy to give us—according to their schedule. If a leader fails to meet our needs, not making enough time to praise us and encourage us, if they're too busy caring for a new baby or teaching another student, then even though we can perform the skill safely and correctly, our success file will be low, and we won't be able to perform the skill comfortably and confidently.

Giving us independence without giving us self-confidence feels like abandonment. Not giving us independence when we're ready and able feels like confinement. Either way we will want to avoid leaders. But avoiding leaders will prevent us from getting the information and supervision we need. And if we're lucky success will still follow. But if we are not, injury or death may follow instead.

Recognizing when an individual is in the first phase will assist a leader in discriminating between habitually dependent people—people who are always scared and nervous—and motivated learners who will move on to competing and creating as soon as they've learned what they need. The Division of Motor Vehicles does a good job of meeting first-phase needs of drivers. The Division requires us to obtain a permit to learn, stipulating that we have a licensed driver with us until we demonstrate we can drive safely and correctly—with a state examiner sitting beside us. First-phase professional training programs teach us what we need to know to be licensed. They prescribe necessary course work, internships and residencies and require us to pass written and oral exams demonstrating we know enough to practice independently—whether we're drivers or doctors or we plan to sell insurance.

Filing your first-phase successes

Your first-phase successes are the completions you've had while following a leader. Let's recall some of your early successes—learning to walk and talk, learning to use a potty, ride a bike, skate or scooter. Going to school the first day, learning to write and do math, taking your first spelling test. Learning to change classes, learning to play baseball, basketball or hockey. Trying out for a team the first time. Learning to please new people— teachers, friends, bosses, dates and mates—learning their likes and dislikes, their rules and requirements.

What first-phase successes have you been having lately? Maybe you're learning to use a new program. Or you're in the process of being certified in acupuncture, dentistry or law. Perhaps you're learning to snow ski or water ski, studying for your pilot's license or learning a new language. Maybe you're taking an aerobics class, a class in Chinese cooking, or xeriscape gardening. Maybe you've just moved to a new city. Or bought a new car. Or started a new job, relationship or marriage. Maybe you're pregnant or you've just had a baby. Or you've gotten divorced. You're doing something new, experiencing unfamiliar reactions and feelings, developing new responses to old situations, exploring new ways of being who you are. These are all first-phase successes you've put in your success file—just by having noticed them.

Word cues to first-phase success

Here are some word cues that tell you when you are in the first phase of success: right/wrong, good/bad, should/shouldn't, have to/must, always/never, safe/dangerous, correct/incorrect, dependent, needy, insecure, scared, worried, doubtful, nervous, hesitant, anxious, frightened, fearful, guilty, trying, pleasing, obedient, loyal. When you hear yourself using these words, you will know that you are in the first phase of success.

Shifting into second: Succeeding at competing

We are shifted into the second phase of success when our leaders give us independence from constant supervision, and we have to begin making decisions on our own. In the second phase we begin to practice the new skill on our own, whether it's medicine or driving, diving or computing. Licensed and certified, having completed basic training, we begin competing with others who are developing that same skill. Then our leaders begin accelerating the requirements for success. Quantity is increasing. Quality is increasing. Hours are increasing. Pressure is increasing. Everything is increasing except the time we have to do it in.

With more independence and less supervision, we must begin to develop our own decision-making strategies. To decide on our own, we have to look back in our memory, reviewing past experiences, successes and failures, recalling rules and requirements. And we learn to rely on our experience instead of our leader's experience. In the second phase we begin deleting beginners' rules—the old rights and wrongs, always and nevers. We start cutting corners, experimenting and improving so we can outperform others.

In the second phase our confidence is still a fragile seedling, easily squashed or bruised when our leaders don't approve of what we've done or decided. The decisions we make aren't always the same ones they would make, given their level of skill and experience. We don't always do what they tell us to do—or believe they have told us. We don't always know what they've got in mind. Sometimes they are helpful in correcting our mistakes, but sometimes they shout and punish us, alarmed at how little information we have "on file" for use.

Second-phase driving

In the second phase, I had my license and I could drive on my own—provided my parents would lend me their car, provided I got it back on time, provided I followed their rules and limits. Shifting and stopping had gotten much easier. Now I was paying less attention to the way I was driving and paying more attention to where I was going and who I was going with, chatting with passengers, figuring out shortcuts, venturing out farther and farther.

Some of my friends wanted to go even faster so they got into drag racing. On the racetrack they were starting faster, breaking street rules, souping up and modifying, crossing to the left, racing and risking, stopping in a second-saving screech. But then they got into trouble when they tried to do the same things on the streets.

Second-phase scuba diving

Certified for open-water diving, I decided to take the advanced training. Something wonderful happened as I entered the second phase. The fish reappeared. There hadn't been any fish in the waters of my first phase, only regulators and buddy breathing and flooded masks to clear. I was so busy paying attention to what I was doing that I couldn't look out.

I was excited when I entered the water more easily, swimming down without panic overtaking me, calm and able to think straight and clearly, to check with my buddy and write notes on our slate. Now we had assignments, courses to plot, longer distances to cover more quickly. There was a wreck at 90 feet to explore, cabins to enter, passages we could barely fit through. I got caught on my tanks and had to be freed by my buddy. And our competitive spirit had reappeared too. We tried to swim faster, to reach the destination first, to use less air so we could stay down even longer. My buddy and I success filed all the way home. "We did this, we did that, we did it all better. We were the best ones."

Second phase on the computer

Back home at my computer, the editing was moving ahead faster and easier. I was using more skills like saving and filing, copying, cutting and pasting, finally feeling the computer was useful to me. I was beginning to take short cuts and develop new methods and understandings. During a thunderstorm I forgot to file and save, and a sudden power failure wiped me out. I never forgot to file and save after that. As my dad always used to say, "The school of hard knocks is a very good teacher."

In the second phase we use leaders' measures to acknowledge ourselves

The second phase is a stressful phase. We want independence but we resent it when we get it. At the end of the first phase, our leaders were there too much, making us feel hot-housed and confined. But now when we're striving for more-better-faster, when we're learning to make decisions and needing their advice, our leaders are nowhere to be found. And we especially resent the times that they tell us we did something wrong without bothering to tell us what they wanted exactly.

With less and less supervision, with evaluations as much as six months apart, we are forced to find other ways to feel successful, seeking peer approval, trying to beat yesterday, judging ourselves according to scores, charts and graphs: "I got the only A." "I had the best time." "I scored second highest." We try to build up enough confidence to offset the failures and disappointments that are coming with our experiments. In the first phase we needed our leaders to acknowledge us. In the second phase we need our leaders' performance measures for us to acknowledge ourselves. Now we put our confidence in their measures.

Our leaders continue to give us independence unless we have an accident or our performance starts to drop. Then they take over, shifting us back into first again, watching everything we do, measuring our results more carefully and specifically until they see our performance come up again.

When I do seminars for corporations, I hear "war stories" about what happens if we don't do what we're told to do. These stories are the hobgoblins of fear and conformity. "His boss found out he wasn't following procedures and immediately fired him. It took him eighteen months to find a new job. And by the time he did, the mortgage company had foreclosed on his home."

Or, "He wasn't working fast enough so they transferred him to a department he really hated. But he had to stay in that job because he had a sick wife and four little children." To reinforce this punitive mythology even further, every once in a while, management makes an example, sacrificing an individual to keep everyone else in line.

Whether we experience such tactics directly or we hear about them through the grapevine, it's easy to decide we have to do what we're told. We have to avoid leader scrutiny at all costs, secretly knowing we've made changes ourselves, we've altered and improved things, no longer following procedures exactly ourselves. So asking fewer questions and volunteering fewer answers, we begin to keep quiet. Yes, we want our results to be noticed but our methods not to be noticed. We will use their systems correctly, interfacing appropriately with other teams and departments, but we want to choose our own methods. We assume that what they don't know won't hurt them—or us.

Listen to the secret confession of an entrenched second-phase employee. "When new employees come aboard, I tell them how the job ought to be done, but I never tell them the way I do it, lest I create a competitor, especially if I think there's a chance this one will be good."

So he sharpens his competitive edge, seeing everyone as a threat and no one as a teammate. It's every man and woman for himself or herself. In the second phase, competition rules and we constantly weigh quality against quantity. Second-phase customers always want more—more quantity, more quality, more service, more quickly. Marketing departments keep upping their expectations, but sometimes we're the last ones to know what they have promised.

But regardless of the cause, whether illness or injury, mismanagement or tragedy, any drop in our performance is seen as a failure. And satisfaction drops too. (Remember, *satisfaction* comes from the Latin, to do enough.)

We can't do any more, any better, any faster. We're up against a wall, nearing 100 percent efficiency, more and more effort producing less and less until we eventually break down from the accelerating effort and pace—or, we learn how to shift into third.

Filing your second-phase successes

Our second-phase successes are better scores, better times, greater quantities, higher qualities, more responsibilities, going faster and farther, doing more with less, winning prizes, meeting quotas, earning bonuses and promotions, doing better or best.

What second-phase successes have you produced in your life? What plaques, prizes and bonuses have you been able to earn? What scholarships and competitions have you won? Trips, mixers and microwaves? Dinners on the company? Increases in responsibility? Who have you outperformed? What standards have you exceeded? What charts have you topped? What quotas have you met?

When did you win your match at the gym? What positions have you served with the PTA, Scouts or Town Council? When did you win a prize for your gardening or cooking? When did you make your child the best Halloween costume? Or send the best cookies or cupcakes to school?

What have you done even more of, even better, even faster? What obstacles have you managed to overcome? Who tried to stop you but couldn't? What scarcities have you coped with? What breakdowns have you recovered from? What stresses and illnesses have you suffered and surmounted?

Which relationships are working better? Who are you spending more time with? Doing more things with? Communicating more fully with, understanding instructions better with? Arguing less with? Are you working out more these days? Or losing more weight? Or taking more vitamins? Are you writing more checks? Making more phone calls? Or seeing more movies or planting more begonias in the garden? These, and similar second-phase successes, belong in your success file.

Word cues to second-phase success

Here are some word cues that tell you when you are in the second phase of success: more-better-faster, win/lose, better/worse, more/less, competition, beat, overcome, effort, struggle, responsibility, hard work, secrets, explosion, ammunition, campaign, deadline, battle, burnout, bonuses, money, scores, charts, graphs, quotas, prizes, plaques, promotions, quantity, quality, stress, illness, disease, drugs.

Shifting into third: Succeeding at creating and leading

Effective, efficient, self-confident and decisive, we now shift our attention from learning skills to using them—creating solutions to problems we've noticed, discovering new methods for producing the same result, developing new systems, new products and services.

In the third phase we teach others what we've been learning, encouraging those who follow us to go even further. In the first and second phases, we succeeded as individuals by doing what others wanted us to do. In the third phase we succeed at doing what we want to do, choosing the dreams we want to complete—the jobs we want, the homes we want, the partners we want, the experiences we want to have.

In the third phase we assume responsibility for the creation of our lives. No longer needing to prove we can do it all by ourselves, we begin sharing our dreams with others and asking for assistance, respecting what others have learned, beginning to cooperate and succeed with a team.

New questions emerge: "What do I want to do with this skill?" "Where will I drive?" "What's the purpose of this scuba dive? Taking

49

pictures, recovering treasure or mapping a reef. Or asking myself what I'm going to write on my computer.

Third-phase driving

In the third phase, I drive to work thinking about the meeting I'm on my way to attend, calling to confirm other members are coming. Planning the rest of my day, reminding myself to stop to pick up Chinese food for dinner.

Third-phase scuba diving

In the third phase of scuba diving, having completed the advanced course, I decided to look for the rockfish I heard about when I first learned to dive. I selected my own team and we planned our own dive, talking about the outcomes we each had in mind and figuring out ways we all could be satisfied. It would be a night dive.

We left the dock one pitch-dark night without even a sliver of moon, moving through the channel out into open black seas. The engines stopped, and the captain dove to check our position over the wreck. It was good, the waters clear, the currents acceptable. So we began diving, mystically moving toward the light, heading steadily down, though down felt like up. It was so peaceful and calm that I understood how divers could forget about time and air, captivated by this serene narcotic beauty. In the area where the light shown, we all came together. Fish circled slowly around us as though they were sleepwalking. A rock wall, nothing special, passing it. Suddenly a rockfish swam out from it like a lizard in an Escher drawing, popping out three-dimensionally from the flat surface. We moved closer to inspect these "rocks," noticing their eyes and the details of their bodies. A mouray eel sprang out from the wall like a jack-in-the-box, retracting after warning us that this was his territory. Everywhere we looked there were fish, even a small shark eyed us from above. Time was up, and we signaled each other to begin the return to the surface.

Back on board, we realized all our procedures had been performed smoothly, easily and invisibly. We were no longer preoccupied with how and how well, we could now use diving to do what we wanted.

Third phase on the computer

Now at the computer I just sit there and think. My fingers take over and do all the rest. And I automatically stop and save every few minutes or sooner if the weather looks threatening. I no longer think about cutting and pasting, spelling and filing—I just do it. I no longer have to fumble through a manual—the skills are all mine. I know how to do it.

Filing your third-phase successes

Let's stop to file thousands of successes, most of which you probably haven't recognized as yours until now. In the third phase you can include in your success file the successes you've had in creating. And you can include the successes you've had in leading—your children, your students, your employees, your fellow citizens, multiplying satisfaction and fulfillment. It's certainly a lot easier to keep your success file full every day when you have lots of other people filling it up for you.

What new methods or new systems, what new products and new thinking have you shared with others? A new recipe, a new method of cutting the yard or cleaning the car? A new product or a different way to distribute it or market it? A new theory or perspective? What creative projects have you been working on? Have you been expressing yourself through painting or building, or through gardening or traveling? What future successes are you dreaming of now, alone or with others?

Word cues to third-phase success

Here are some word cues that tell you when you are in the third phase of success: respect, cooperation, communication, interest, compassion, caring, sensitivity, teamwork, mission, service, appropriateness, certainty, health, balance, holistic, healing, integrity, choice, parenting, teaching, managing, governing, leadership, creativity, confidence, satisfaction, fulfillment, flexibility, simplicity, ease. When you hear yourself using these words, you will know you are in the third phase of success.

When your success file is full, you feel success-full
When the success files of those you lead are full, you feel full-filled

What successes have your children had? In school, in fairs and productions, in athletics, in hobbies you've taught them? In their work? In their community? What successes has your mate had at work, in sports, in the community? Which of these successes are you the most proud of? Which ones inspire you the most?

What successes have your students had? In the first phase, when you were totally responsible for them? In the second phase, when they were learning to be responsible for themselves? What improvements have they made on what you taught them? What creative ideas and inventions have they contributed? What have they gone on to do in their lives? Are they now leaders—parenting, teaching, managing, or governing?

What successes have your employees had? Have they increased production, provided better service and faster results? Have they devised creative new ways of doing things, like working more closely with other departments, cross-training and developing more responsive organizations? How have you brought your team into greater alignment? What changes have you made? Which team members have you supported and encouraged especially?

What have you done to create a healthier society and a healthier environment? What have you done for children? For education? For the arts? For sports and recreation? What have you done to bring about better understanding between the peoples of one country and another? One industry and another? One culture or ethnicity and another? How have you contributed to a better life here on Earth?

Life, like success, has three phases too

In infancy and childhood we are in the first phase in all areas of life—in an immature body needing to be cared for. Whenever we want something, we have to count on someone else to do it until we can learn how. We have to trust them to be wise enough to teach us the things we are ready to do and to keep us away from the things that might hurt us.

In the second phase of life—adolescence and young adulthood—second-phase successes motivate our lives. Competition and productivity become our obsession. We don't want to follow leaders now, instead we avoid them, confident we know better than they do. We're hanging out with peers, hoping to get along but needing to outdo them.

In the third phase of life—our mature adult years—we finally have the opportunity for satisfaction and fulfillment. Cooperative and creative, we enter the world of wanting and dreaming. Skillful and experienced, we begin creating solutions for ourselves and our planet, developing teams and helping them flourish, nurturing inventions, new methods and technologies. And finally allowing those who have led us, our parents and teachers and managers and leaders, to harvest the fruit of all their tending and tilling.

On the way to our dreams, we shift from one phase to the other, shifting into whichever one is appropriate—up-shifting and down-shifting as needed. We recognize the feel of each phase, each phase's timing and use.

But no matter what age we are, we can create and lead in all phases of our lives, not simply waiting until we reach the third phase of life. We can start to build our third-phase abilities even before starting school. First we learn to color in the lines. Second, we win stars for coloring better. Third, we go on to use our coloring skills to express the way we feel about a hurricane. First, we learn to ride a bike with our parents holding us up. Second, we ride around the neighborhood with friends. Third, we plan a bike trip for the family. Even a two-year-old can bang on a pot with a spoon and then show a little sister how to do it. Or a first-grader can play with clay and lean over to a friend and explain that fat legs on clay elephants make them stand better.

When I was a child, there was a special desk in the hall outside my classroom where I was regularly sent to sit. I was too curious for my over-worked first-grade teacher, asked too many questions, was too eager to share what I was discovering with others. And so I was banished until, "You can come back and obey." And I've met many thousands of bright employees whose overworked bosses punished their suggestions, restricted their interest in why and how, ignored their suggestions for far better methods than the ones they were using.

The first phase of almost everything

Ideally, we learn one skill at a time, mastering that one before going on to another. But it doesn't always work out that way. When my daughter Margaret was in the first year of her radiology residency, she was simultaneously in the first year of her marriage, her first year in Miami, and her first year at a new hospital. Suddenly she began to feel frightened and uncertain. The confidence and security she had felt in medical school while she was single in Richmond, stood in sharp contrast to the way she felt now. And she began to question everything in her life—her choices, her marriage, her career—believing something was drastically wrong. Even when she did something as simple as buying clothes, she would second-guess her decision and end up returning them.

She had not anticipated what it would feel like to be a third-phase adult down-shifting to the first phase of almost everything in life. But as she moved into the second phase of almost everything, her confidence rebounded, her decisions looked better. Her marriage felt good again. Her residency became the opportunity she had wanted. And Miami transformed into a great place to live.

My grandmother, the gourmet, could down-shift to teach

Most of us know how to cook successfully—in one phase or another. We can follow a recipe or microwave a dinner. We can improvise and experiment, adding this or that. Or we can turn out a meal with an aroma that calls the guests.

Gourmets are third phase. They break beginners' rules, not measuring ingredients, not following recipes, not doing the same things over and over. They know that they know how to cook.

My grandmother was a gourmet. She cooked in pinches and handfuls. She had a real feel for it. If the flour was too dry she knew what to add. If the eggs were too large she knew what to cut. I was taking seventh-grade home economics, and I wanted to learn to cook exactly the way she did. But when I tried using pinches and handfuls, I failed every time. I didn't have her instincts for which eggs and which flours.

I got upset with my grandmother and the methods she used. "You don't know how to cook right," I told her. "You don't even measure." And she chuckled to herself, inviting me back to cook again the next day.

This time I watched as she felt her ingredients, picking up a proper handful and putting it in my cup. Then she told me to measure it. Ingredient by ingredient, step by step, I wrote down her recipe and learned how to follow it. She was delighted when my cakes turned out right. She said someday I'd be the better cook. And that seemed to be exactly what she hoped for. But not understanding the ways of gourmets, I gave her my recipe and insisted she use it.

A generation later when my daughters learned to cook, I laughed to myself when I realized that I too was cooking in pinches and handfuls, sensing and knowing each and every ingredient. And I heard my grandmother's chuckle again. She had known how to cook. In fact she had known so much about it that she'd gone past the phase of needing to use recipes. She had gone past the phase of measuring precisely. She had arrived at the phase where she just knew how to do it. I used to tell my daughters and their friends when they sat down to eat, "Enjoy this meal, my dears, because I'll never make it exactly this way again."

We need to lead differently to develop "gourmets"

We need to lead others not just to follow, not just to do more and more-better-faster, but we need to encourage them to go past what's known, to adventure into the dreamt about and teach others how to journey there.

We need to parent differently to develop "gourmets," encouraging them to move past first-phase compliance, past second-phase competitiveness, all the way into third-phase creativity and leadership.

We need to teach differently to develop "gourmets," encouraging them to move past sticking to the book, past obeying outmoded rules, past working for grades into third-phase expression, into dreaming, inventing and leading.

We need to manage differently to develop "gourmets," giving them independence as soon as they're ready, letting them break beginners' rules, committing them to outcomes and freeing them from methods.

We need to govern differently to develop "gourmets," allowing those who perform safely and correctly more independence, more access to support and expertise, giving third-phase citizens the freedom to create new ways of living happy, healthy lives here on Earth.

With our world changing as rapidly as it is, we need to aim early for third-phase successes, no longer preferentially rewarding recipe-followers or cutthroat competitors, but rewarding early creativity as well, celebrating each sign that the seeds of the future, theirs and ours, are coming up.

The choice of the leader: Throwing up a dreamer's hook

In the third phase we have three choices about how to make decisions. First, we can compare what we're considering doing with what didn't work in the past, telling ourselves we shouldn't do those things again. Second, we can compare what we are considering doing with what did work in the past, with the successes we have on file, telling ourselves we should do those things again.

Or we can use a third choice—the choice of the leader. We can compare what we're considering doing with the successes we want in the future, throwing a dreamer's hook up high on a mountain, then anchoring it in firmly and pulling ourselves up to it. We can fill our success file full of future successes, experiencing ourselves as already there, feeling the excitement, the fulfillment and the pleasure these successes are giving us. And once we've added future successes to our success file, our inner computer will bring them to mind whenever something seems similar, motivating and inspiring us to take action in that direction.

When we were little, our parents used to say, "Look both ways before crossing the street." This is also good advice for when we're making decisions. "Look to the past and look to the future." Think about what happened before, noticing especially all the things we learned since then, noticing especially the skills we've developed, the expertise we now have available. Look to the past, then look to the future—to the successes we want.

The third choice, the choice of filing future successes, frees us from the past, hooking us to our future and allowing us to steadily pull ourselves up as individuals, as organizations, as a nation and a world. Allowing future successes to give us the confidence and motivation we will need to get there.

Finally understanding the elusive nature of success

Success has been elusive because we didn't know what we wanted, having gotten in the habit of pleasing other people, doing what they wanted, "pleasing" various systems, grades, scores and graphs. The question we asked ourselves in the first and second phases was, "What do they want?"

Finally as we shift to third, we begin asking ourselves the most important question of our lives. "What do I want?" And we begin to get answers, usually different answers than the ones we got when we were trying to please others— parents, teachers, bosses, mates—different answers than when we were trying to satisfy quotas and raise salaries.

Our dreams begin to change. They get clearer and more exciting. Our energy comes up. Our enthusiasm is on the rise. We feel more alive and well than we've ever felt before, a little scared perhaps, but very much in charge. The key question— "What do I want?"—allows us to begin doing things that make our hearts dance. Things that make our minds sing, our bodies feel young again. The people we begin choosing are a different sort of people, people who are also asking themselves the same question, people who have moved past competition, past effort and struggle, having shifted into the third phase of relating as well, wanting to be true to who they really are, to be healthy and happy. And wanting us to be true to who we are too, no longer prostituting ourselves to be in charge, to be independent or best, but committed instead to balancing our lives. Committed to making our unique contribution on Earth.

We need to know two points to navigate—where we are and where we want to be—whether we're charting our course on a sailboat or deep underwater or plotting our way toward success. By recognizing the success phase that we're in, we identify our current location. Once we know that, we can begin to dream our destination, eager and excited, setting our sights, sounds and feelings in tune with that reality, correcting as needed when the winds change direction, when the tides run full and heavy with the moon, when sandbars and obstacles unexpectedly impede our way. And we can replot and rechart, holding our destination clearly in mind.

Success has been elusive until now because we didn't understand the whole process of success. We didn't know we needed to file and save our successes. We didn't know success was continuously shifting and changing, and we couldn't recognize our own successes even when we looked for them. And we had unrealistic expectations that made success unattainable, expecting instantly to be able to do what our teachers could do, not realizing they had already shifted through first and second and were now operating in third.

We have judged ourselves harshly when we felt afraid and doubtful, dependent and needy. And because of these feelings, we sometimes decided we just weren't cut out for a particular skill, job or relationship, quitting the success process entirely and giving up what we wanted— instead of stopping to reassure ourselves these feelings were a natural part of it. Many of us have become afraid of the first phase, wanting to avoid the feelings of stupidity and ignorance that come up in us, uncomfortable with resurfacing childhood fears and doubts about leaders, preferring to keep on doing what we've been doing and so missing the opportunity to be a creator in life, a contributor in society.

Understanding the three phases of success will allow us to venture forth more skillfully and confidently now as mature adults. Knowing if the leader we are following isn't meeting our needs, we can find another leader. Knowing if we can't find another leader, we can lead ourselves.

Possibilities emerge in the third phase of success

Entering the third phase, we begin dreaming again, big potent dreams like the ones we used to dream as little children, dreams about the future, how we'll change this and invent that, thinking about the experiences we want for ourselves, our children, employees and customers, for everyone on Earth. Dreaming about new products and services and technologies, new health and new joy.

Now we are led by our dreams, relying on them instead of on our leaders. Is this on the way to where I'd like to be? We compare each step we take with our goals and destinations, recognizing each success we have along the way. Self-acknowledgment is the key to third-phase success.

When we begin our lives we learn from our parents. When we master our lives, we learn from everyone we meet and everything we do. We know what we know and we know what we don't know, and knowing all that gives us a new sense of certainty, allowing us to use others' expertise. Allowing us to use the wisdom all around us. Allowing everyone to show us the way, learning from their example, from seeing them do what they dreamed they would do.

The shifting responsibilities of a leader

Our first responsibility as a leader is to create an attractive dream, to proclaim a destination, communicating it in detail to others who might be interested in joining our expedition. When we've chosen our team and they have chosen back, then we have to down-shift to get our dream started, teaching each other basic skills, sharing rules and requirements, understanding fears, needs and doubts we all have, and filing our successes to build up team confidence and team spirit.

Getting a project started is like moving a ship. It takes a lot of energy to build up momentum. Sometimes we get impatient with those still in first phase, those who don't seem to be moving yet when we've already shifted into second and third, wanting to move ahead more quickly than they're able to, annoyed with their questions, their anxieties and fears. Sometimes we get stuck in second or third, unable to shift back to know what they need from us.

When we're impatient with beginners around us, we would do well to sign up for a class in scuba diving, ballroom dancing or anything else totally brand-new for us. Then we will feel the child within us, stepping to the forefront, to control our bodies and minds—scared and frightened when there's no one beside us to tell us what to do and how to do it. Then in the first phase again, we need to listen carefully to our own questions: "Is this right? Can I do that? What's wrong? Will you help me? Are you sure that I'm ready?" And having geared back to first, we'll be able to understand their needs and figure out ways to support them.

**What we mean by success
keeps changing.
What we have to do to succeed and
lead keeps changing too.**

The Third Success Skill

HOLOGRAMMING

What we think is what we get— like it or not

Scientists are now teaching us the science of wishing and dreaming, having discovered that, in actuality, dreams do come true. Have you ever wondered why some people get what they want time after time, while others never do?

Some people are doing a different sort of dreaming, consciously or unconsciously using a method I call hologramming that increases their chances of getting what they want. Hologramming is a way to make plans and dreams much more powerful, increasing the probability of their coming into reality.

Brain research indicates that thoughts are quite literally attractive, even measurably magnetic. Thoughts generate an electro-magnetic force field that attracts to us the things we think about. The more detailed the thought, the more power it has. If we use this attractive force field properly, it can increase the probability of getting what we want. But if we use it carelessly, this same force field can increase the probability of getting what we dread. Now creation is a learnable skill.

Adults who had their dreams consistently squashed as children, adults who have been disappointed over and over, often try to ward off further pain by giving up on dreaming, not wanting to risk feeling disappointed again. Not realizing that when they begin to limit their dreaming, they begin to limit their success too.

Physicians are discovering that "wanting" is essential to good health. Surgeons in my seminars told me about patients, going in for surgery with next-to-no chance of survival, who pulled through miraculously because they had something to live for—seeing their daughter graduate from college, holding their first grandchild, moving into the home they had dreamed of for years. And they lived to experience what they had wanted so much. Then those same surgeons told me about very depressed patients who, in for minor surgeries, died on the table. They seemed to have given up on dreaming—and living.

What is a hologram?

Holograms are three-dimensional images created by using two or more laser beams. Dennis Gabor was awarded the Nobel Prize in 1971 for his work with holograms. Most of us have seen them at Disney World, in science museums or on credit cards.

There are two types of holograms. Some holograms appear as flat images that swell in or out three dimensionally. Other holograms appear as images projected volumetrically in space, like crew members beamed up on *Star Trek*, or R2D2's hologram of Princess Leia pleading for galactic assistance in *Star Wars*.

A participant in one of my seminars waved at me frantically as I talked about holograms. He was eager to share an experience he'd had at a World's Fair. Sitting cross-legged at a campfire he listened to a Native American talk about the Indians of the Northwest. His family was descended from the tribe being discussed so he was eager to ask questions. He waited while the rest of the crowd left and then headed toward the Indian. But as he reached out to shake hands, the Indian vanished in front of his eyes. He was dumbfounded until he heard a closing announcement, "The Indian was presented courtesy of a holographic projection."

The negative of a holographic image is quite different from a regular photographic negative. If we cut a regular negative into sixteen pieces and project one of those pieces, then we will see one-sixteenth of the picture. The other fifteen-sixteenths of the image will be missing. But if we cut up a holographic negative and project one-sixteenth of it, we still see the whole picture—the whole but less clearly. As we project more and more parts of the hologram, we see the whole picture more and more clearly. Holograms are quite literally whole-o-grams.[3]

The Einstein of brain research: Holographic brain theory

Dr. Karl Pribram, a neurosurgeon/physiologist at Stanford University and Nobel nominee, has been called "the Einstein of brain research." After the Korean War, Pribram began re-examining brain theory. Existing ideas about how the brain stores and accesses information were refuted by findings made while treating brain-injured soldiers. The old brain theorists had mapped the brain into parts. They assumed memory was stored the way it is on a regular photographic negative. If one part was destroyed, then the corresponding part of memory would also be destroyed. But it wasn't. These soldiers were remembering things and doing things they shouldn't have been able to do.[4]

Instead Pribram proposed that memory is recorded holographically, recorded as a whole in each cell. When many cells are destroyed the memories remain but are re-experienced less clearly and easily. According to Pribram, the hologram is a model of how visual and sensory information is received, stored and recalled by the brain.[5]

Holograms are created using two or more laser beams. Holographic brain recordings are created by two or more laser-like inputs from our senses—seeing, hearing, feeling, tasting, smelling, touching or doing. These holographic recordings of events we've experienced constitute memory. Under hypnosis we can access memories we can't remember otherwise. The recordings are all there, in living color and sound, complete with all the things we've felt, and all the things we've done. Our memory gives us access—consciously or unconsciously—to everything that we've ever experienced.

Telling time: The perspective system of the brain

Our brain has its own holographic perspective. Unconsciously we know when something happened a long time ago by the quality of the stored hologram. Holograms that appear smaller and dimmer, signal that the memory was recorded a long time ago. Holograms that appear larger and brighter are interpreted as having been recorded more recently. This gives us our sense of time.

As the brain ages or degenerates, the ability to record is often reduced. Then poorly recorded recent memories appear dim and faded. While the old memories seem as clear as a bell. I knew an old woman who was totally disoriented in the present, not remembering breakfast or what she had just said. But it was wonderful to talk to her about fifty years ago. She could tell me all about her holograms from childhood—the clothes she wore, the foods her family ate, the rooms she lived in. I cooperated with her memory and we thoroughly enjoyed journeying through her past.

Comparing holograms so we can decide what to do now

As we think, we are constantly accessing and re-experiencing holographic recordings. Whenever we sense something new, we instantly and unconsciously begin searching and comparing what's coming through our senses with what's stored in memory. What does this look like? What does this sound like? What does this feel like? What does the same things? Using all our senses, we analyze and match so we know what to do now.

My daughter Cathy was preparing to assist with a hip replacement surgery. The doctor briefed her on the patient's condition. Cathy gasped when the doctor mentioned the patient's name. Where was he from? Miami Beach. What was his age? Sixty-three. What was his wife's name? And all the answers matched, so she concluded the patient must be her uncle. The doctor called the patient to say his niece would there for the surgery. The patient was delighted. Cathy called her cousin to let him know his father was in the hospital.

Her cousin called the patient. The same name, the same age, the same city, the same wife's name, a niece who did the same work, but the similarities ended there. The patient was not his father. The son knew it as soon as he heard his voice. The voices didn't match.

We can also holographically record future events seen with our inner eyes, talked over in our minds, anticipated and savored in our daydreams. We can build holograms of whatever we want—even if it has never existed, even if no one's been able to do it, even if everyone agrees it's impossible.

But what was impossible ultimately can be. We are the designers and the architects of the future, creating blueprints in our minds. Sitting on our bed or standing by the ocean, we imagine we are there, doing it, being it, having and enjoying it. Knowing the end in advance allows us to move past the scariness of the beginning and the struggles in the middle.

Remember the day you first learned how to drive, when you took the keys in your hand and slid in behind the wheel, eagerly steering and turning, imagining you were a skilled driver already. You were hologramming then, attracting the experiences you now have every day.

The more detailed the hologram is, the more charge it has

Dr. Pribram goes further in his research. Some thoughts, he said, are more powerful than others. To create powerful thoughts we must think in great detail and involve all the senses. We need to see those thoughts, hear them, feel them, even taste them and smell them. Our thoughts and their generated force fields provide the steering mechanism of our lives.[4]

When we wish for something, we begin to attract it by dreaming it completely in advance—the actual scene, full of sound and feeling, with full sensory palette, all the colors and textures, the tints and shades, all the sounds and pitches, the volumes and tones. All the feelings and sensations we want to include. We become artists mentally sketching and then painting in the details—each rich color, each subtle feeling we want in the finished experience.

We are also the sound men, mixing the narration and music, allowing sounds to swell and fade, creating the sound track of the experience we want. We feel the feelings in advance. Proud. Happy. Enthusiastic. Teary-eyed, remembering all the times it seemed impossible along the way, all the times there wasn't enough time, money or skill. The moments when we didn't have the foggiest idea how to do it but we still held onto our dream, held fast to our hologram. Methods will come later, but first we need to focus on creating and energizing the force field that will attract us to what we want. We don't have to do it all by ourselves. We can hire experts to do what we want them to do.

Many people decided long ago to stop dreaming, hoping to avoid the painful differences between what they wanted and what they got.

65

Constant disappointments, caused by rejection and negativity, drug and alcohol abuse, illness and calamity became more and more intolerable. Gradually they began to tone down their holograms, imagining their futures would look pretty much like their pasts. Imagining what they thought they would get instead of what they wanted, becoming "realistic" instead of being creative.

They can't imagine getting what they want anymore. They can't even tell themselves they'll be able to get it. Their dreams have become sketchier and sketchier. Imagined colors have dulled, details have disappeared and blurred. The sound tracks and their rhythms have slowed and become threatening. They've stopped anticipating and looking forward. Their dreams have lost power, but their dreads have become much more powerful and magnetic.

The Reticular Activating System: The "Razz"

Once we have chosen the way we want to go, another part of our brain helps us stay on course, alerting us to take action. The reticular activating system is part of the brain stem—a bundle of nerve fibers about the size of a little finger, connected to the eyeball. When we think back over holograms we have three ways of searching for the information we want—we can look back over it, we can listen back over it, or we can feel back over it.

Research says our eyes act as a switch. When our eyes automatically move up to one side or the other or, we stare straight ahead, then we are "seeing" the data we access. When our eyes move from ear to ear, we are "hearing" the data we access. When our eyes move down to the right, we are "feeling" that data, remembering the actions we took and how we felt then—or anticipating our dreams and how we'll feel then.

The Razz alerts us when what's coming through our senses matches a future hologram, alerting us when something's incomplete, letting us know when to take action, assisting us in completing our dreams. If we've told ourselves we'll get toothpaste the next time we go food shopping, then when we're in that aisle, toothpaste will pop into mind. "Oh, yes, toothpaste. I need to get toothpaste." The Razz may even wake us up in the night when we didn't do what we said we'd do. Most of us have found ourselves suddenly awake in bed thinking, "I was supposed to but I didn't." That was "the Razz" working toward completion.[6]

If we take time to holographically program our outcomes, to see what we want, to tell ourselves and others what we want, to feel what we want, to even smell and taste it, then the reticular activating system will assist us in seizing opportunities for success we might otherwise miss.

The black plastic flower pot

Early one morning I was sitting on my balcony planning my day when I noticed the flower pot my lady palm was in had a huge split in it and couldn't hold water. Summer was coming. The lady palm would die without water. I would be passing a hardware store on the way to my meeting, so I measured the pot to know what size to buy.

My list was complete so I went down the elevator out onto Brickell Avenue. I loved jogging along the bay at sunrise. But this morning I noticed a lot of trash on the bay. Mumbling to myself about the whole human race, I continued to run. Then looking at the bay again I noticed something more. Floating among all that trash was a black plastic flower pot. I looked at it carefully and it seemed to be the exact size I needed.

I couldn't quite reach it by leaning out over the seawall. But when I looked behind me, there was a large palm frond lying on the ground. That frond would be the perfect tool for fishing my pot out. The pot looked brand new and it was just the right size. Chuckling to myself, I walked the rest of the way home with my black plastic flower pot tucked under my arm.

Then I thought back over what had just happened. The first time I looked at the bay, all I had seen there was trash, a lot of stuff floating. If I hadn't had a hologram, if I hadn't known that I wanted a flower pot exactly that size, I would never have noticed it. I would have driven to the store and paid them my money, missing the opportunity to get it more easily.

Nothing but sticks

We can look into our future and dream elaborately the life we want, living in our dream until we can build it. I bought my huge run-down old house. As I walked into it, I saw past what was there to my dream. I saw a pond in the center of the house. I saw palm trees and waterfalls. I saw bright-colored fish meandering among water lilies in bloom. I saw huge lush bananas and heliconias, low-sprawling rocks with crevices filled with mosses. I bought that dream. I bought that house. And I lived in my dream while I renovated my house.

The people who came to see me couldn't understand my love affair with my house. They saw it as it was, while I was seeing it as it would be. For a moment one day, I could see what they saw. Out front, I had put in a row of what would be huge variegated green plants. They would be high, wide and wild. They would shield my house from the street, giving me privacy. I had stripped all the leaves off the branches to force them to grow roots and put out new leaves. In that moment, talking with my neighbor, I looked through my dream back into my present. And I saw—sticks. A long row of sticks. I started laughing and laughing and laughing and crying. No wonder my friends were reacting the way they were to my house. That was all there was—a row of sticks. The rest of it, all the leaves, the variegated patterns, the richness and the fullness, was growing in my mind.

It took two years before the sticks blossomed into my luxurious foliage shield. The pond shimmered with bright-colored fish and the waterfall played its timeless melody. Until the bananas were heavy with sweet golden fruit hanging in bunches. Until heliconias sketched over the details of the wall, blurring out the neighbors and fusing me into the tropics. The world of my dreams had become real. And finally everyone could see the dream I had bought.

What we think is what we get—like it or not

We can create the life we don't want, blaming others and complaining bitterly about what fate has so cruelly imposed on us.

Let's try an experiment. Follow these instructions: Don't think about a hot fudge sundae. Don't think about that warm rich chocolate melting over two scoops of your favorite kind of ice cream. Don't think about the large spoonful of whipped cream just prepared in the kitchen. Don't think about a generous scoop of walnuts in delicious maple syrup. Don't think about a cherry on top, with its stem still attached. Some of us are salivating now, planning to get up and go to the kitchen.

Despite the fact that we were told not to think about it, we did. That's because we have a Positive Command Brain.[7] To understand what's being said, first we take the "not" out of the sentence. We understand it as a positive statement—think about a hot fudge sundae. Then we consider the "not," and we go back and insert "not" creating resistance to doing it. This is the thought, but don't do it. Awakened in the night, we hear the caller say, "Don't worry. Nothing's wrong." And we immediately begin worrying, wondering what's wrong.

My mother was a master misuser of the Positive Command Brain. She knew how much I loved eating chocolate pudding as it got thick on the top cooling in the refrigerator. She knew she could count on me to stick my finger in and scoop off the thick part. She unknowingly was the very one who advised me when to do it. Even if I didn't know that she'd made chocolate pudding, even if I hadn't seen it cooling already, she'd come out from the kitchen and point her finger right at me. "Susan, don't you dare mess up that pudding that's cooling for dinner."

Don't play with matches

Unfortunately some of our Positive Command errors are not quite so innocent, causing much greater damage than just an ugly pudding. A sales manager at Kimberly-Clark told me a story that tragically reinforces the attractive force field of a negative hologram—like it or not. He and his wife had a babysitter for their six-year-old son just before my seminar in Atlanta. As they were leaving home he heard his wife tell their son not to play with matches while they were out. She made him promise he wouldn't. That was a peculiar thing for her to do because their son was afraid of matches, he'd never even lit one. But they were late to meet friends for dinner and the father didn't say anything.

As they drove away he asked why in the world she would say that. She said she had seen a TV show that afternoon about children setting fires while staying with sitters. She was frightened by what she'd seen. It stuck in her mind and she kept seeing it over and over. She felt she had to say something to her son. Her husband understood.

When they returned home, they found fire trucks on their lawn. Their son had followed her Positive Command. He had played with matches. He'd set fire to the drapes. They rushed to the hospital where he was being treated for serious burns.

Good intentions must be communicated correctly

In the first phase of learning we developed a habit of giving many negative instructions to children, to students, to employees, to citizens. I don't want you to. Don't ever. You can't. Thou shalt not. Don't drink and drive. Don't do drugs.

As leaders, are we inadvertently creating the very thing we don't want by the instructions we give them right from the start? Yes, we certainly are. Our language is based on holograms. We see it, hear it and feel it—in order to understand it. And when we see it, hear it and feel it, we begin to create it unless we are monitoring our thinking and switching when we notice it.

The Catholic Church understood this when they made it a sin to be thinking about sinning. They wanted to prevent the inexperienced programmer from getting caught in this trap. As parents, as teachers, as managers, as those governing, we need to be skillful hologrammers aware of the Positive Command Brain. Aware of what we are programming on TV, in movies, in the instructions we give.

The little boy in the bathroom story

During a seminar for customer-service supervisors at Florida Power and Light, we were talking about the Positive Command Brain. One of the participants wanted to get input on a problem he and his wife were having with their six-year-old son. He thought it might be relevant. He and his wife were worried about their child. They thought he might have a learning disability. His teacher was concerned too. I asked him to be more specific about the problem.

"What exactly does your son do? Give me an example."

"Well, every night before bed, we make him take a shower. He does the same dumb things over and over. He leaves the wet towels in a pile in the middle of the floor. He leaves the shower curtain hanging outside the tub so the water pours out all over the floor. A few months ago we had our dining room ceiling replaced because water had poured down through the plaster. Then he leaves the soap afloat in the tub, melting into a thick sticky goo. We go through a bar of soap every couple of days."

"What do you and your wife do when your son does all of this?"

"Well it goes pretty much the same way every single night. First we get mad. We just can't believe he's that stupid. We can't believe he does the same dumb things over and over. And that's what we say to him. "We can't believe you're so stupid. You must really be slow. How many times have we told you not to leave the curtain out? Then we see the pile of towels and we yell about that too. It's really frustrating and then the soap is the topper. He starts crying when we yell and then we send him to bed. Do you think our son is retarded?"

"Well, I have good news and bad." I said. "The good news is that based on what you've said, I see no reason to think that your son is retarded. The bad news is that you and your wife have been responsible for creating the problem he has. Remember the Positive Command Brain? Think about the instructions you've given him. He has done exactly what you told him to do, if you just take the 'not' out of each and every sentence.

I asked the group what they thought this father could do to begin leading his son to success. We hologrammed together. We suggested he start by having a meeting with his son, telling him he had learned some new things in a course he was taking at work. Telling his son he was sorry and explaining that he understood now that he had caused the problem. We suggested he tell his son that he wanted to start over, doing it right together this time. They suggested he tell his son that he loves him. That he's smart, so smart in fact, that he had been doing exactly what they had been telling him to do all along—except for the "not." From now on, he should promise that he would tell him what he wanted instead of what he didn't want. Things would be a whole lot easier.

The next day we were all eager to hear about his meeting with his son. "It was amazing," he said. "I told him I wanted to teach him how to take care of the bathroom. I said I was sorry that I had forgotten to teach him all that in the first place, but I'd be happy to do it right now if he'd let me. I was sure he would be able to do it perfectly from now on. First I showed him how to use a shower curtain. Turning the water on, I pulled the shower curtain inside the tub and turned the shower head in the direction of the curtain. The water ran right down the curtain to the drain. "Did you see that?" "Yes, Dad I did." OK, next I lifted the shower curtain outside the tub and turned on the water. The water ran down the curtain right onto the floor. He quickly pushed the curtain inside the tub.

"Good, you've got it, son. You're a very quick learner. My son was beginning to breathe normally again. He had looked very scared at first. Anything to do with the bathroom had certainly become traumatic. But he understood the shower curtain perfectly now, he was smiling and proud. He was glad to be finally doing things right.

"Next I took a towel down and told my son he could choose between two ways of folding it. I'll teach you both methods and help you practice them until they are both easy for you. First there's the one-fold method." I laid the towel on the floor and folded it down the middle very neatly. Then I picked it up and carefully carried it to the towel bar, putting it over the bar, pulling it down and evening out the edges. My son was nodding yes. He understood how to do it. He laid the towel down folding it neatly along the middle, carried it over to the towel bar, pulled it down and evened out the edges. He could do it perfectly. His confidence was growing.

"Now the second method. I laid the towel on the floor again. This time I folded it twice, one-third and one-third. This I called the two-fold method. He was delighted with this method, liking it even better. He did it easily and quickly. We were both smiling.

"Now there's only one thing left—taking care of the soap. How about this? Could you figure out a way to have one bar of soap last for a week if I took you out for ice cream when you succeeded in doing it?"

"I sure could. And if it lasted two weeks, would you get me two cones?"

"I sure will provided you still manage to get clean."

"OK, Dad. Then take me out to buy a soap holder with the points on the top and the points on the bottom. I'll use it to keep the soap very dry."

"OK, good idea. Let's go get it.

"Then my son started crying and I got worried."

"What's wrong, son?"

"I thought you didn't love me, Dad. You always said I was stupid. You said I couldn't do anything right. I'm a good boy, aren't I, Dad?"

"Yes son. "

"I love you Dad."

"I love you too, son. You're a very smart boy. You're a very good boy.

"I put my arms around him. We hugged each other hard. We both felt a lot better."

"Let's go get your soap holder now."

We were all weeping. His story had touched us. We spent hours talking about how supervisors could use these same understandings in supervising their teams. The father said this experience would help him a lot, he had been doing the same things with his employees he had been doing with his son.

Creating objections

Salespeople often unknowingly create the very objections they then have to work hard to overcome. How do they do that? By misusing the Positive Command Brain. When completing the sale, the salesman starts closing, wanting to reassure his customer, he says, "I don't think there'll be any problem getting this delivered in time. "

"What? It won't be on time. I can't take a chance on that. I'm going somewhere else."

"No, No. I didn't say it would be late. You misunderstood me."

But he didn't misunderstand. He had paid attention to the hologram, to what he had shown him, to what he had told him, to what he had felt. He wanted his merchandise to be delivered on time. Who created the customer's objection? Yes, the salesman had inadvertently put doubt in his customer's mind. If he had wanted to reassure his customer, he could have said, "I know you'll be delighted when all your furniture is in place in plenty of time for a wonderful party. I look forward to hearing how much your guests liked the new room."

If we don't know what we want, we'll probably get what somebody else wants

We live in a marketing world. Everybody is selling products. Everybody is selling ideas. If we don't take the time to build the holograms we want, detailed the way we want them to be, then others will fill in those blanks for us. And later we'll wonder how we got what we got, and why in the world we ever went along with them. We will blame them for pressuring us, but it was really our own pressure that pushed us to agree with them—the pressure creation creates. We didn't know what we wanted in that moment and their hologram seemed clear to us. Their arguments sounded so convincing to us. Their thinking was so detailed and so multi-sensory and so powerful and our thinking wasn't. So we decided in that moment to use their well-constructed hologram. Their thinking became our thinking, at least during the time we were both standing there.

We are the architects and designers of our dreams. The job we have, we holo-grammed. The home we live in, we hologrammed. The car we drive, we holo-grammed. Or someone else hologrammed and sold us their hologram. When we decide we are going to buy a certain model of car, then we start noticing that car everywhere we go.

That hologram is so powerful to us then, it sounds so good to us then, it is so well programmed in our Razz, that we notice it over and over and over. We don't notice equally other cars on the road. Our attention is riveted on that particular model, that color, that style. We want it. We are attracted to it. If our sound track agrees, if our energy agrees, if our budget agrees, if everything else lines up with that picture, then we have the energy to go out and buy it. And instead of being our dream, it becomes our reality.

It's not my bag

Sometimes we settle for things that aren't what we want. Maybe we think it's close enough. Maybe we're afraid there won't be another one.

Maybe we just want something now, something to fill our need, to reduce the creative tension. Maybe we're in a hurry and we aren't paying attention.

A director at American Express traveled at lot in his work. He had been in and out of airports all day. He was particularly tired after delays and bad weather. He stood exhausted, waiting for his luggage, eager to get home. The sound of the conveyor belt lurched on, the baggage was coming. And there was his suitcase. He grabbed it and ran for a cab.

Arriving home he wanted to shave. Reaching in the suitcase, he pulled out someone else's shaving kit. Opening the suitcase he saw someone else's clothes. Then he had to call the airline to report his error and he ended up waiting until the next day to get his bag.

Sometimes we accept something much too quickly—jobs, relationships, purchases—without matching holograms completely. And after we've committed to it, after we've said yes, after we've sold our home, after we've moved, after we've begun work with our new team, then we figure out it wasn't our bag. Then it's not so easy to return.

We need to examine what we take carefully, looking for identifying tags, unique scrapes and nicks, using all our senses to decide if this is exactly what we had in mind. And if it's not, we need to let it go past us—saying no—and waiting for the conveyor belt of life to bring along the reality we want.

When we can choose from our past and our future, we can steer our own course, no longer anchored to our past, held back by the things we were taught to do, by the things we can never get past. Now we can throw anchors out toward the future, allowing us to pull ourselves forward. We can search our memories, choosing among methods we've recorded, ones used by our parents, teachers, managers and friends, choosing to use one of their methods again.

Or we can search the holograms of our future, the outcomes we want, the things we are looking forward to, listening forward to, wanting to feel and do—choosing the methods we know or choosing to use experts.

When we can think backwards and forwards, we have access to the best of both worlds. We can use the wisdom of our past without getting stuck in it, and we can use our dreams of the future to pull us, to attract us, to magnetize us to the realities of the world that we want.

My three Bernies

In my life there have been three Bernies—Bernie the doctor, Bernie the lawyer and Bernie the communicator. I shared more with my third Bernie than anyone before him, but the one thing I could never do, that became the most important thing I ever wanted to do, was to dream with him, and, together, make those dreams come true. My beloved Bernie was married to another set of dreams, tending another crop and enjoying that harvest. And he didn't want to let go of it. So, with great regret, I let go of wanting to dream dreams with him.

Love is like a plant needing to be continually watered and fed. Honest communications are their water, but their food is the completion of dreams. Without food and water, the love stays but the relationship withers and starves.

Life is a journey. Many people come aboard our ship, sailing for the moment along the same course, completing the same dreams, arriving at the same port. But then when we get ready to set out again, when we start to chart and plot the next course, they become restless and resistant to going further, needing to move in a different direction, needing to find a different inner answer. And, with tears in our eyes and heaviness in our hearts, we wish them farewell, loving them enough to send them on their way to wherever they need to go, knowing that if we keep them with us, if we prevent them from climbing the mountain their heart is hooked onto, we will become not their lovers, but their keepers and restricters.

"What do I want?" becomes our centering device, the compass that guides us in the direction we need to go. By asking others to ask themselves that question, we are finally able to know who they really are, discovering their special gifts, their uniquenesses and talents, instead of asking the usual homogenized questions like "How are you today?" or "How are you feeling?" And getting the usual homogenized answers, "Good" and "Fine."

"What do I want?" is the dream maker. Asking that question, over and over, day in and day out, will lead us to the most precious successes of all—the successes we really want.

Getting the impossible

We have all had the experience of getting what others think is impossible. When we think back, we were sure in our minds it was possible. We saw it happening time after time, we told ourselves we would get it over and over. We were excited and enthusiastic whenever we thought of it. We took all the actions we needed to take.

And we got what we wanted. Even though they had told us over and over it was impossible. Even though they'd said we'd never get it. "There's no way." "You're in for a big disappointment." Even though they tried to talk us out of our dream. But no matter what they showed us, no matter what they said, no matter how they felt, no matter what they did, we continued to believe. And for us, their impossible was possible. We could create their impossible dream.

What we think is what we get— like it or not.

The Fourth Success Skill

COMMUNICATING DREAMS

The more detailed the communication the more power it has

In the first phase of life, we told everybody everything. Our parents were embarrassed at the things we blurted out. "Mom wears a wig." "Dad has on striped underwear." We said what we thought, and that was all there was to it.

We doggedly persisted when we needed others' help. I remember trying to bake a cake when my three-year old wanted ice cream. When I was busy, my typical response to her was—later. So then she would start, "Can we go now? Is it time yet? Can we go now? Are you ready yet?" I was remaining fairly calm, until I noticed I had put the vanilla in the refrigerator and the butter with the spices. Her persistence had won out, and as soon as I finished, we jumped in the car and went to buy ice cream.

But in the second phase of life, we learned not to ask or tell anybody anything, for fear of being punished, restricted or confined. What they didn't know wouldn't hurt them, or us. In order to do whatever we wanted, we pretended to do whatever they wanted. We had to please them to get their permissions and promotions and so we began fudging our communications, shaving a little bit off here and there, manipulating the details of the holograms we shared.

And then our holograms began to lose their power, no longer clear and focused but becoming blurry and confused. Saying what we thought others wanted to hear, but not what we were telling ourselves. Telling others we were feeling one way when we were really feeling the other. These communication habits began affecting our relationships, forcing us to hold back spontaneous reactions until we could think through the reactions we thought they wanted. So in the name of competition we gave up our integrity. The word *integrity* comes from *integer* which means one.

Business today is pushing us into a stressful corner, expecting us to give others what we aren't giving ourselves. Customers are no longer satisfied with just getting a product. They want us to be interested, they want us to discover exactly what they have in mind—the details, the quantity, the quality, the service and delivery. Third-phase customers don't want us to tell them, they want us to ask them. And then follow through.

We're beginning to give others what they want, becoming sensitive to their feelings and needs. But we're not doing the same for ourselves, giving them more than we're giving ourselves, smiling when we'd like to yell, saying yes when we feel like saying no. Our second-phase communication habits are getting in the way of creating what we really want. Our holograms have become confused, two or more versions of the "truth" fusing together, diluting the power of either one. Like people holding hands but pulling in opposite directions, we're creating powerful holograms pulling against each other and canceling each other's force—and ability to create.

Here are some ways we've reduced our creative power: Lying, exaggerating, downplaying and omitting details

Let's review the guidelines for building powerful holograms. The more detailed the hologram, the more power it generates. The hologram must involve two or more senses. We have to see, hear and feel what we want in great detail.

The first block to communication is lying. Who me, lie? Yes, we all lie when we intentionally misrepresent the details of our hologram, showing different pictures than we see in our minds, telling others different stories than we're telling ourselves, acting as if we feel ways we don't, saying we did things we didn't really do or vice versa. Then communication becomes obscured and confused. (From the Latin *confusere*, to fuse one thing with another.) Classic lies we all know are: "It wasn't that way when I left it." "No, I never said that." "The check is in the mail." "Oh, I didn't have time."

Communication is blocked when one person tells another the thing they have in mind is bigger than it is. The listener records and then uses inaccurate information. Comparisons become distorted. Something that sounds larger, really will be smaller. Something that sounds smaller, really will be larger. Then these two people aren't really talking about the same thing and are unable to work toward completing the same dream.

Sometimes one person downplays a hologram, showing a situation as less difficult than it is. The amount of work it will take to complete it is distorted. Planning is inappropriate. The very foundation the plan is built on is flawed and inaccurate.

Integrity is the key to successful communication. What we show must equal what we see. What we tell must sound like what we hear. What we tell others we feel must be the way we feel. What we communicate we're doing must be exactly what we're doing.

The director who couldn't speak up

In the name of politeness or competitiveness, we've learned to remain silent when we need to speak up. Refusing seconds of mashed potatoes even when we're hungry. Saying no to help when we need it. Saying we agree when we disagree emphatically. Knowing but acting as though someone else knows better. Following but not leading.

A director of a major corporation attending a meeting on an upcoming project realized the plan wouldn't work. But when asked how she felt, she pretended to be enthusiastic and eager to get going. Then for fourteen months she couldn't sleep, seeing her dreadful premonition coming closer and closer. The system she thought would fail was failing. In the next meeting she tried to sound the alarm, but her boss, sensing disagreement and knowing his own boss was expecting alignment, ignored her raised hand and moved on to the next one, someone he knew would sound positive and enthusiastic. Fifteen million dollars later, the whole project fell apart. And in the post-mortem, everyone on the team said they were concerned about that system right from the start. But no one had spoken up, afraid that speaking up would affect their evaluations, making them appear negative or nonsupportive.

I was called in by a city government to look at communication problems city managers were having. One of the complaints was their employees couldn't write effective memos. After discussing the problem with all those involved and reading writing samples, I discovered they could write very well. But they didn't want to put their ideas down clearly, fearing they'd be held responsible if anything went wrong, creating unclear messages so others could be blamed for misunderstanding what they meant.

Record and playback: The first step in communicating holograms

When we record a message on an answering machine, we play it back to hear how it will sound to callers. If it sounds the way we want, we use it to answer for us. But if it doesn't, we record the message over and over until it sounds right—the right words, the right tone, the right pitch, the right energy and enthusiasm, giving the right impression.

As we listen to a conversation, we are recording that other person's message—their request or plan, their instruction or experience, the words that they said, the way they looked and sounded, the way they used their bodies, the energy they put out. And we are responsible for playing their message back in full holographic detail. Is this what you have in mind, is this what you want me to know and to use? Playing them back let's them know that we're really interested in knowing exactly what they want. If the message we play back isn't complete and accurate, then we need to ask specific questions, recording and playing back until the hologram in our mind matches the one in theirs.

The salesman didn't play back

A car salesman lost his sale because he didn't spend that crucial minute or two playing back his customer's message. His customer was an executive who told him immediately that he'd be using his new car for business. He wanted a mobile office that was luxuriously spacious and comfortable. And quiet enough to easily discuss important plans and agendas on the way from the airport to important management meetings.

But that salesman missed his first opportunity to satisfy the customer, failing to play back what his customer had said, failing to confirm the specific details that he'd heard. All he had to say was, "Let me make sure I understand exactly what you want, George. You want to use this car for business. It will be your mobile office. You want it to be extremely comfortable, spacious and very quiet for when you're meeting with passengers on the way from the airport to meetings. Is that right?" "Yes." "And what else do you have in mind? A specific color or style? A four-door, I imagine. Is that right?"

If he had taken those few minutes to let his customer know he'd recorded his instructions, he would have been clear about exactly what to do. But instead, he took that customer outside to the car and showed him the engine, pointing out the details of the exterior and giving him a long list of performance statistics.

And his customer was upset. He hadn't been heard. He hadn't been responded to. He turned and left, heading directly across the street to another car dealer, telling his story to the salesman over there.

That salesman played the information back, asking additional questions. Then he did what he'd been asked to do. He took him out for a test drive. He closed all the windows and asked him to listen to how quiet this car was. He pointed out how comfortable "this meeting" they were having was, how quiet the interior was, how spacious and comfortable it felt. Then he turned on the stereo and put in a tape. They talked about meetings he would have in the future, or how if no one was going with him, he could listen to a tape of the previous meeting so he could follow-up on what had to be completed.

The customer was delighted with this salesman. His communication had been received and acted on. He had gotten what he wanted. They were both satisfied. One got the comfortable mobile office he wanted. And the other got the sale and a customer who referred him ten other people, telling each of them what a great salesman he was.

The word *interest* comes from the Latin *inter*, within, and *est*, to be. To be interested is to be within someone else—within their pictures, sound tracks, feelings and actions.

Good friends and co-workers know how to play back exactly what we tell them. They are interested in every little detail of what our child did at school, telling us about the time their child did that too. They keep our recordings stored in their memory, remembering our successes, replaying them for us when we forget them, success filing for us when we've switched into failure.

We are used to playing back our recordings before going into action, taking a minute to agree on our plan. "OK, then we'll meet at five in front of the school." "Is that OK with you?" "No, on second thought, it would work better to meet out back by the parking lot. So if it rains, you could sit in your car until I come with the umbrella."

Two La Glaciers

I have a friend Julia who is as prompt and precise about agreements as I am. If one of us is late we know that something came up. We always laugh as we arrive simultaneously exactly on schedule. We agreed to meet at a restaurant called La Glacier, Wednesday at noon.

Wednesday at noon I was there, and Julia wasn't, the first time in years. Meanwhile Julia was also at La Glacier precisely at noon, saying the same thing about me. And both of us at the same time walked up to the hostess, each asking about the other. And the hostesses provided each of us with a crucial bit of information—there were two La Glaciers, one near her home and the other near mine. We were both at La Glacier, but the La Glaciers were not the same A quick call by the hostess got us together. Our holograms hadn't matched, the right name, the right day, the right time, but in not the right place.

Fortunately we knew each other well, and it wasn't a first date or a very important meeting with someone we didn't know who would have made a very different assumption about our absence.

Playing back angry people

People who are upset literally scream to be recorded and played back. They tell us their story over and over, wanting us to tell it back to them accurately and in detail. And when our playback exactly equals their story, then the upset is completed. And we can both move on to solution.

But alas, woe befalls the person who does not play back that upset three-dimensionally and in living color, who leaves out a crucial detail, who tries to go on before the replay is agreed on, who argues that the story is wrong. That one will get the upset turned back on him. That one will unleash all the pain that person has ever felt. That one will be hung up on or have doors slammed in his face. Hell hath no greater wrath than the wrath of someone who wasn't played back!

Sharing the details

I was fortunate to have taken a circuitous route to get where I am. One stop on the way was a master's degree in design. That turned out to be one of the most important steps in my training for success. When I first began designing houses and buildings, I got terrible headaches whenever I had to detail complicated plans in my head. When I had to think about each corner, each overlap, each connector, each contour, each shape and material. It was hard for me to manipulate all those details in my mind, seeing each one, deciding and remembering. But my headaches got better as I got better at hologramming. I was able to design unique summer homes, drawing plans from every angle—site plans, perspectives, floor plans and elevations. After I put down every detail I could think of, I was always amazed by the questions the contractors still asked me. I was even more amazed when they would come back with an even larger set of questions after talking to carpenters, plasterers, electricians and plumbers. Some of the details they asked me to specify, I hadn't thought through. I had seen the whole picture, but I hadn't looked closely at every part until they needed to know whether a door opened right or left, whether corners were butted or mitered, whether lighting was recessed or surface-mounted.

After we create holograms, we often have other people complete those holograms for us. More detail will be needed by the ones who will follow through—building, making, marketing and distributing. As the designers of the future we need to share what we're thinking in full holographic detail, staying in close touch with those who are doing it, answering their questions and sharing exactly all the way through.

Sensory fill-in

Think about what you do in your mind as you follow these instructions. Picture a red-brick cottage. Now put one window on each side of the door. Make it two stories high with another window above the door. Put on a pitched roof, high in the middle and low on the sides. Now paint that house a soft gray green, adding dark green shutters on each of the windows. Stop now and notice what other details you've filled in automatically. Maybe a brass doorknob and knocker, or a globe light above the door. Or five steps and a porch. Were your windows casements or double-hung? Large panes or many small ones? Was it out in the country or lined up in a city?

As we communicate we see, hear, feel and do in our minds, sketching and erasing the details of our holograms, amplifying or diminishing their sound tracks and lighting. These changes can be exciting, challenging, even frightening. We want those who are listening to be simultaneously altering their holograms and sharing their reactions to the change. "Yes, I see what you mean. That sounds good to me too. Now I have a sense of why you want it that way. I agree with the change. Or, I don't agree. How about doing this instead?" We are working to match holograms so we can work in alignment, together or apart, having precisely the same thing in mind.

Sensory fill-in occurs when a communicator doesn't provide enough details for the person using their hologram, a child, a student, an employee, a carpenter or plumber. The doer then has to decide—without asking—about the unspecified details, filling in whatever was omitted from their own data base. Sensory fill-in is what creates arguments. "But I thought you wanted." "But I was sure you meant." "But that's what you told me to do last time."

Words are only 7 percent of communication. In the third phase we need to understand people not words. We need to record everything, not just what they say, but how they look and sound, what they feel and do. We may hear their words but completely miss their message.

The young broker and the young lawyer

A young broker was in love with a young lawyer. They were struggling to stay together, both having grown up with parents who put a lot of energy into politeness, smiling pleasantly even when they were upset. Both of them as children had wanted to know the truth about what was going on in their families. But the words they were told didn't match what they sensed within them.

When she wasn't picked up at school as a little girl, she wanted her mother to tell her she was sorry she'd forgotten her. But her mother always rushed her into the car saying she was busy, that something had come up. But it seemed to her that her older sister was never forgotten. Nothing ever came up when she had to be picked up. She wished her mother would just tell her the real truth, "My dear, I'm terribly sorry. I don't know why this is, I just prefer your sister over you." It would have brought her some peace, validating the feelings that ate away inside her, letting her know at least she wasn't crazy. She needed an integrity between what she saw, heard and felt. But all that her mother ever said was, "You know that I love you and your sister exactly the same way." And her father would add, "Don't upset your mother with anymore of that talk."

And the young broker who loved this young woman had a mother who took him to the hairdresser every morning as a boy, parking him there with a huge pile of toys, while they prepared her for her day. He never wanted to go there. He hated his mornings.

He dreaded his nights too, when his busy doctor father took him off to the hospital, leaving him with nurses while he made rounds. Finally one morning at age four, he threw himself in the swimming pool hoping to drown the pain he was feeling. But he didn't drown. Instead his mother scolded him for having been careless, spanking him for getting too close to the edge. Then she packed him up for another trip to the hairdresser.

Now the broker and the young lawyer were playing out their childhood communication patterns in their relationship. She wanted desperately for him to be really honest with her, making her first. And he wanted to be able to do whatever he wanted, not having to always do what she had in mind.

One evening she was depressed about her job and needed him to spend time listening and comforting her. He wanted to do that, but his old pain started coming up, feeling once again pushed into doing what others wanted but not what he wanted. And she could feel that he didn't want to be there with her. She asked what he really wanted to do. He answered very honestly that he wanted to go work out at the gym but he had decided it was more important to support her.

The only thing she heard was that he wanted to go work out. Now her old pain rushed up. She never heard the rest of his sentence—his statement of love and support. Those first words had confirmed inside her that he was just like her parents, polite but insensitive. So she ran out of the restaurant nauseated by that familiar repulsive feeling, wishing he had just said he didn't want to spend the evening with her. At least she would have believed him then. At least there would be integrity.

Ninety-three percent of the message comes through the voice and body

We sense, and check, the integrity of the communications we receive. If someone is standing with arms crossed, face flat and low energy, then the words "I'm really excited" don't match what we're experiencing. We hear those words but believe what we're sensing instead. Words communicate 7 percent and voice and body communicate 93 percent. We need to record and use that unspoken 93 percent.

In one of my seminars, I asked a young man to get up and change seats with the woman who last spoke. I asked him to play her back—sitting as she sat, speaking as she spoke, using his voice the way she did, the same volume, tone, pitch and pacing. I asked him to feel what she was feeling, to do the same things with his face and body. I asked him to play back her whole person—starting his playback with, "I am." Saying her name and playing back her story as though it were his. I asked him to be her instead of talking about her. Not "She felt." But "I feel." I wanted him to go beyond the words to her whole message.

I often do this playback exercise in my seminars, and the seminar energy shifts at this point. Everyone knows they could be asked to be anyone at any moment. They learn to communicate, not just to listen, becoming creative listeners, asking whenever they're not sure, wanting to know more, wanting to be certain when there's confusion. And they tell me they hear their families differently from then on. They hear their employees

87

differently. They hear their friends differently. They sense messages they never sensed before. They pick up on things they never used to notice, a change in someone's sitting position, a different tone of voice, an eye that's more closed. And they ask because they really want to know.

We communicate through our bodies, letting others know when we're feeling open—sitting with our shoulders, arms and legs back and open. We let others know when we're feeling closed off, shoulders, arms and legs covering our soft places like shields. We signal others when we change how we're feeling—opening about this or closing down about that. We can sit as they sit. We can stand as they stand—first closed then opening up little by little, following their pace, allowing them to sense that we're respecting their boundaries.

Since 55 percent of communication comes through the body, 55 percent of what people sense about us comes from our bodies. We need to be conscious of what our bodies are doing. We need to use that 55 percent of communication to let them know we're interested. And get them interested in us and our dreams.

Three brain languages: Learning to speak the same language

As we think about our holograms, we have to decide how to talk about them. Shall I talk first about what I am seeing or what I am hearing? Or should I talk about the feelings and actions?

It's like talking about a movie. We describe what we saw—the vivid imagery, countryside and costumes. We talk about what we heard—the conversations and the way the sound track amplified the mood. We talk about the feelings the actors had, the places they went, the actions they took. And we reveal the way we were feeling and whether we walked out disgusted or we stood spellbound in tears all the way through the credits.

Sometimes a powerful movie gets us so fired up that we leave the theater on a campaign to right wrongs. The pictures they show us and the sound track they play for us, plus the holograms we access internally, lead us to experience our past and our future. And we react and emote— recommending the movie to friends we know will also respond.

Here in Miami, people look at you and try to decide whether to speak

English or Spanish. When you respond to them in English, they know which language to continue to speak in. Similarly when someone asks us a question, we need to listen to which brain language they ask their question in. Then we will know which brain language to answer in.

If we speak "visual" to someone who's speaking "audio" it's almost like someone speaking English to someone speaking Spanish.

People give us word signals: Show me, tell me, or give me a feel for it

Even if we are all speaking English, we still speak English in three different brain languages—visual, audio and feeling/doing. We signal which brain language we want to use by the words we use. **Show me** what you saw. **Tell me** what you heard. **Give me a feel** for what it was like.

Show me tells us they want to see a picture. They want to see what we're seeing. They want an image, an illustration, chart or graph. As we communicate with others, we can show them—in words—the mental pictures we see. The car salesman can describe the impeccable dove-gray leather interior, seats that adjust up and down to just the right angle, the charcoal-gray control panel with factory CD, and a pull-out cup holder.

Tell me indicates that the customer wants to be told about the car. They want us to tell them what the experts have said. What they've heard from satisfied customers. They want to record those sound tracks. That customer may tell us, "I'm a concert pianist. And I was absolutely astounded by the concert-hall quality I experienced when the windows went up, and the CD began to play. Bravo!"

Give me a feel for it indicates that they want to get a sense of the car. They want to know how it will feel when they drive it, what it will do on the highway. They want to go for a test drive, sit in the seat, try out some corners to know how it handles, stop it themselves to feel how it stops. "I loved the ABS brakes, stopping smoothly even suddenly."

People ask questions precisely the way they do to assist us in knowing how to correctly communicate our answers. We have to be conscious not only of what they're asking for, but how they're asking for it. We must be aware of all the brain languages and fluent enough to respond in any one of them.

When they say show me, we need to say, "I'm going to show you..." When they say tell me, we need to say, "Let me tell you..." When they say give me a sense of, we need to say, "I want to give you a sense of..." Then they know we've recorded not only what they asked for, but the way they asked for it. Then they feel we understand them.

Brain preferences: People prefer one brain language over others. Take giving directions, for example. Some people want us to **show them** how to get there. They need to see signs, landmarks and pictures. A visual thinker wants to know there's a firehouse on the corner where she'll need to turn. To know there's usually a fire engine parked out in front—but that the fire engine is pea green, and not red. She will miss the turn if she doesn't see what she expects to see.

Some people prefer audio instructions, short and sweet little audio loops they can remember quite easily. They want us to tell them, "two rights and three lefts. 1603 Elm."

Some people want to be given a feel for how to get there. They'll want to know where to hang a corner or how close they'll be when the traffic slows down. They need to know how many traffic bumps they'll bump over as they are coming down our street.

And people give us eye signals as to brain language as well

Remember the Razz? The part of the brain that alerts us or wakes us when something's incomplete, when we didn't call our mother back or we forgot to mail our taxes?

The reticular activating system has a second function. Not only does it help us take action to complete the future holograms we have in mind, but it also assists us in communicating with others. The Razz acts as a sensory switch.

Eyes up or focused ahead shows us a person is seeing, operating in visual. Eyes ear to ear shows us a person is listening and hearing—operating in audio. Eyes down toward their body, shows us a person is feeling or thinking about doing.[8]

We need to think the way other people think. If they are seeing what they have in mind, we need to see what they have in mind. If they are hearing what they have in mind, we need to hear what they have in mind. If they are feeling what they have in mind, we need to feel what they have in mind. We need to do exactly what they're doing.

If we pay attention to others, they will tell us how to think the way they do. A confused employee might say, "I just can't **see** how we are going to do the project in the time frame we've been given." By saying **see**, he is letting us know that he wants to be **shown** a picture of how it will work. He needs to see how the time frame can be met. And he needs that picture in order to take action.

Another team member might say "I need to **hear** more about it. **Tell** me how you think we can get it done in that time frame." He wants to hear an explanation. Tell him. Talk him through it.

Still another team member wants to get a feel for how it could happen. Give him a sense of it, help him feel how it will all be accomplished. Give him your plan of action. Step him through the process of getting there.

Selling in the three brain languages

I taught the sales team at Levitz Furniture how to sell in all three brain languages. When a customer said she wanted to see a piece of furniture, the salesman knew he should take her over and show her. And he said right away, "Let me take you and show you." When a customer said he wanted to hear more about a sofa, the salesman said. "Let me tell you more about this sofa." When a customer said she wanted to get a feel for a chair, the salesman responded, "I'll take you over and let you sit in that chair." He suggested she get comfortable and relax, taking all the time she wanted. And with his assistance, she quickly sold herself. And she told him the chair was just as comfortable as her friend had said it was.

Upsets occur when someone asks us to respond in one brain language but we respond in another. Couples in counseling frequently argue in different brain languages. She says, "He never sees things the same way I do. We don't see eye to eye." And he says, " She doesn't listen to me. I've told her over and over what I wanted, but she just doesn't hear me."

He needs to see what she's showing him, beginning her playback with "I see that you…" She needs to begin her playback with "I hear you saying that you…" When they can fluently speak each others' brain languages, they will begin seeing, and hearing and feeling the same way.

Most people think visually. We were trained as children with flash cards, growing up on a steady diet of TV and movies—a visually oriented society. The way something looks, matters a lot.

Some people talk to themselves as they think. They hear what they're thinking. They make decisions by talking things through. They need to be told the facts and information. Graphs only work for them if we tell them what the graph says.

Other people learn by doing and feeling. They need a feel for it. They have to get up and go do it in order to learn it.

Our schools need to teach teachers how to teach in all three brain languages. Many low performers are students who need to get a feel for what they're learning. They end up successful in sports but not academics. Their teachers are probably teaching them in video or audio, but they're needing to learn in feeling and doing.

Speaking the same brain language when we don't speak the same language

A manager at Digital was transferred to Amsterdam. He called to let me know how valuable these communication skills had turned out to be. Though he wasn't fluent in the Dutch language, he was fluent in their brain language. Knowing about brain languages was allowing him to establish rapport with his customers and staff, using their eye signals to know how they were thinking. When they looked up as he spoke, he knew they were picturing what he was saying. He knew in their brains they were seeing what he was showing them. He quickly learned the words for seeing, describing and picturing so he could begin his response to them appropriately. When their eyes moved from side to side, from ear to ear, he knew they were talking to themselves about what he was saying. They were thinking in audio. He learned the words for telling, talking about and discussing.

When their eyes went down as he spoke, he knew they were feeling or thinking about action. He learned the words for feeling, sensing, doing and action. This communication skill made a difficult assignment far easier than it would have been otherwise.

Look at me when I speak to you—an old error

One of the mistakes we've made in the past was demanding that people keep eye contact as we talked to them. "Look at me when I'm talking to you." Fathers said it. Mothers said it. Teachers said it. Bosses said it.

But when we made them look at us, then they couldn't access the information they needed. They felt confused and couldn't carry out the thinking. But we thought they were looking away because they were being rude or even insolent, when in fact they were trying to understand our communication in detail.

If we want someone to think about what we're saying, then we have to allow them to look up or look off. Watch your child. Watch your parent. Watch your employee. Watch your neighbor. Any age, any stage, all people think this way. That's how the brain works.

A father got his son back

After I did a seminar on practice management for health professionals, a doctor wrote that he got the increased profits he had come to the seminar to get—and he got something else he valued far more. He got his son back. He'd never been close to this son, they just never seemed to see eye to eye. He had always tried hard to share his visions and perspectives but nothing looked right to his son. He discovered in the seminar that he had a preference for thinking visually and when he got home he listened and watched for the signals his son would give him.

He discovered that his son preferred feelings and actions—not visions and perspectives. His son had tried hard to get a sense of things from his dad, to understand his feelings, to have his feelings understood. The seminar had helped his father become fluent in all three brain languages. Recognizing the problem, he explained the three ways of communicating he'd learned to his son. They practiced them together.

93

Then his son summed it up in a nutshell— "You know Dad, we never saw eye to eye because you never saw how I felt. And I never felt how you saw. Now after all these years, I'm learning to see what you see and you're learning to feel what I feel. It's good to know you Dad."

I was called in to solve a communication problem at Ryder System. In their graphics department, there was one person who didn't communicate well with the rest of the team. She was their computer graphics expert, so this was a problem they really needed to solve. I talked to the team members one by one. Graphic arts. Yes, as you might suspect they were all primarily visual—except for the one who wasn't getting along. Her complaints were what I needed to hear. "They always try to show me diagrams and pictures of this, that and the other. I keep telling them that's not what I need. I wish they'd just tell me what they want. If they'd take a few minutes to explain their needs, I would be glad to do whatever they wanted." She was an audio. She wanted to be told what to do, she needed spoken instructions. Without them, she felt irritated and annoyed. Pictures didn't work for her. It was only through conversation that she got herself organized and into action.

We all talked about the three brain languages. I demonstrated the different ways of thinking and everyone practiced them. She practiced talking visually over and over. The others got a kick out of her efforts— for them it was easy—until they began to try to speak audio, to tell her exactly what it was they wanted. She laughed then. That was so hard for them. They kept whipping out a pencil and a paper. "See, that's what I mean." But with these new understandings and a month's practice behind them, they began communicating as a team. They could all tell her what she needed to hear to see what they wanted.

The '90s are about people skills

Third-phase businesses expect to communicate, they expect to meet our needs. As we train employees to satisfy customers, we are training our employees to satisfy everyone—our families, our friends, even those we don't know yet, seeing the value of every single one of us. Today's competitive marketplace is making us people-oriented. The '90s are no longer about technical skills, about having the best machine, the latest model, the newest technology. Everyone has access to all of these. This decade is about people skills, about how we're treated while we're getting the products we want, after the sale is closed, when we call on the phone, when we stand in line, when we ask questions, when we have a problem. Technical skills make the products we need. People skills deliver the products we make.

We need to know who has what and who wants it. We need to ask questions, recording and using the answers we're given. Our global marketplace is teaching us to be interested not just in our own families and communities, but in everyone on Earth—the whole family of man.

Communication skills are the skills of today's business "gourmets." Others come with their measuring cups and spoons, eager to discover how we do what we do. They will write down exactly what we said and what we did. But what we did wasn't it. There was no magic formula, no step-by-step procedure. The main thing we had was a genuine interest in what someone wanted, in completing their hologram with them, sharing the excitement and satisfaction and fulfillment of a dream coming true.

The parrot on the mantle

Customers want more than our product or service. They want us to be interested in who they are and the unique circumstances of their lives and dreams. Having worked with customer-service organizations for many years, I've heard some unique stories about the unusual needs of customers.

A Florida Power and Light customer-service rep responded to a call that an electric meter wasn't working. He went out to check it, but the meter was working fine. The old woman thanked him for coming so promptly, asking him to look at something in her house. Once inside, she told him that he seemed to be a very kind young man. She had a special problem that was the real reason for her call. She walked him over to the fireplace and pointed to a parrot perched on her mantle. For many years this parrot had been her beloved pet. When he died, she had him stuffed. All these years since then, he had been perched on that branch in the center of her mantle.

She loved her parrot dearly, but he was keeping her awake lately. She was very ill and whenever she'd fall asleep, she would dream she had died and someone was taking the parrot down off the mantle and throwing him in the trash. Just talking about that scene made her weep, and she begged him to take her parrot home and always keep him on his mantle. And he did.

A "bad" customer

"Bad" customers may have special needs. The collections department had a customer who didn't pay on time. Months would go by before they would receive her payment. This time a rep was being sent out to either collect what was owed or cut off her power. It was an unfamiliar neighborhood but the rep finally found the number on an old apartment building. Climbing three flights, she knocked at the door. A weak voice invited her in. As she entered, she saw two silver oxygen tanks and a frail old woman lying flat on her bed, struggling to breathe. The rep was shocked by what she saw. But she had a job to do, so she asked about the bill. The old woman said she was terribly sorry for paying so late, but she lived here alone. Her son was only in town every couple of months to bring up her mail and write out her checks. The rep promised to call social services to get someone to assist her.

Customers are more than "problems" in our system. They are people with incompletions who need to have completions. The upset person in fact has two problems—the way they are feeling, and what they want us to do.

Handle first things first. Complete the upset, playing back their feelings, detail by detail, until they know you've understood. Then they'll be sorry they yelled and thank you for listening. Having completed their communication, then you may also be able to complete what they need—taking home the parrot to preserve peace of mind or calling social services to assist with her mail. Sometimes our job is to follow procedures, and sometimes our job is to follow our hearts.

Solving the wrong problem

Time-driven customer-service reps feel pressed to solve a problem in a certain number of seconds, but that pressure sometimes drives them to solve the wrong problem. These incorrect solutions result in hours of escalating complaints. Customers get mad when we jump into action without hearing their whole story, thinking that we know exactly what they mean when we don't.

"No, that's not it! And this is the fourth time I've called. None of you will listen to me, and this time I'm fed up. My lawyer is filing a complaint with the FCC." And your supervisor gets involved and your manager and director and the CEO is told. And everyone files reports. And hours and hours and hundreds of thousands of dollars later, it would have been far more efficient to have taken a few minutes to hear the whole story.

In the first and second phases, we were taught how to use communication loops—"If they say, then you say." We didn't know enough to analyze the whole problem. We only knew a few methods and we hoped one of them would work, listening just long enough to pick the one to try. We wanted to be right. We wanted to work faster, listening to ourselves, but not hearing our customer.

The new waiter in the restaurant had just memorized the menu. Like a robot he presented the specials for the night, playing back what he'd just memorized. "And tonight we have..." We could sense his brand-newness and self-consciousness and we didn't dare interrupt him, fearing we'd throw him off if we asked him to stop long enough to give us the information we wanted.

We've all been stuck in our own performances at one time or another. People complained that we weren't listening. And even though we denied it, it was true. It was impossible to get through to us, no matter how hard they tried. We were so busy listening to what was going on inside ourselves, rehearsing and critiquing, that we couldn't hear anything that was happening outside of us.

Communicating about the future

Unless we learn new skills, our loyalty to the past will continue to pull us back to the way it was before. The older generation has held onto the power, keeping things their way, demanding our respect. They assumed they knew what's best for us.

Yes, the past has its wisdom, but it is the wisdom of the time that was then. Our present requires wisdoms we haven't had yet, haven't needed up until now, and won't even get used to before we make the next change. This present requires levels of consciousness and communication the past cannot provide. The rate of change in our world is continuing to accelerate. We are communicating more and more about everything—using global systems, global skills and production. And creating information overload.

Our technology pulls us ahead in spurts. The computer is introduced but it takes time to get used to it. The CD player is introduced but it takes time to get used to it. The microwave is introduced. And the ATM. Our technology advances but old habits hold us back. It takes time for things to become familiar and useful. It takes time to get them recorded in everyone's memory. It takes time for people to use them until they become comfortable. Some people resist change, getting out of sync with the process, growing more and more rigid and old until they die.

We no longer want to keep fixing what's broken, old systems that won't work. We need systems that can be updated and expanded, instead of systems that need to be updated by the time they're completed. We need to explore new options instead of relying on old ones. We need to ask the questions we were told not to ask, challenging situations we were taught weren't our business, that were put in inner-boxes marked "Don't Talk About" and "Don't Bring Up." We need to stop telling ourselves "They" will take care of it.

With today's levels of instant communication we can't keep the old ways together anymore. Walls are coming down. Ideologies are breaking open. New life is springing forth. We must look, listen, feel and decide what we want, communicating dreams and developing the self-confidence we will need to undertake them together.

We must create a Big Picture that is so desirable for all of us, so attractive to each of us, that we are enthusiastic about creating it and living it. It may be a long journey. And we must notice where we are along the way, staying healthy and balanced, modeling communication skills we would like others to use. We will need skilled leaders and so we will have to raise them and educate them, manage and govern them so they can lead in the future. We are about to shift into the third phase.

We know some things. Others know some things. All together we know everything. We need to talk. We need to ask questions to find the missing pieces. And as we put more and more pieces together, the Big Picture emerges more and more clearly and distinctly. We beg to hear and feel and know what everyone on Earth wants, what everyone on Earth has, what everyone can do. The Big Picture is the hologram of the collective dream we'll only see completely when we all become a part of it.

Leaders of the future

Leaders are visionaries. They see the outcome. Leaders are communicators. They tell us what they're seeing. They hold the dream, letting us feel that it's possible. Our minds open up to what they show us could be. We dream with them. We get excited with them, drawing on all our abilities to create the future.

When a society shifts from one phase to another, they do so because of leaders. Together they dream the new way so clearly, so specifically, in so much detail that they begin to live it, breathe it, and taste it. They talk about it with so much eloquence, with so much passion, with so much desire that they experience it in advance. They commit to that reality.

Then leaders ask their citizens how to do it. Then managers ask their employees how to do it. Then teachers ask their students how to do it, and the ones who have those skills step up and say, "I can. I will." And others eagerly join in to do their unique part. The excitement and enthusiasm attracts everyone and everything it takes to build that new phase of society.

Shifting to the third phase

In the first phase we begged to be told what to do. In the second phase we avoided being told like the plague. We did things in secret, in private, in confidence—pushing the limits, taking our methods way past the rules, well beyond the boundaries of propriety. We didn't care what others thought. Or what they had to say. We were paid for results, and results were what mattered. Isolated, alone, afraid others would find out exactly what we were doing, whether it was a special technique we used to produce results a little faster, or a not-so-OK method we employed to stay on top.

99

People didn't matter. It was every man or woman for himself or herself. We were disillusioned with ourselves and others. Humanity had gone to Hell—or so it seemed from the extreme realms of our race through the second phase.

Finally we broke free into new territory. We have found there are people here. Others we can work with, others we can talk to. And taking a deep breath for the first time in a long time, we look around newly at life. We reach out to be comforted, needing to rest, wanting a massage or a day at the spa.

We looked again at our priorities, at what mattered and what didn't. We sold possessions we were struggling to afford, reducing huge credit card balances, lowering our blood pressure. We reintroduced ourselves to our spouses and families, taking time to rediscover who they had become. We met our friends newly—amazed at all we hadn't noticed in the blurry years of achieving.

This third phase requires us to approach ourselves and others more openly and skillfully. We've been disconnected, we've resisted needing anyone, even the ones we admit we need. We've had legitimate reasons of course—no time, no energy, no money.

But now we want to be with others again, making the time, taking the energy, spending the money. We want to live, not just work. We slowed—down. We—slowed—way—down.

It feels strange going slower. We have real conversations, not just leaving instructions about who has to pick up the kids or fix dinner. We're taking a new interest, caring and listening, recognizing ourselves in others, sharing concerns about our future, about children and parents, about security and retirement, even about fun.

It had gotten confusing, smiling when we were crying inside, saying yes when every fiber of our body wanted to scream "No!" We had been putting up a good front, but feeling separate and lonely, longing for family, friends and community. To re-establish our integrity (remember, integrity comes from integer, meaning one), we have to begin sharing exactly what we're thinking and feeling and doing, sharing our holograms specifically and precisely so together we can finally begin to create the life we all want to be living.

Completing our dreams

To complete all our dreams we will have to use the skills of everyone on Earth, available for the asking, available for the hiring. In the third phase we don't have to know it all. We don't have to do it all either. We can use the knowledge that others have gathered, the skills they have practiced and mastered already.

Earth is a planet of commerce. Our work here is the completion of dreams. In return for completing others' dreams, we are paid money. Then we can use that money to complete our own dreams.

To work successfully with others, it is essential that we distinguish between our outcome and our method. The outcome is the experience we want—the destination we've set. The methods are the ways we can go about getting there—the actions we'll take, the corrections we'll make, the journey from dream to reality. If we are going to Chicago, Chicago is our outcome. The bus, the train, the plane, the car, the motorcycle are methods we can use to get there. We need to commit to our outcomes. And stay flexible about our methods.

How successfully we work with others depends on how well we communicate. In communication we access and transmit the details of our holograms. How well can we show each other what we are seeing? How effectively can we tell others what we're telling ourselves? How skillfully can we give them a feel for the experience we want? And how willing are we to trust that another human cares enough to carry out—exactly—our innermost dreams?

The more detailed the communication the more power it has.

The Fifth Success Skill

USING EXPERTS AND MONEY

An expert is anyone who can already do what we want to do

I had been creating a detailed hologram in my mind ever since the first day I walked in my house. I had bought it because of the pond that would be there shimmering and glistening, the waterfall that would soothe and relax everyone who heard it, the huge colorful fish that would lunge up through the surface with mouths open wide, waiting to be fed.

A year later the renovations were complete, and the whole house was furnished using my "everything-for-nothing or next-to-nothing" strategy. It was time to build my pond—an unusual pond, irregular in shape and depth, unusual in flow and construction. I began searching for experts to assist me in building it, inviting them over to stand on the spot with me, to visualize the details I had in mind. I could show them exactly what I wanted if only they would listen and imagine with me.

Each time someone came, I would sketch the pond out in words for them, then watch and wait. Could this one grab on to my idea, creating my pictures in their mind, talking it through positively and specifically? Did this expert have the construction skills and expertise to do whatever it would take to complete the whole project?

Many came. And many went—the ones who told me it was impossible, it couldn't be done, it wouldn't work. They would walk around the yard nodding "No" in advance, mentally focused on the difficulty, impossibility and high cost. Whenever I recognized that an expert couldn't hold my hologram, I thanked him for coming and let him know this wasn't the job for him. The person for this job would be able to see it, believe it and do it successfully.

My search continued for almost six months until one day a man came who saw my hologram and immediately got excited. "Something unusual," he said, "something creative. These are the projects I like." And he quickly began asking questions to get the details of my hologram, walking around the yard "seeing" my pond with me, noticing how wide it would be, its depth here and there, walking off its exact size and shape. Then he began telling me how he would build it—the steps he would take, the materials he would use, the tentative schedule.

He was creating my hologram right along with me, owning my dream and making it his own. The first test was passed. Now for the second. Did he have the construction skills and experience that were needed? He showed me pictures of other projects he had done, huge houses with waterfalls and unusual form-poured concrete staircases, architects' jobs not exactly like this project but requiring the same construction skills and creativity. He was as eager to build this pond as I was, asking if he could take pictures of the completed job to add to his portfolio.

For weeks before we started to dig, we poured over books and videos. I took him to visit huge ponds in jungles and botanical gardens, smaller ponds tended and tilled by my friends, with soft fuzzy mosses growing on coral rocks, ferns springing from pockets and crevices, lily pads and lotus leaves floating on the surface. I wanted to give him the experience of what my pond would be like when it was finished. We carefully walked all around these ponds, lifting foliage here and there to examine their edges. How high above the water, how rounded or rough, how thin or thick. Then we made sketches of especially pleasing rock groups, how they were piled up, the way water moved through them, the sounds and the eddies they created. I pointed out right edges and wrong ones, right waterfalls and wrong ones, right rock placements and wrong ones, right waterfall sounds and wrong ones, detailing out the differences I experienced specifically.

He was readying himself to manage his team, creating certainty within himself about the way he would direct them, the ways he would proceed when things were happening fast and furiously. I had pointed out many times how much easier it is "to move furniture in your mind than to move it in reality, how much cheaper it is to make mental mistakes than to pour them in concrete." By now he was quite comfortable asking questions whenever he thought of a detail we hadn't talked through, aligning up front to eliminate sensory fill-in that would create upsets later on. With each passing day our holograms were coming more and more into alignment. He thought he knew what I had in mind playing it back frequently, checking it out with me.

Then we spent time looking at the things we thought could go wrong, so we'd be aligned on how he should handle them. We developed contingency plans in case of bad weather, in case of bad workers, in case of bad luck. We aligned on everything we could imagine needing to be aligned on.

When the action began and everyone was working at top speed, it was so noisy we couldn't ask questions, drowned out by backhoes and loaders, concrete trucks and high-pressure hoses. By that time he knew what I knew and he did what I wanted, and it all went like clockwork. After the pond was finished, he brought his friends over to see his success and I invited mine. We all stood admiring what we'd created together, a success that was even more than we each had in mind.

Experts need to be co-programmers

In the third phase we are responsible for programming ourselves for success. And we are responsible for programming our experts as well, for letting them know exactly what we have in mind—the pictures, the sound tracks, the feelings and actions. As a co-programmer, our expert is responsible for making sure the pictures, sound tracks, feelings and actions they have in mind match ours, by asking and questioning, recording and playing back over and over to assure precise alignment, mentally adjusting their hologram—bigger, smaller, higher, lower, changing the details of color, texture, shape and construction—until we both feel confident we have the same things in mind, remembering that past programs will click into action in unspecified areas.

Most people expect experts to spend all their time taking action and if there are mistakes they blame their experts for having made them. But in the third phase, we're responsible for those mistakes ourselves. It's up to us to spend as much time as necessary hologramming the outcome up front, sometimes even more time than the action will take, knowing the faster the action, the more precisely programmed that action must be. And building this pond was a very good example, for once the concrete trucks were on site, once the laborers started playing their past programs on how to build swimming pools, it would be too late and too expensive to explain it then. They had to know up front that this project was different, their old ways were great but not here, not now.

Creative success requires that we build our projects in our minds before we build them in reality, making mistakes mentally, correcting and realigning. Then when it's finally time to take action it feels like a dance or a dive, flawlessly executed and even more. The most well-disciplined and well-rehearsed performers in the world live for the wonder of those moments when choreography becomes dance, notes become music, brush strokes become art, the planned becomes creative.

Picking the right expert in the right phase

Money is the medium of exchange between experts, allowing us to trade what we do for what others do, freeing us from our dependence on family and friends. The wife in the last generation who had to wait for her husband to fix a broken pipe can call a plumber today. The husband who used to ask his wife over and over to starch his shirts can get his cleaner to starch his shirts light, medium or heavy. Even a child tired of waiting for busy parents to help with homework after school can ask for a tutor. Using the right expert allows us to get what we want easily, instead of having to beg and argue endlessly and pointlessly. The effective use of experts gives us back time and energy to do other things.

Remember, an expert is anyone who can assist us in doing what we wouldn't be able to do by ourselves. The things we can't do because we don't have the skills or time.

105

But we need to know how to find the right expert. **First-phase experts** can do what they're told to do—a maid or a laborer, an untrained apprentice or a willing pair of hands. **Second-phase experts** can do the job we want efficiently and independently—an electrician to put in a light or a carpenter to build a fence. And **third-phase experts** can design or invent what we dream of, even something unusual, doing it effectively, efficiently and creatively themselves or by managing a team. An architect or designer can explore what we have in mind for the new wing of our house—the style, the details, the feel of the space—and then take our rough sketch to a whole new creative level. Wisely chosen experts assist us in moving past our personal limits to success.

Then why do so many people avoid using experts?

Depending on experts may have left us with a bad taste in our mouth early in our lives. When we were children, our parents were our only experts. Whatever we needed, we went straight to them. If they didn't help us, we couldn't get what we wanted. But as our skill levels increased, as we learned and practiced, our requirements for expertise went beyond what our parents could give us. We needed more skills and more time. By then we were in school with other experts assigned to us, a teacher, a counselor, a principal, plus new friends and their parents. And we were old enough to be able to communicate effectively, asking for whatever expertise we needed or wanted.

Earlier in our lives, there were lots of things we wanted our experts to assist us in getting and doing, but sometimes they wouldn't share their expertise with us, disagreeing with what we wanted and so refusing to help us—like when we wanted to build a birdhouse and they wouldn't let us do it, going on and on about how we'd get hurt or get dirty. Or, when we wanted to choose what to wear to school, but instead of teaching us how to choose, they told us that the outfit we had so carefully and eagerly put together didn't match, the patterns all clashed. And we had to change. Or, when we wanted to buy our first car and they told us we couldn't, forbidding and prohibiting instead of assisting or planning to buy it later. Or, when we asked advice from our boss and that got us into trouble because they felt we were stupid. In the first and second phases our leaders were our experts and they were more concerned with our safety and competence than the details of what we wanted. Their choices and tastes carried more weight than ours.

Then we didn't want to use experts. Instead of our experts they were our obstructers, telling us what we shouldn't do if we knew what was good for us. So we learned to keep our wants and desires to ourselves, withholding our holograms, not sharing their details, figuring out our own ways of doing what we wanted so we wouldn't get stopped. Some parents, in order to maintain their authority, blocked us from seeking help from other experts, not wanting us to tell the teacher or preacher what was going on at home, protecting their image more than our well-being. We were forbidden to talk to relatives and counselors, prohibited from getting help for problems we were having at home—alcohol abuse, drug abuse, spouse or even child abuse.

Many of us decided using experts wasn't worth it. Because whenever we used them we had to give up what we wanted, give up our own methods, our own unique expression. Whether we wanted to sing in the choir if that was our passion, or study ballet, or learn to fly a plane, we didn't get their help unless it was what they wanted. So, we developed a secretive attitude whenever we were around experts, preferring to get advice from those who didn't know much but wouldn't stop us.

If our parents had recognized our need to be supported—not in something dangerous or harmful of course but just in something we wanted—if our parents helped us find the experts we needed, then our growth and success were greatly accelerated. And our enthusiasm for using experts expanded each time we got what we wanted with their help.

Picasso and his father

The skill levels of parents or parent substitutes are the skill levels a child aspires to unconsciously. The fortunate child has highly skilled parents—teachers or business people, artists or musicians, builders or craftsmen. Familiar with that skill level, hearing it, feeling it, expecting it all through their lives, they become the Wolfgang Amadeus Mozarts. The Jean Michel Cousteaus. The Natalie Coles.

Picasso's father was a highly esteemed art teacher, but when Pablo was only ten his father told him he could no longer be his teacher. His son, and everyone else, wanted to know why not. His father's response was a very profound and wise one. He told his son, "You already know more than I do. You need a teacher far better than I am."

As we become more skilled, we need more skillful experts as well—tutors and coaches, music teachers and art teachers, diving instructors and flight instructors. Our parents are responsible for finding these experts, for discovering programs for us to attend, asking teachers and counselors who the experts are in computers, photography, gymnastics, counseling, swimming, dancing or voice, or whatever else we're interested in. Participation in group activities often facilitates our being noticed by even more skilled experts.

Our parents' ability to find expertise may depend on how much money they have available. The more money they have, the more experts they can hire. Our parents' ability to find experts may depend on the people our parents know, experts they work with, teach with and play with. But our parents' ability to find experts depends most of all on their ability to dream about our success—becoming inspired by the things we'll end up doing some day, finding experts to assist us in getting there.

Childhood is the time when we're subsidized by our leaders to learn to use experts. That's when we're recording our data base, copying in parents' and teachers' input and playing it back for them to check, grade and update. Our main responsibility as children is acquiring skills. The more skills we acquire and master, the more easily we can acquire other skills. Learning to learn—succeeding through the three phases of a skill—is a skill in itself. Mastery is knowing we know how to learn.

Once out of elementary school we're required to use more experts, better and faster. Instead of having one teacher, we have five teachers a day, plus coaches and bosses after school. We have to be able to move beyond our fear of experts, developing the willingness to ask for assistance whenever we need it, the willingness to use feedback and to cooperate with others who are more skilled and experienced.

Are we leading or following?

When we use experts we have to decide who the leader is, who's following who. Sometimes experts are also leaders—like electricians, plumbers, consultants or nutritionists—telling us what we ought to do and how to do it. Other times we lead our experts—painters, laborers, or maids—telling them what to do and how to do it. We have to be clear which position we're in, thinking through the relationship before we begin, recognizing which success phase we're in, how much we know, and how much we need them to know.

Sometimes we only know what we want—a new roof, a pipe unclogged, a painful tooth repaired. Those are the times we want our expert to lead us. We sketch out the hologram we have in mind, and then wait for our expert to do all the rest, as long as their price and timetable are affordable and acceptable.

These are the times when we need to check experts out carefully, getting their references and credentials and letters of recommendation, because we don't know enough to evaluate their price, plan or work for ourselves. We're easily "had" and easily taken. We are like children. They are like parents. Good ones are great. But unskilled or uncaring ones can be painful, frustrating and disappointing. Even though we asked, even though we expected, we still will not get it, if they don't have the skill, if they don't make the time, if they don't have the willingness to support our success.

In areas we know more, we can lead our experts more. We know what we want, having built our own hologram. We know one method that will work but we're willing to learn a better one, sharing the leadership—but still holding the deciding vote. In the second phase of working with an expert, sometimes we find ourselves arguing over what, when and how. "No, I don't think you should do it that way, this way would work better. No, I don't really want that. I'd like this better." Now our experts begin to feel our competitive edge, having to spend time and energy struggling with us. Some experienced mechanics have signs in their shops increasing their prices for people who watch.

Sometimes we clearly know we are leading and we let our experts know we're in charge from the start. We want them to assist us, discovering our hologram instead of creating one themselves, or simply using an old program they learned in their trade. We share our hologram in full multi-sensory detail, asking them to play it back so we know they're seeing and hearing and feeling the same things that we are. And we notice the places where they've changed things a little, the places where our two holograms aren't yet aligned, taking the time before taking the action to get all the details the same.

If alignment comes, then we're eager to hire this expert. But if resistance continues, if our differences persist, then we let this expert go and look for another. On this project, we want someone who can "mind read"—asking us questions, finding out our meaning, putting aside their preferences and judgments—aligning with our thinking and dreaming.

In the third phase the details of our hologram are important to us—the design, the execution, the exact details and specifications. To be useful as experts, these details must be just as important to them, asking when they're not sure what we want.

Some experts may resist following directions, insisting on leading even when that's not what we want, unwilling to follow us—even though it's our project and we're the ones paying. We need to choose carefully the experts we hire, avoiding the ones who try to make us feel like we're little children who have overstepped our bounds because we want what we want and insist it be done our way.

If you are the expert and you feel that what we want, or the way we want to get it simply won't work, then sell us your ideas. Explain how what you have in mind will give us even more of what we want, even more easily. Then let us choose. If we choose to do it our way, then let the consequences of our actions teach us to choose more efficiently the next time, and let it go gracefully. Experts can sell their ideas but they shouldn't impose them.

The red ZX

When my daughter Cathy was twenty she wanted to buy a red Nissan ZX. She had seen it, driven it and fallen madly in love. Then she came to me for advice and expertise. I asked why she wanted a ZX, what her specific car needs and desires were. She explained what she wanted and the options she'd considered. I asked her how much of what she made she wanted to spend on a car. Based on all of that, I recommended she pass up the ZX and buy herself a Jetta. I told her the insurance on a sports car was higher than she probably wanted to pay.

I told her a red sports car would attract a lot of attention, maybe even tickets. I told her all the reasons I was making my recommendation. And then I reminded her that she had asked for my advice. It was only my opinion—for what it was worth—and I wished her well with whatever decision she made.

She decided to get the ZX. A year passed, and we spent lots of time together, but the subject of her car never came up. One day my phone rang, "Mom, I just traded in the ZX and I got a new Jetta. I want to thank you for the advice you gave me last year. But even more than that, I want to thank you for letting me do what I wanted. That way I discovered the value of your advice. I did get noticed. I did get tickets. And it did get to be too expensive. And when my insurance came due, it wasn't what I wanted anymore. I love you, Mom. And thanks for your expertise."

Mother birds are experts

A mother bird is a parenting expert. Watch her as she flies over there to her nest, her mouth full of worms, swooping in and landing gracefully. Watch as she looks over her brood, deciding which ones she will feed. Oh, how very simple she makes it seem, feeding only the birds with their mouths open, only the ones who are hungry and eager, not wasting time prying and force-feeding the others.

Many times in our lives we've tried to force-feed those who didn't want our expertise, those with their minds tightly closed. We've pushed and pried, shoving in information only to have them throw it back in our faces. Experts—like mother birds—must only feed those who have their minds open, those who are asking and wanting advice.

Getting on the same side of the table

In the second phase we're competing even with our experts, blocking their input, having to know best, needing to be right, picking apart their methods. In this competitive mode we seem committed to thinking of all the reasons why their methods won't succeed, why they won't be of use to us.

Instead of sitting across from them, judging and vying, we need to imagine getting up, walking over to the other side and sitting down beside them, facing the problem together. In the second phase we've tried to win so often, wanted to be better so intently that we developed a strategy for withholding information, keeping it to ourselves. Hoping that when others don't know all the information, we'll end up on top—in class, in sports, on the job. But when experts don't have all the information, they can't help us.

And as we begin moving toward team, we still sometimes find ourselves on opposite sides of the table, stuck in our old habits, withholding information to appear smarter and better, still pretending we've got everything under control—even when we don't. When we don't give full and factual information to doctors, insurers, workers, to anyone who is serving us—yes, they will slip up but that slip up will be our responsibility, preventing our own success.

Cows and corn—the shift from farming to commerce and industry

Earth used to be a planet of grazing and farming. When someone needed a cow, they found someone nearby. Then they loaded the corn into their wagon, hitched up the horses and traveled to where the cow was. After the farmers looked over what they each had, they made an agreement—this cow is worth this much corn. Then they unloaded the wagon and loaded on the cow, climbing back onto the seat of their wagon and heading home satisfied.

Today the purchase of cows and corn happens quickly and easily through a broker on a phone, using checks or credit cards. If there's a delivery, it's arranged through an expert. But many exchanges occur each day where there is nothing delivered, simply exchanges back and forth on paper or computer.

When we observed our world from high up in a plane, we saw ships and trucks crisscrossing oceans and land masses, carrying raw materials to manufacturers, product-parts to assemblers and distributors and on to customers. We saw rows and rows of boxes stacked one on the other, filled with people, products and services. We saw people moving fast and furiously across the surface, selling what they have and buying what they want.

But the movement is slowing. More and more people are staying put, using communication systems and delivery systems to get what they want without ever going anywhere. Through computers and faxes, telephones and modems, we can locate and purchase goods and services anywhere in the world—the best place to buy almonds or soy beans, the best source of lumber or oil, the right place to go skiing or purchase computer software at the right price, the right quality, the right time. We live on a planet of commerce and industry, a global marketplace connected by information technology.

What do customers want?

The real outcome of a business is to satisfy customers. The real outcome of the busy-ness of a planet is to satisfy its citizens. And we are all the customers of Earth.

Without satisfied customers, businesses fail. Without satisfied customers, planets fail too. How can we satisfy ourselves with the expertise and resources available? What new products and services are needed by the citizens of Earth? What expertise is your corporation or business contributing to the care and keeping of our planet? Does your business provide the power to energize homes and businesses? Does your business provide the telephone equipment to expand communication and cooperation? Does your corporation facilitate safe and efficient movement of money? Does your business care for children while those people work to provide for the rest of us?

Spending money is how we vote in the marketplace. By spending money on a product, we communicate approval to the experts who supply it. "Yes, this is what I want. "And as long as we keep buying their product, we let them know we're satisfied. "Yes, keep making it." But when we buy something else, we're voting "No"—putting them on notice that we've found something better.

Business is an arena for practicing our balancing acts. We lease ourselves out to produce others' outcomes. Then with money coming in and money going out for mortgages, health care, clothing and education, we have to learn how to keep our balance. How do we know when our balance is off? Pain, upset, effort, struggle, fatigue, illness and death are alert messages, red blinking lights.

If we spend too much time and energy in business, then we don't have enough for ourselves and our families. If we spend too much time and energy on ourselves and our families, then we don't have enough for making a living. Then monies coming in are not enough—for leasing plumbers, electricians, health professionals, food suppliers, clothing providers, child care specialists and entertainment professionals.

We've got it better than kings and queens

When we look back in history, we see people relying on their families for expertise. Only on rare occasions did they use money to buy anyone else's assistance. Even as recently as our grandparents' generation, a father or grandfather, a brother or an uncle did the repairs for the whole family. A slice of pie and a glass of milk were their payment for services rendered.

Systems were simple and few. A fuse and a washer handled most plumbing and electrical jobs. A handsaw, a hammer, a pair of pliers and a screwdriver could fix almost everything. Problems about parenting or relating, food, clothing and health care were matters for the females in the family—mothers, grandmothers, aunts and great aunts—while disciplining was handled by fathers after they returned home from long days of hard work.

When a relative became a lawyer, he became the family lawyer. When a relative became a doctor, he became the family doctor. The level of expertise a family had, was the level of expertise of its most skillful individuals. For better or for worse, families stuck together but rarely did anyone go further. And if they ever did, they were thought of as black sheep.

Kings and queens, on the other hand, operated very differently, using advice from all over their realms to build Taj Mahals, temples and pyramids, using the best craftsmen their money could buy. Kings and queens shared their dreams with their people. And everyone with those skills assisted in making them come true. But even their experts weren't as skilled as experts are today. And their experts weren't as available as our experts are today. Kings and queens couldn't pick up phones and call anywhere, charging that advice, product or service on a credit card.

Our own parents' generation depended on family much less than our grandparents did. Getting ahead in business became more important than living near family. When a husband said yes to his company, then his family could be pulled up by the roots and plunked down anywhere industry wanted him. Wives reoriented and resocialized the family in the location assigned them, maybe thousands of miles from parents and relatives—the experts they were used to.

And long hours and competition changed our parents' lives even more. Dad was married to work. Mom was married to the children. And there wasn't much time and energy left to be married to each other. Dad couldn't even make it home to have dinner with the family. The kids were in bed before he came through the door. There was no time for chatting while washing evening dishes, no energy leftover for sharing dreams. No Sunday dinners with family together. No ball games on athletic fields with guys in the neighborhood. All that was replaced by watching TV.

Family structures began loosening and divorces began increasing. Families were split apart. Kids spent every other weekend with Dad or Dad's new family. Moms mothered and worked to make most ends meet. Dads tried to be fair to two separate families competing.

115

Our dependence on family experts quickly broke down. Instead of asking Grandpa or waiting for Dad, Mom called in a professional and paid for those services. She was pleased that the job was done right and right away. With Dad busy more and more, she bought more and more expertise—carpenters, plumbers, electricians, counselors, lawyers, support groups and AA. Moms were becoming independent and more aware of their choices.

Now the Baby Boom Generation is shifting into third

Knowing how to use experts today is essential for success. Families still live apart. Fathers still compete. But now many mothers are out competing too. And there's less time than ever to do the things they need to do.

Women today live very different lives than their mothers and grandmothers, still wives and mothers but using different methods, expecting different things from husbands and families—80 percent of American women will be working by the year 2006, one-third of U.S. doctors, lawyers and managers will be women, 60 percent of the mothers with young children are working today. Child care is a necessity. Two incomes, the norm. Life insurance companies are now selling more policies to women than men. Women's incomes have become a necessity, families need their income to qualify for mortgages.[9]

By 2010, the oldest of the Baby Boom Generation will retire. A full one-third of our population will be over sixty-five. Active and healthy we will probably live twenty years in retirement. Will pensions and Social Security provide enough money? Will health insurance cover our costs of staying healthy? Will the experts we need be available to assist us? Will we have money to pay them? Will we be able to take care of ourselves? Will our families be able to take care of what we can't? And how well will our government oversee the whole thing?[10]

The structure of family has changed. Single mothers. Remarriages. Families of blood and non-blood members. Families are more diverse now—men raising children, men staying home, women living with women, men at home with men. The job of parenting is being done, but done very differently.

Working men and women have to use more experts. We can't do it all and our families aren't able to pick up the pieces. We're spending more and more money for child care, for fast foods and deliveries, for maids and lawn cutters, pet walkers and groomers, hair stylists and manicurists, doctors and chiropractors, nutritionists and weight-loss consultants. We're ordering more from catalogues. Hiring personal trainers to keep us in shape. Even hiring personal shoppers to go out and shop for us. The Baby Boom Generation is moving more and more toward interdependence.

We buy the technical skills we need, as well as the people skills we want. The experts we hire are professionals—as effective, as efficient, as creative as we select them to be—in the business of serving our every holographic need.

What we need to know is different than in generations before us. We don't have to know it all anymore. We know it's not possible with a data base this large. We expect to use experts and also to pay them. We expect to serve as experts and also be paid.

We know what we know and we know what we don't know, and this gives us a new level of certainty. Each of us has the skills to do some things. All of us together have the skills to do everything. We're becoming much more skillful at communicating what we want—face to face, through representatives and brokers, over phones and via faxes.

We've got a lot of stuff

Our ancestors didn't have much when they came to this country. Everything they owned could be jammed in a few trunks. Many relatives lost everything in wars and migrations. Most never had much, used to simple lives on farms and in small villages. Glad to be alive, happy to be free, they had to start all over when they came to this country. They needed stuff, so they designed things and built things. Everyone needed basics. Demand was very high.

Our parents' generation expanded the production and distribution of almost everything—radios and TVs, washers and dryers, mixers and blenders, refrigerators and stoves, houses and autos, clothing and shoes of all kinds in all sizes. They built more-better-faster, meeting the needs of millions of people. Massive fortunes were made by some families—Fords, Dodges, Chryslers, Vanderbilts, Astors, Rockefellers and Kennedys, to name a few.

But the Baby Boom Generation has always had stuff. All the stuff our parents had plus VCRs and CDs, food processors and microwaves, large-screened TVs, Walkmans and Talkmans, alarms in our home and our cars, beepers and cellular phones we carry everywhere with us. We're focused on organizing all our stuff—computerizing it, systematizing it, ordering and delivering it, storing and insuring it, maintaining and repairing it. And we're having to reach out farther and farther to find new demand for it.

The challenge of the Baby Boom Generation is to stay conscious. We must organize massive quantities of information coming via faxes, voice mail, media and modems—so it remains accessible.

We can't hold it all in our own memories, so we need systems with memories. And we hire experts to extend our consciousness further— lawyers stay conscious of legal matters, accountants of accounting matters, financial advisers of financial matters. Instead of going straight to our data, we go straight to our experts, calling or faxing them to access our data and interpret it for us. We are managing more and more by managing more experts.

The Gate to the Third Phase: Entering a holographic world

We're beginning to take responsibility for everything on Earth, noticing things prior generations never wanted to discuss, the things they used food, alcohol and drugs to avoid. We're taking responsibility for things they didn't feel responsible for, things they felt were outside their territory, none of their business. They were taught to keep their noses out of other peoples' business, to "Never trouble trouble till trouble troubles you. You'll only double trouble and trouble others too."

We are facing—head on—the dilemmas created while we were preoccupied with only ourselves and our families, only taking responsibility for our part of things, our part of the whole. We are learning to live in a holographic world, a world where everyone and everything matters. Where we're responsible for all of it. Where when anyone is abused, everyone is affected. Where when anyone is deprived, everyone is affected—whether Nazi Germany or Bosnia-Herzegovina. In a holographic reality, where what happens to one of us happens to all of us. Where what we change in our lives, we change for everyone. Where what we heal in our lives, we heal for everyone. Where changing our part changes the whole.

We live in a global marketplace—depending on each other for raw materials, products and services. We can get anything from anywhere overnight—by air, fax or courier. When the market here is soft, we sell our products elsewhere. Our shows, our sales teams, our franchises are international.

Media instantly creates one reality. As events happen, everyone knows where the flood is, the hunger is, the fighting is, the opportunity is. We're beginning to recognize that we're citizens of Earth—all faced with the same needs for fresh air, nourishing food, full communication, health care, education and security. The same team with the same dream. We are beginning to see it, to hear it, to feel it, and hold it as possible. Beginning to discover the expertise we've got to do it with.

A pan of water sloshing

But seeing ourselves as everyone and everything is a challenging hologram to hold. We begin by denying parts we don't see in ourselves and seeing those parts as only happening to others. How could "they" have done that? "They" must be bad people. We include and then deny, we include and then deny—like a pan of water sloshing back and forth. The realization of it all pushes us into denial. The remembering of it all brings us out to look. The seeing it all pushes us into denial. The growing willingness to include brings us back out again. Back and forth, back and forth. And over time, we see we're sloshing less and less, centering more and more.

Where in our lives are we doing the things we once said only "They" do—where in our families, our schools, in the places we work? Where have we, as parents, abused and neglected our children, putting our needs ahead of our responsibilities as leaders? Slapping, withholding attention or food to force them to conform? Where have we, as teachers, taken advantage of our power, making our agenda more important than our students'? Whipping and punishing, blaming and denying, ignoring their needs while attending to ours? Where have we as bosses ourselves punished people cruelly, blaming them for mistakes we had made, withholding promotions when they didn't agree with us, fearing creative ideas, their growing skill and power? Where have we as those who govern, treated people unequally, protecting some and not protecting others, supporting some of their needs but not others? Black rights, minority rights, gay rights, women's rights, children's rights, disabled citizens' rights.

We have trouble owning the things that we do. But now we're seeing it all in the media, caught on home video. Parents starving children because they were crying, drowning them in toilets, burning them with cigarettes, leaving them alone while going on vacation. Children shooting baby ducks, torturing puppies and kittens. And killing other children. Teachers molesting students. Police brutalizing citizens. Bankers embezzling funds. Mayors doing drugs.

It hurts. It's confusing. (Con-fusing, from the Latin *confusere*, to fuse one with the other.) We see goodness and we see badness. We see workability and unworkability. We are sorting and labeling and organizing our experiences all over again, noticing what we noticed but didn't want to know. Accepting the realities we didn't want to be conscious of. Taking responsibility beyond where we've ever taken it before.

We've developed through the three phases as individuals, and we're developing through the three phases in society as a whole. It's time to assure first-phase freedoms for everyone on Earth—the right to self-confidence, health, security and education. It's time now to assure second-phase freedoms to everyone on Earth—freedom of choice, freedom of speech, freedom of opportunity and expression.

And as we stand at the Gate to the Third Phase, we are looking at freedoms we want now: the freedom to solve problems we face, the freedom to talk openly about whatever is bothering us, the freedom to solve problems beyond national boundaries, the freedom to use available expertise and information, the freedom to create fulfillment for every single citizen.

We're challenging our first and second phase leaders to shift into third now—our parents and caretakers, our teachers and preachers, our bosses and managers, our organizations and governments. Anyone anywhere who is still holding back.

And we're looking at the thinking that kept us from knowing—separate homes, separate schools, separate businesses, separate governments. It all started at home when we taught children to be obedient, to be seen and not heard, to see but not tell. Yes, children should have respect for their elders. But their elders should first have respect for their children—their needs, their rights, and their expectations that elders will take care of them. Yes, children should respect their elders, but not when their elders aren't doing the right thing, not when they're abusing them and teaching them not to call out for help.

A Declaration of Inter-dependence

We are feeling a new interdependence, feeling the need to support everyone in being safe, healthy and effective, mastering the first phase. To support everyone in being skillful and productive, mastering the second phase—linking systems, creating compatibility, continuity of information, production and delivery.

We are eager to solve problems we've never looked at together, talking about things we've never discussed before. AIDS has got us talking about sex in all its varieties. Our needs for child care and assistance in parenting has got us talking about family in all its varieties. Our vantage point on what's happening around the world has got us talking about leaders in all their varieties. Talk shows facilitate exchanging experiences. And we are sharing our dreams, showing, telling and feeling them altogether, acknowledging they're possible. Millionaires are sharing how they started out with nothing. The lives of the rich and famous have been made public.

Some people are uncomfortable with all this new openness, pushed against the first-phase rules that limit their lives—things they're not supposed to tell strangers, things they're not supposed to do in public, things they're always supposed to do for themselves. In the third phase, identity isn't attached to what we do. We can do anything. We can be anything. We know who we are. In the third phase we become human beings instead of human doings.

Finally becoming human beings

We no longer have the time or need to do it all by ourselves, even though that's what success used to mean. Our dreams now require us to journey beyond the lonely waters of independence along to the newly marked trade routes of interdependence. Our success is no longer limited by what we can do and what we know. We are starting to reach out to everyone on Earth, establishing a data base of who has what skills and knowledge, and when and where they're available.

Being able to shift into all three gears of success allows us to serve the needs of anyone on Earth—whether they're completely dependent on us as experts—or, whether they're competitive and independent, struggling to let us know they can do it too. Or whether they know exactly what they want and even how to do it, and they simply want our alignment in carrying their plan through—communicating so effectively, hologramming so completely that their dreams become our dreams. And their success becomes our success, allowing us to experience not just satisfaction but fulfillment.

An expert is anyone who can already do what we want to do.

The Sixth Success Skill

UPDATING THE PAST

By completing our past, we recover lost power

A rotor-rooter is designed to clean out clogged pipes. When a roto-rooter goes in, it releases built-up sludge, increasing the flow. Updating is a roto-rooter designed to clean out your emotional "pipes," clogged by pains and disappointments over the years, releasing the built-up emotional sludge that is blocking the flow of your life now.

In this chapter you will develop the skills needed to change old habits. You will learn to update your life the way a computer programmer updates a program, recognizing errors that come up on the "screen"—things we say, things we do, things we don't say or do, and experiences that aren't the ones we want. Having consciously updated these programs, when they go back "off-screen" into memory, they will unconsciously run our lives in a more up-to-date way.

Many past experiences are still incomplete—unacknowledged or unfinished—left hanging there suspended in time, trapping our energy, bringing pain to our chests and tears to our eyes whenever they come to mind. This is an opportunity to satisfy the frustrated child or adolescent still alive within us—the one that wasn't heard, the one that couldn't choose, the one that didn't get what was wanted.

This chapter has three parts. The first part is the recipe, a step-by-step procedure for how to update. In the second part you will learn how to clear away fears. In the third part, you will look at life's changing expectations, updating what matters now, updating what you want.

Knowing how to update will allow you to begin following your heart, moving past old rules and limits, the reasons why you couldn't, shouldn't or didn't. Moving past the belief that you can't get what you want. What you think is what you get—like it or not. By changing your thinking you can begin liking what you get. To start the process, I will tell you stories so your own stories will come to mind.

Scared puppies and alley cats

I live with two large dogs, Mica and Mango. Whenever it rains, thunders and lightnings, Mica sleeps happily wherever he is. But Mango immediately begins panting and shaking, slinking to find where I am, his tail between his legs. Why does one dog have fear and the other have none?

Mango is my daughter Margaret's dog and when he was a puppy he stayed outside in a pen while she spent long days at medical school in Virginia. He had a huge luxurious dog house, but he wouldn't go in. So whenever it stormed he was outside alone through the worst of it. And apparently he still relives those cold scary, wet days whenever it rains here in Florida years later. In external reality, Mango is a house dog now, warm, safe and cozy, but internally he's still alone in his pen in the rain.

But sometimes instead of searching for someone to help us, we try to avoid help that is offered. At the start of an extended trip through the Everglades, I stopped to pick up a friend. As I waited for her to complete last-minute packing, I noticed a cat in her glass-enclosed courtyard. She was allergic to cats so I knew it wasn't hers. "Did you know there's a cat in your courtyard?," I said. "No, but I heard cats fighting on the roof before dawn. That one must have escaped by jumping down here."

Jumping in had been easy, but jumping out was impossible. It was a very hot day and there were no trees for him to climb, no way for him to get back up on the roof. This cat was in serious trouble. I looked in my friend's refrigerator to find a little milk or a tiny bit of tuna to lure him through the hall and out the front door. But despite my tender offering, he backed farther into the corner, hissing and spatting at me—a mistreated alley cat attacking the hand that feeds it. Afraid to accept help based on earlier experiences, he was determined to stay put and handle things on his own. But on his own, he would die, so I went into the kitchen and got a broom, swooshing and sweeping as he ran angrily away from me right down the hall out the front door, running to safety despite contrary instincts.

There's a scared puppy or an alley cat alive in each one of us—a frustrated child bent on survival, a self-appointed preventer of future pain and bad feelings. That child rides along content inside, trusting our adult-self to manage things for us until our adult-self gets scared. Then the child-self is frightened too, doubting us because we're doubting ourselves. Like a child scared to death or one throwing a tantrum, our frantic inner-child experiences a fear that takes over our adult mind and adrenalizes our adult body, creating "fight or flight." And sometimes "our scared puppy" or "alley cat" prevents our adult-self from responding appropriately.

Our early fears were about survival—living and dying, eating and breathing, being taken care of or abandoned. Later we developed fears about our ability to perform, our ability to compete with others. But whether we are stuck in obedience or competition, the most fearsome fear of all is the fear of taking charge of our lives, of going for what we want.

Dreads instead of dreams

Some people are vivid dreamers but they do their dreaming in negative, majoring in nightmares—dreading instead of dreaming—not understanding their nightmares are attracting what they dread. In biblical times it was said, "Your fears shall come upon you." That was the Positive Command Brain working back then.

In our memories we've all stored holograms of what we should and shouldn't do, what was right and wrong, safe and dangerous, possible and impossible back then. Some of those old memories are excruciatingly painful, the old pain recorded right in with the memory—slaps, burns, falls, cuts, losses, failures, criticisms and embarrassments. And some memories are quite pleasant but inappropriate now.

Bunny, bunny, bunny

I remember when my mother used to take me to the park as a child. There were lots of acorns and lots of tame squirrels. "Bunny, bunny,

bunny," my mother called. And the squirrels came running, eating bread from her hand. Then when I got up the nerve, I fed them myself. Day after day we brought bread to the park. "Bunny, bunny, bunny," And the squirrels always came.

Twenty years later I took my husband to that park. "Bunny, bunny, bunny," I called and the squirrels all came. Then my husband laughed, "Why in the world do you call a squirrel a bunny?" I hadn't heard what I was saying. Of course, I knew the difference between a squirrel and a bunny, but that was the label that popped up from my memory.

Memories are permanent unless we update them, allowing more recent successes to erase our past failures, allowing our present abilities to replace past inabilities. We often hear ourselves saying things like, "This is just like the time that..." "This always happens." "Or, here we go again." These phrases take us back into our old files, reactivating a flood of memories, reactivating our old insecurities, fears and expectations and bringing them up into the present.

Let's review. When we detail a dream or a plan in our minds, we program it. The more detail we imagine, the more charge that dream has. That energy is set aside for that program making that energy unavailable for other use. As long as we don't complete or delete the dream, the energy is held and the program keeps operating. And our Razz continues trying to complete that incompletion.

But now is not then

What is happening now never happened before. Things, though similar, are never identical. If we take the time to look closely we can find the differences. The only part that's identical is the way we're reacting.

Different circumstances require different responses. When we react the same way, we let our past run our present. "Doing unto others what we hated having done unto us" is the unfortunate result of running the past in the present—like it or not. When we have our own children, we catch ourselves saying the same things our parents said, reacting the same way our parents reacted, doing the same things our parents did. Our habit of remembering keeps bringing up old data. But each time it comes up on the screen of awareness, we have the opportunity to update the errors we find recorded there.

Always/ever/never and sometimes

Why hasn't our past just been updated in the process of living life, of learning more and more day after day, year after year?

Let's look more closely. Whenever our leaders—parents, teachers, managers or those governing—have taught us something new, they've started out with a black-and-white recipe. The goods and bads, rights and wrongs. "When you do this, you always..." "When you do that, you have to or must..." Their first-phase program was entered in our computers and locked in, made permanent and unchangeable by the words always/ever/never. Then other behavioral variations were punished until they were extinquished, until our behavior was consistently pronounced right and good.

Then we practiced and practiced, and when we were doing it safely and correctly consistently, our leaders unlocked the program for us, inserting a new instruction—"sometimes." Sometimes they let us do other things, other ways. But some of their programs were never updated, and those old "always/ever/never" programs still run our lives.

The Safe Zone, The Danger Zone or The Potential Zone

In late childhood our parents began to teach us to rely on our memory instead of on them. They were preparing us for when they wouldn't be there with us. They taught us to always look back in our minds, asking ourselves, "What happened before?" "What did I do then?" "Was it safe or was it dangerous?" And then redo what was safe and avoid what was dangerous. So then we were programmed to stay in our Safe Zone.[11]

Then our parents further amplified our fear of The Danger Zone by associating yells, slaps and punishment with doing things that were dangerous. This system worked well for keeping us away from hot stoves, dangerous streets, bad things and wrong things. This was an effective operating system for a child, but not appropriate for adult use.

So like cows trained to stay within electrified fences, humans are trained to stay within The Ivory Tower of their lives, doing what they know how to do, seeing from the same angles, using the same scripts— bored and disgusted and apparently safe. But never allowed into the zone where they could leap, dance and fly, where dreams can come true, where the impossible is possible. I call this area of our lives The Potential Zone.

Old fears hold our energy trapped, blocked and unusable. But behind our fence of fear is everything we haven't done, everything we might love and enjoy, everything new and exciting, everything we could do if we weren't afraid to try. But in order to enter this verdant virgin territory, we have to walk toward our fears, conversing and learning from them, making them a wise and valued part of us instead of something to be avoided or evaded.

Looking closely at the word emotion, we see it contains motion. Like a human body that has completely stopped moving, past experiences that have completely stopped changing their meaning ought to be pronounced "dead."

My grandmother used to say, "There's no wind so evil it doesn't blow good to someone." Some of those worst-thing-that-ever-happened situations will in the long run be relabeled the best things. Fortunately there's a wisdom in the universe that knows more about what we need than we do in the moment. Sometimes we have to "wait and see" what that wisdom is all about.

I realized my incomplete experiences were a reservoir of energy I could draw on. Each year since I've known this, I've made up a list of things that still frighten and upset me, things I don't do for one reason or another, things I've caught myself making excuses to avoid doing or experiencing completely. And I update one per year. What are the current items on your Most Dreaded Fears list? What items have you completed that used to be there, now able to drive, scuba dive or use a computer?

But our reliance on our past has become entrenched and habitual. We're still avoiding methods we got hurt using way back then, even though why we got hurt has nothing to do with that method. Maybe we weren't ready or our timing was off. Maybe our leader didn't supervise us well enough. And so we got hurt physically or emotionally.

Sent off to court alone

A young lawyer fresh out of law school was sent off to court alone her first time. Her busy insensitive boss simply handed her a scribbled diagram of the courtroom showing her where the judge would sit but not preparing her to present the case. The busy and insensitive judge proceeded to make her look foolish and stupid. That first embarrassing failure tainted her professional confidence so badly that she decided to abandon law.

Memories are like witnesses. Things look different depending on where we stand. When we are standing in a new place in our lives, reviewing old experiences, those experiences look different. Their meaning has changed, and we need to put those experiences in a new file and attach a new label. "In retrospect; you know, that wasn't all bad. I really learned a lot. And the next time that happens I'll..." The old thinking is updated.

By completing our past, we recover lost power.

Updating: What to do step-by-step

Sitting at a computer we update a program at the insertion point, the point where the cursor keeps blinking. But we update our lives at the point where we're hurting. That is our insertion point, the place that's alerting us, that's telling us we need to change and correct. Of course we can choose to ignore that alert, but then we'll just continue to feel pain and confusion, or, even worse, move into numbness.

But once we've updated our data, it returns to unconsciousness, operating our lives without our knowing it, increasing the probability that we'll get what we want. And having updated that error, when we recognize another one, we'll be more able and likely to correct that one too. And the next and the next, day after day.

Remember, Earth is a correctional institution. We're here to correct and correct and correct all of our programs until they produce desired results. In the third phase we are programmers, programming our own lives holographically.

But we weren't programmers in first and second. We were programmed by others, dependent on their praise and acknowledgment, their input and updates, waiting for their permission to shift into second. But we don't have to get their permission to shift into third any more. We can choose for ourselves the exact moment when we are willing to be responsible for updating our own programs. And that moment might be now.

By the end of this chapter you will have the skills and experience you need to update pain, confusion and numbness whenever it occurs. You will be able to correct anything that's been entered in your data base so far—by you or anyone else.

Neutral: Out-of-gear

As we drive, forward gears are essential parts of the transmission, and there's another crucial part, neutral. Sometimes we need to let a car idle, or we want to rev the engine to check how it sounds before we start driving.

Sometimes we need to shift into neutral in our lives too, shutting down the transmission of instructions to our bodies, thinking without having to feel or take action, allowing us to test ideas without carrying them out immediately, allowing us to pre-feel and pre-do so we can choose.

Up above the car

At this point in one of my seminars, a participant shared that she was excited to hear about this because it made sense of an experience that had made her feel crazy. She and her husband were in their convertible stopped at a light, when a man ran up and began striking her husband over the head with a pipe. The man kept hitting him over and over. She was sitting in the passenger seat of the car screaming at the top of her lungs when she suddenly saw that scene from a different perspective. She was up above the car watching herself scream as the man kept hitting him. She could see a policeman running to the rescue. Then when the man was securely handcuffed and the situation was safe, her perspective went back to normal. She was back in the scene again watching the man being arrested, knowing her husband was alive and an ambulance was on the way.

Now having heard about out-of-gear, she understood what had happened that day. She realized she had used an emotional protection device, an automatic jumping out-of-gear that allowed her to avoid the intense shocking pain she was experiencing. Similar to how a circuit breaker shuts down the power when a circuit overloads.

Hot-wired, turned-off, or having a choice

In the first phase of our lives we were always in-gear, sensing and doing except when we slept. Reaching and touching, seeing and tasting, wanting and getting. Think-do. Think-do. With no way to break the connection. Hot-wired and always-on was exciting, or painful, depending on circumstances. Sometimes we got so overstimulated that we ended up having tantrums. Always-on was very dangerous, requiring someone with us to keep us from doing unsafe or inappropriate things, to distract our attention and refocus it on what we should do instead.

Then as we shifted to second, we learned how to operate in neutral more and more—waiting, delaying, thinking what others wanted, doing what others wanted, keeping our own ideas to ourselves. We became appropriate and political and neutral, pushed into secrecy and out of integrity. The thrill was gone. The excitement and enthusiasm seemed to be something only remembered from childhood. Instead of direct-wired, we were usually turned off. But turned off was dangerous too. We had gotten so detached and so distant from our experience, from our own wants and needs, that we'd started asking, "Is that all there is?"

As we shift into third, we can turn ourselves "on" again, taking over at the controls of our lives. But now we find ourselves stuck with our internalized parents, their old holographic programs, the old scary scenes we lived through with them. Plus all of our old delayed gratification programs, the ones that keep telling us we have to do what we're told to do, we have to wait until later to do what we want.

As you've been reading this book so far, you've no doubt experienced many emotions. This book has been designed to bring to awareness old scenes you may want to update. As I've shared the updates that I've done, you've probably done ones of your own. You may have had moments when you put the book down or tears came to your eyes because a resonant chord was struck deep down inside you. Because you re-experienced something that had caused you pain earlier. Maybe you hadn't thought about these experiences for years. Maybe you were shocked that the feelings were so strong.

Think back over some of those moments, thumbing through the pages and making a list of your old incomplete scenes. Now is the opportunity to begin completing and releasing them. This chapter will teach you how to manage your emotions by doing this work in neutral.

Start by comparing the difference in the amount of emotion that you feel as you read these two different versions of the same scene.

Locked in a suitcase: A painful story from my past told in-gear

I remember the day when I couldn't find Cathy, then four. I had been calling her and calling her. Two-year-old Margaret was standing in the hall all by herself looking sad and dejected. I asked where her sister was, but she didn't look up. Something was wrong. I began searching through the house, but Cathy was nowhere. Finally I looked up toward the attic, and the door that was always locked was wide open. My heart was racing, my face flushed and hot as I ran up those stairs. Muffled sounds were coming from a locked blue suitcase, moving and shaking. One latch was unhooked and one small arm had pushed its way out, swollen, lined with deep red ridges. She had tried to break free. My younger daughter must have locked her in while they were playing, but one latch was broken, thank God. I unlocked the other one quickly grabbing her limp blue body, running with my two daughters in my arms down both flights of stairs, out the back door into cold winter air. Her color was returning, she was starting to cry weakly. Margaret cried too. And fear-driven words sprang out of my mouth. "How could you have done that! You almost killed her! That was really stupid!" I was blaming my two-year-old as I stood clutching her recovering sister in my arms.

Telling you this story in-gear, even in the past tense, brings tears to my eyes and panic to my heart. This is the way we usually review scary experiences. I can choose to get out-of-gear and into neutral by stepping out of the scene, becoming an observer, seeing it happening from a distance. Read through this version told out-of-gear and feel the neutrality this method will give you.

The same story told out-of-gear

Looking at the scene from a distance, we see a young mother asking her two-year-old where her older sister is. The mother had checked all the usual places, called and looked everywhere, but there was no sign of her. The two-year-old looked dejected and silent. Something was wrong. The mother looked up to the attic. The door which was usually locked had been left wide open. Her heart pounded, her face was flushed and hot. She heard muffled sounds and looked for their source. A locked blue suitcase was moving and shaking. The older child was in there, probably locked in accidentally as part of their play.

She saw that one arm had pushed out. One latch was broken, unlocking the other quickly she saw her limp blue child. She ran down both flights of stairs with her two girls in her arms. Out in the air, her daughter's color was returning. She was cold and began to cry. Her mother could see red swollen ridges where the edges of the suitcase had pressed into her arms as she had worked to get free. That distraught mother screamed at the younger girl, saying she might have killed her. That was really stupid. How could she have done that. And then that young mother broke down and cried.

We have just viewed the same scene from a different perspective, from outside and not inside. It feels different from this angle, more detached and impersonal. Less intense and emotional, easier to look at. This change in vantage point is the first step in an update.

Step one: Recall the situation from now instead of then

Shift into third-phase thinking, feeling confident and successful, remembering all the things you've completed since then, all the people you've interacted with successfully. Notice your current ability to communicate wants and needs, your ability to use experts instead of relying on unwilling or unable people—whether parents, teachers, bosses or those in government.

Note that the prefix "re" always indicates an update—re-do, re-think, re-construct, re-engineer, re-train, re-marry. Listen to others who are wanting to update, asking us to recall, rethink or redecide.

Step two: View it taking place up on the screen

Imagine sitting in the audience viewing that scene up on a movie screen, watching the "younger you" going through what happened back then. And what the others in the scene were experiencing too, knowing that everything looks different from different angles at different times. You are watching and listening to your past, seeing that scene from the outside not the inside, from now instead of going back to then. This advantage point gives you the kind of wisdom you have when you give advice to a friend. Give yourself this same perspective and wisdom seeing neutrally from this distance what happened back then, whether back then was when you were two or ten, yesterday or the day before. If you find yourself getting sucked back into the scene, feeling the old pain and losing perspective (starting to talk in the first person, I, instead of the third, she/he) then step out of the scene again and go back to your seat. Review the whole scene several times following these instructions.

Step three: Take over as the director, making and remaking the scene until it's a success

Now step into the role of the producer/director who is creating this movie. This movie is supposed to be about success and satisfaction. What does that younger you want? How can you rewrite or recast this scene so it will indeed turn out to be a success. Imagine this scene working in as many different ways as you can think of, loosening up the idea that this was the only way it could have happened. Think about other options and possibilities.

As directors what could we change in this mother-child scene? First let's change the ending, allowing the mother to be supportive instead of blaming, having her comfort both of her girls, making sure she reassures the younger one that it was only an accident. "You are both fine now and a whole lot smarter."

We could change the beginning, installing a lock on the attic door so whenever the parents leave the door will lock automatically. Or we could have inspected the attic for dangers a long time before then, keeping all suitcases locked, removing all potential threats to their safety.

We could change the middle of the scene, telling her not to try to run all the way down two flights of stairs, instead lifting her daughter quickly out of the suitcase but staying right there, comforting and reassuring, reducing the fear sooner, asking her what happened, acknowledging her bravery, letting go of the upset. Telling the two-year-old Margaret that she loves her and everything is OK, hugging and touching.

It's pretty simple to see ways to change this update, but sometimes what we have to change in the scene isn't so obvious. If we can't think of any other ways to play it out, then we need to ask experts how they would handle it, remembering that an expert is anyone who can do what you want to be able to do—whether an expert in parenting, counseling, communication, negotiation, time management or auto mechanics. Experts know

135

many ways of solving the same problem, skilled in many methods and different approaches. And if one way doesn't work, then they switch to another and another. So if you're not an expert in this skill area, go ask what an expert would do and hologram yourself using their input to complete that scene successfully. Remember success is completion—or deletion. Find ways to complete it or ways to delete it.

Who else was in the scene? How skillful were they in communication? Were they upset? Or under great pressure? How satisfying were their relationships? Were they feeling nurtured and satisfied or frustrated and angry? What about their jobs? Were they satisfied and appreciated or did they dislike their boss or feel unappreciated?

The higher the frustration level people have and the lower the level of communication and expertise they have, the more likely they are to take their frustration out on other people—their children, their family and co-workers. If they couldn't talk to their boss or spouse, then they probably couldn't talk to their children. If they had no time for themselves, then they probably have no time for others. If they had nothing for themselves, then they probably had nothing for anyone else. Other peoples' expectations probably feel like too much for them, especially if those other people are needy and demanding little children.

As the director, you can increase the other participants' skill levels so everyone in the scene can communicate more skillfully. You can mentally substitute an actor instead of the real person until you can imagine the actual person being more skillful. Direct that actor to stand the way you want, move the way you want, talk in the tone of voice you want, touch you the way you want. Direct other participants specifically as to how they can satisfy you.

Even a death can be updated and completed. You can allow that person to still be alive in your consciousness, allowing yourself to imagine sitting down with that person catching them up on what's happened since then, what you miss and you don't miss, what you disliked or hated, even telling them how angry you felt when they died and left you here all alone. You can do this in one sitting or in several sittings over time, ultimately bringing that relationship up to date. Or you can imagine having had more time before the death to get your communication complete, knowing in advance and saying everything there was to say, making sure you let them know how much you loved them. Living out that scene from a distance if it's painful, and then stepping into it when it feels safe and loving.

It is important that you update old scenes in which you decided you wouldn't ever be able to get what you wanted. Or you decided that things would never turn out for you in relationships, jobs, sports, music or dancing. And you locked those decisions in with always/ever/never making those reactions permanent, repetitive and never-ending.

A wise teacher of mine once told me I could assume I was attached to a point of view unless I could think of at least two other ways I could view it. To free ourselves of old pain and disappointment, we have to let go of the certainty that we were absolutely right back then, that we really did know exactly what was going on for our parents, teachers, bosses, or others involved.

In remaking the scene, your desired outcome is for that younger you to feel heard, responded to, appreciated, satisfied, happy and complete. The method you use can be usual or unusual as long as it works.

Step four: Get into the scene and enjoy that success

Then shift back in gear, stepping up into the best version of the scene, getting on stage, speaking in the first person (I am), living this successful experience now, recording it holographically, giving your brain a better more up-to-date option, a more satisfying choice to use the next time, then filing that completed scene in your success file.

One day I can't find my girls. I am looking room to room. Finally looking up I notice the attic door is open. That is their playroom now. We have a doll house set up for them. All their toys are up there too. It is their special spot, safe and well-organized, with all of our junk stored in a partitioned-off part. I love going up there and peeking around the corner to see them dressing or undressing a doll or seeing her in a high chair with tea cups all set.

Reprogramming our inner computer

When we update what appears on a computer screen, first we locate the error. Then we decide what we want to insert there instead, entering that data in place of the data we want to delete. As soon as we insert it, we delete what was there and then that updated data comes up on the screen the next time we access it.

In our inner computer, the old memory is not deleted, rather it is preceded. The updated scene is put in front of what happened further back in time. It becomes a better choice, a more up-to-date option. Our inner computer doesn't update totally the first time, requiring repetition before updating is complete. Repeat that new scene in your mind, reliving it a few times to make sure it's holographically recorded and accessible.

Truth is a very funny thing. It looks different depending on where we stand. It's the old blind man and the elephant story. An elephant is as big around as a tree trunk. An elephant is as thin as a rope. An elephant is as rough and leathery as an old shoe. What an elephant is like depends on where we stand.

It takes twelve people to determine the truth in a courtroom, but then we never know if twelve others would have drawn the same conclusion. So why did we insist that the way we saw that scene back then was the truth? The real truth is that whenever we look at something newly it changes. Try out this new version in your life, and if it produces more joy, health and happiness, then proclaim it "your truth."

You may want to ask a friend who understands updating to play out your scene with you. Let them assist you in having that success, "really." Direct them so they will do it all just the way you want them to, and then enjoy the success that you've created together. Let them be the patient supportive parent, your encouraging teacher, your acknowledging boss, the government that assures your health and security. Allowing this new holographically constructed memory to attract more of those successful experiences in the future.

The three phases of updating

When we begin to update we usually start with things that happened in the first phase of succeeding, when we were infants or young children, when we were just learning at home or in school, when we were new on the job, relying on others to teach us, to build up our confidence. When we needed others to tell us what to do, dependent on their availability and interest, their skill and sensitivity as leaders. And so our early updates usually involve changing what other people did. Changing a parent who yelled when we asked questions. A teacher who told us we were hopeless in math. A boss who told everyone they were incompetent and stupid. A government that took over everything we owned, running us out of our own country with nothing. When we suffered loss or death. These are the first updates we need to do. Maybe for months we'll do first-phase updates, experiencing scenes where we were led much more successfully, where we were given what we needed.

Then after that, we'll start updating scenes where we felt we weren't as good as others, not as able. We just couldn't learn or we felt hurt, angry or embarrassed. We wanted to do something just as well as the others could. Maybe we were ignored, put down or criticized, told we were terrible, too dumb to learn. Or our leader lost confidence in us and told us to quit. Or our peers made fun of us, refusing to choose us or let us be a part of the gang. We wanted them to cheer us, knowing we would do better and better with their encouragement.

Then after doing second phase updates, we'll want to start updating the things we've done as leaders. The specific situations where we failed to praise and support. Where we gave inadequate directions. Where we yelled about failures. Where we put down their ideas. Where we held the control and wouldn't let them have it when they were ready.

Updating: Erasing fears, doubts and limits

To begin to change, it's important to be able to recognize which phase of fear has us stuck. Did our failure occur in the first phase, in the process of getting started, when we were dependent, when our skills were undeveloped, when we needed a coach with us? Or did it occur when we could already do it, when we were competing with others, but not doing enough, fast enough or well enough? Were we criticized or put down or avoided by our peers? Or are we afraid to let ourselves dream and get what we want, having it and deserving it?

First-phase fears: Fears of loss or abandonment

First-phase fears are—I'm afraid I'll get hurt or killed. Or someone I love will. I'm afraid I can't do it. I won't know how to. I can't do it safely. I'm not allowed. I shouldn't, it's wrong or disloyal. I don't understand the directions. I won't do it correctly. I'll be abandoned or left. And we start remembering back to when our parents told us to never do that, we looked stupid when we tried, or we'd be punished if we did it. We just weren't cut out for it. We didn't have what it would take. Or a teacher told us we had some sort of deficiency—a learning disability, a block to learning math, science or even art. Or a guru told us wanting money was evil, having material things wasn't right—that taking charge of our own destinies meant that we were spiritually defiant.

Second-phase fears: Fears of competing and failing

Second-phase fears are: "I'm not as good as. Not as smart as. Not as attractive as. Not as able as." Afraid to be compared, criticized or made fun of. We say to ourselves: "I won't measure up. I've tried and tried and I won't try again. I'll get the worst grade. My peers will exclude me or make fun of me. I'll be the only one who fails. If I do it my way, I'll get in trouble. Authorities will stop me. Or criticize me in front of others. Hold me up as an example, someone who hasn't done enough, well enough or fast enough. Or a person who was caught in a lie or a secret."

Third-phase fears: Fears of dreaming and leading

Third-phase fears are the fears of imagination, our limitations to dreaming. "I can't imagine doing that, owning that or living that way. I can't see, hear and feel that it's possible. I can't give myself permission to believe I'll ever get it. I can't introduce myself, ask, apply or take action. I'm afraid of leading, of assuming responsibility, of being the one in charge."

Fear of loss: The little-orange-kitty story

Notice what fears of loss and abandonment come to mind for you as you experience this story and make a few notes on what you want to update from your past. The little-orange-kitty story can guide you to recover energies you've had tied up for years, allowing you to release that energy for creating dreams in the future.

Little did I know that one of the great teachers of my life would come to me in the form of a little orange kitty. One day as I sat at my computer, the phone rang and I heard my friend Sharon's voice. Someone discarded a large box in her yard Wednesday, but it wasn't until Saturday that she finally had time to drag it out to the trash. She was shocked to discover the box contained four little kittens, less than a month old. Two were dead and crawling with maggots and the other two were screaming loudly for help.

Now she had a problem because the kittens needed to be fed every hour and a half, with a tiny nursing bottle and mother-kitty-replacement milk she had bought at the pet food store. But she was busy at work these days. So she called me, the home of the strays and the homeless, and somewhere in the conversation she mentioned the magic word calico. A calico kitten I had was hit by a car, dragging her broken body almost up to my door dying in the bushes unnoticed. I was still feeling incomplete, wishing I'd known and could have done something to help her. But I couldn't.

So based on the fact that one of the kittens was a calico, I said I would take her. But she explained that they only came as a pair. They'd had so much trauma that she didn't want to separate them. And so a little begrudgingly, I said I'd take them both for now, provided she'd take back the other one when they were old enough. And she agreed. She brought them over in their own new blanket-lined box, and, sure enough, the calico was exactly like the one I had lost, and my heart felt warm and full toward her. I was certainly nice to the orange one, but I felt no special connection. I fed him, I cared for him, but only as a second. A "me too."

Early one morning there was a violent thunder storm and all the animals in my house piled on my bed with me, the two little kitties were at my head on a pillow. Finally the storm passed and we all slept a little. Around six I got up to make breakfast for me and my flock. But when I called the kitties, only one of them came. And I had a sick feeling inside me as I went to my bedroom to search for the other one. And there on the floor at the foot of my bed was the other kitty writhing and convulsing. The calico kitty was dying in my arms. I drove frantically to the vet and with only one block to go, she went limp.

As I walked into the vet with that dead kitty in my arms, I felt alone and helpless. The attendant looked knowingly as I turned to leave, saying I would take her home to bury her. And out near the pond under the tallest bananas trees, I laid another calico kitty to rest. And with my shovel in my hand, I wept.

As the day drew on, the little orange kitty was getting mad, furious in fact, and directing his full fury at me, biting me and scratching me as if I had intentionally taken his sister from him. I felt the way a distraught mother must feel when she recognizes that she isn't able to love her surviving child. Why are you here, little kitty, and not my little calico? And I judged myself harshly for even thinking that thought, hating my feelings, wishing them away from me. But they were real and they were there. And the little orange kitty knew it. He could feel it. He had probably sensed it all along. And so I apologized to him. I told him I was sorry. And the tears streamed down my burning face sore from so many tears already.

We seemed to make peace with each other then. He and I had both suffered great loss. We made a pact, he and I, that we would try to become friends. That I wanted to get to know him. That I needed his tender purring support. And I gave him an extra blue-delft dish full of food, letting him know he was very special to me.

And day in and day out, we learned to know each other. Each day as I sat for 10 to 14 hours at my computer, he slid in behind the keyboard resting on my lap. And sometimes he did it so skillfully that I didn't even know he was there.

He seemed to assume that he was one of the dogs—Mica the 85-pound Rhodesian, and Mango the gentle Labrador mix. Wherever they curled up in the afternoons to nap and dream noisily, moaning and twitching, the little orange kitty was there, nestled in the C that their curled-up bodies created.

And one morning there was another violent thunderstorm and I felt panic rise up in me. It wasn't the storm, it was that old memory flooding in on me. That earlier, similar morning with the calico kitty dying on my lap, finding the first calico dead by the door, feeling the loss and pain. But then I started to laugh, waking from my fantasy, drying tears that had poured out already and reaching down to my new friend right there beside me. And I felt so much love in my heart for him. Little orange kitty, you've done it. You've made me fall in love with you, with your gentle sensitive ways, your quiet attentive tenderness. And I considered calling him something like "Book" or "Success," but those names didn't suit him. The little orange kitty had become "the little man."

And that little man had taught me something most precious. Relationships are built on mutual caring and understanding, getting into each others' rhythms, satisfying each others' dreams. I realized I had updated my old dream from wanting another calico to wanting this kitty sleeping afternoons on the window ledge next to my parakeets, squawking at him noisily. Once he was napping, they pulled fur from his side to line their nest. The little man and I "feed and water" each other every day, honest with how we're feeling, completing the same dreams—six a.m. breakfast, out to feed the fish, settling in on my lap while I'm writing all morning, purring in the kitchen during lunch. And he's settled in his favorite spot now, writing this all down with me, putting in paw marks every once in a while.

xxxxxx   ttttttttt   nnnnnn

I've shared this tender story with you to underline a precious fact I've discovered. Life fills in whatever spaces it creates. If we can trust that our needs will be met, if we accept the wisdom of what's being given or taken away, then we can begin to feel the perfection of life's process. And then knowing that what we think is what we get, like it or not, we need to begin thinking about what we want, even in disaster, even in loss, instead of getting stuck in what we didn't want to happen.

We've succeeded in completing a painful experience when we can write about it or talk about it thoroughly and completely, when we can finally see some good that came out of it, some way the experience has allowed us to grow, some way that experience has allowed us to understand people and life better.

Now we can delete

In the first phase we were dependent on the people we had, our parents and caretakers, always trying to please them, hoping to win their love so they'd continue to take care of us. Our greatest fear was losing them, or having them be upset with us.

As adults, we can succeed by deleting—choosing to leave marriages, choosing to leave friends and family, choosing to leave teachers, choosing to resign from jobs when we've communicated our needs skillfully and frequently and they haven't been met. But we couldn't delete our parents and teachers when we were children. We couldn't even refuse to eat all the vegetables they put on our plate. We couldn't get money when they didn't give us our allowance. We couldn't leave our room when they said we'd been bad. We couldn't move in with relatives even though we'd have been happier and healthier there. We were dependent on those who managed our lives, whether skillfully or not so skillfully. Dependent on their sensitivity, their willingness and ability.

And if they weren't sensitive for one reason or another, we learned to hate the things they always pushed—like broccoli or spinach, like dancing or choir, like homework or bedtime, like taking naps or staying home after dinner, like obeying an older sister who seemed to be their favorite and given all the privileges.

We would have been perfectly happy to eat another helping of green beans or sliced tomatoes, but that wasn't allowed, it had to be broccoli. We would have been fine with going to bed when we were tired, but we had to go to bed when they were tired. We had to do what they wanted, when they wanted it. And we hoped that if we did, they'd do what we wanted. But we seemed to get disappointed more often than not. And we've gotten stuck with some of those disappointments and decisions that resulted. I'll always do this, I'll never do that. They always do this, they never do that. And we've seen the same patterns playing out over and over, year after year. And we've asked the same question, "Why me?"

Sometimes we update holographically in our minds using the four steps we've learned. And sometimes we update in our lives, living out the update, creating the scenes we want in reality, choosing the people we want to coach us and support us, and enjoying the pleasure of that completion success.

Fears of competing: Conquering my most dreaded fear, ballroom dancing

I was still working on my one-per-year list of Most-Dreaded Fears, and the most-dreaded of all was the one that came next, learning ballroom dancing. This story will help you to recall your fears about competing and failing.

You may be a marvelous dancer but, like me, somewhere in your life there's something you fear failing at, something you feel you can't measure up in whether it's making presentations or motivating speeches, hitting balls on the driving range, preparing a large dinner or taking care of a new baby.

My mother was a frustrated dancer, still studying ballet at sixty, seeing an eighteen-year-old girl in the "inner mirror" that she gazed into, feeling her youth as she chausseed and jeteed across the stage, carried by the music, a famous dancer deep inside her. But when the music stopped and the adrenalized passion of her dancing subsided, she saw once again her old image in the mirror.

But this frustrated dancer forced dancing on me, hauled me to ballet studios every week, lined me up on stages with all the lithe and lovely ones, feeling like an ugly duckling, geeky and dumpy and clumsy and slow. Hoping to get me to complete her own dream. As if ballet weren't enough, another day a week she took me for tap. I can still see those netty tutus and sequined Spanish dancer costumes hanging in the attic. I loved them hanging there, but I hated putting them on and prancing on stages.

Where Mom saw a beautiful graceful swan out there, I saw a horse, a slow stubborn mule. And feeling that way, dancing was no pleasure for me.

Then in junior high, it got worse. I had managed to talk my mom into piano lessons instead by then, passionately loving the sounds and the rhythms, the brillantes and crescendos, the staccatos and largatos and, as much as I hated dancing, that's how much I loved the piano. I walked fifteen blocks in the rain, snow or scorching muggy summers to my lesson every week. I taught children in the neighborhood so I could get the money to pay for it.

But then the era of "polite and proper" was setting in, the time for becoming "a young lady," and I had to learn to ballroom dance. My white gloves in hand, I was enrolled in cotillion, like it or not. And I didn't. Once a dreaded week all the girls would line up on one side of the Ladies' Club and all the boys would line up on the other. And then by some amazing pheromone-sensing process, the boys would pick a girl. But I was never picked, probably slumped in a corner somewhere, becoming invisible and undiscovered, avoiding their glance. I must have been good at invisibility, because they never seemed to see me. Or if they did, they didn't look a second time, quite sure they didn't want to dance with me, moving quickly on to the next girl. But if there was an even number, that night I had to dance.

On rainy days in gym class we had to stay inside and dance. There was one boy that all the pretty girls refused to dance with, but the gym teacher always made me dance with him. And I couldn't refuse, even if I wanted to, because I knew how he felt. I knew that not being chosen really hurt. That not being chosen to dance was even more painful than not wanting to dance. And so whenever I danced, whether on rare occasions in cotillion, or under empathic duress in gym class, I was stiff and in rigid resistance. "I didn't want to." "I didn't like it." "And I couldn't."

So at fifty when I made up my list of most dreaded fears, ballroom dancing was still at the top. Approaching this fear now put my old fears in perspective. Scuba diving looked easy, cave exploring seemed simple, rappelling down mountainsides quite manageable and delightful, but ballroom dancing was still as fearsome as ever. And I decided it was time for me to conquer that fear.

That fear was totally irrational now. I was a nationally known speaker, able to hold audiences spellbound with a story, able to whisper and have everyone in the room leaning forward to hear my next word. Able to act out anger and fury so convincingly to make a point, that when I immediately dropped back to my regular voice, people couldn't believe I hadn't been angry and furious. That was all easy for me.

I told my friend Sharon about my list, my plan to find a ballroom dancing class and the perfect teacher. I wanted to learn to love dancing. I was eager but not excited, eager to get it over with, eager to get it behind me, and that was the best I could do at that point. But Sharon loved to dance. Like my mother, when I mentioned dancing classes she lit up, reaching out to embrace me excitedly, telling me that was something she wanted to do too. And she had a friend, Charlie, who taught ballroom dancing many years before and wanted to get back into it now that he was retiring. And my heart pounded. I was trapped. No more excuses. It was going to happen.

We had our first class in her dining room. I graciously offered to push all the furniture back, to find the right tapes and to do anything else to delay the dreaded start. But Charlie was gentle and reassuring and simply started to dance with us, needing to assess what he had here to work with.

Sharon glided easily wherever he led her, smoothly and softly. And I broke into a sweat. "Here we go again, and I bet she was always chosen to dance at cotillion." Then it was my turn, and approaching me exactly as he'd approached her, he hit a stone wall, a solid rigid object, not moving from its spot, even with a lot of pressure. I wanted to move easily, to glide, but I couldn't, feeling stuck in the same pain I'd felt so many years ago. And I started to cry. At fifty years of age, I still had the rejected thirteen-year-old inside.

I sat down with Charlie, explaining the dreaded list and my desire to love dancing some day. "Could you help me? I'm a very good learner." I told him I was scared and that I needed to be coaxed and reassured. I needed him to know that he was teaching the frightened thirteen-year-old still alive inside me. He said that whenever she took over my body, I should tell him right away.

And so the fifty-year-old self-assured speaker embraced her scared inner self. Charlie and I led her through the first phase of dancing, starting all over again. But this time it was safe. I could tell he really liked me and my honesty. And I knew Sharon did. But it was hard to not hate her, to not make myself wrong every time she moved, swiveling her hips in S movements to a tango. My hips were stuck in concrete, and no matter how many times she showed me how to move my knees and feet, nothing would happen. Except tears would come up just short of my eyes, and I would tell Charlie that my thirteen-year-old was in charge again.

He would reassure her, changing the lesson so she could succeed, backing off from the tango, going back to the waltz. Then I found I could feel the rhythms from my years of studying piano, and Sharon couldn't feel them. Now there was something about dancing I could be good at. I felt even. Sharon could move easily, but I could move in rhythm. That was my first breakthrough. My first success in dancing. And my confidence came up one notch from bottom.

We had done the basics—the box-step in all its rhythms—over and over, week after week. I knew what I was supposed to do even though I couldn't always do it, and my panic level was manageable now—not gone but not running me. Until Charlie suggested we go to a dance studio he knew, and join in a class there. I was OK, even a little eager, until we walked in. And guess what I saw? A large room like the Ladies' Club, with all the men lined up on one side and all the women on the other. And I shrunk back immediately to my past. And the class already in progress turned out to be intermediate. I wanted to run. Really, I escaped for a few minutes to the ladies' room, seeing a panicked child's face in the mirror, talking to her, reminding her it was now and not then. And this was Charlie, and this was Sharon. And so I went back into that room, recommitted to my plan to learn to dance and enjoy it.

An amazing thing happened then. I caught on to a sequence, a series of rights, lefts and turns. I got the idea quickly, even faster than Charlie did. And a lot faster than Sharon. Another success, building more confidence.

This new teacher was a showman, enjoying his performance but not noticing his students' needs, a master dancer but not a master teacher. Able to do, but not able to explain. So I started explaining it to Charlie and Sharon now that I'd caught on to it. As astounding as it seemed to me, suddenly I knew how to dance, not that I could glide yet, but at least I knew where my feet were supposed to go and I could get them to go there.

Then another unexpected thing happened. Sharon didn't want to continue taking that class, not liking that teacher, hating that experience. She didn't want to come any more. And I was left there alone to be Charlie's dance partner. And we danced, and he reassured me. And we danced, and he complimented each and every improvement I made. And we danced, and I started to have fun, my body softened up, my hips came unglued, and the mirrors around the room showed me a new picture. A graceful couple, a beautiful responsive woman, following his lead easily and softly. I could hardly believe my eyes. I was seeing a new me, a me who was a dancer. And then the tango played and Charlie swept me up and we moved magically around the room, my skirt swirling, our bodies as one. I was dancing the tango, loving that dance. And I could even see my mother in me, gliding easily and happily.

Four steps to change

Step 1 Seeing where I am now—how not doing this has hurt me.

Step 2 Seeing where I want to be—what doing it will do for me.

Step 3 Developing new skills—learning how to do it.

Step 4 Success filing my progress—acknowledging my success, noticing and recognizing that I can finally shift, no longer stuck outside "the experience," keys in hand but afraid to get in, no longer unable to get it started or accelerate or go the whole distance to where I want to be.

In the process of change, a mirror is an important tool, whether that mirror is a real one—like the glazed glass on a wall in a dance class or gym, or held up in our hand so we can see ourselves now—or another kind of mirror like a photo or video. That mirror can be a person reflecting our progress back to us—a teacher, a coach, a counselor, a therapist, a parent or lover—showing us a new picture of ourselves, showing ability and success instead of inability and failure.

And once we're successful, we begin to enjoy it, looking forward now instead of avoiding, eager instead of dreading, confident instead of fearful. Ready to try something new, something different. And often we outgrow what was so comfortable and supportive in the beginning, when we needed someone to tell us exactly what to do and when to do it.

Updating through divorce: Divorce can be a master teacher

Our first marriages are often re-creations of our relationships with our parents, someone we've chosen to do what our parents did, telling us what to think, want and do. If we failed to learn to think, want and do for ourselves while growing up with our parents, then first marriages often teach us the lesson of dependence more strongly. And we finally leave our "second parent" asserting our in-dependence—becoming dependent inside ourselves instead of dependent on others.

But once we're independent of our mate, once we've gotten away from the most recent one we'd allowed to run our lives, then we come up to an even more powerful preventer, our addiction to the first and second phases of success. Our old beliefs and assumptions. Our old fears and limits. Needs and dependencies. And we discover that we've known what we didn't want for a very long time, but we haven't ever known—dreamed and imagined—what we did want instead.

This discovery presents a new challenge. And another temptation. Will I find myself this time? Or will I try once again to find myself in another, someone else to tell me what to think, want and do. A new boss. A new religion or master. Someone else to control my life. Someone else to fight against. Instead of someone to create with, dreaming and sharing the journey.

As adults we can understand success not only as dependent beginners do, not only as struggling competitors do, but also as creative leaders do. We need to understand the whole process of success. But as long as we're dependent on others to fill our success file, dependent on their praise, recognition and approval to feel successful, then we can't take the risk of stepping out beyond their rules, beyond what they know and they're comfortable doing, beyond what they like and believe. So then we can never do what we want in our lives, express what we came to express, never contributing our own gifts and perspective.

Updating the fear of dreaming: I can't until I remarry

When I wanted to buy my house, I found there was something else I needed to update. Many times I heard a voice in my head that very strongly and convincingly talked me out of things I wanted to do. That voice always told me, "I couldn't until I remarried." I couldn't go on long trips, or so it told me. I couldn't have big parties. And of course, I couldn't have the house of my dreams. But this time something powerful rose up inside me, and I stood challenging that voice I'd so often listened to and believed. I doubted that voice, and I wasn't willing to listen. "That isn't true," I told it. "That just isn't true."

Fears, I've discovered, are like black clouds—very scary from a distance, but whenever we approach them, moving close to them, there's nothing really there, only a mist or a vapor. And I've learned to walk up to my fears, talking directly to them, doubting them, and with my hands firmly gripping the rope attached to my dreamer's hook, continuing to climb up instead of going back down to where I've been before.

And so whenever I've heard that "finally recognized voice," I've argued, disagreed and continued to take action. I bought the house knowing, "I can have whatever I want and whatever I am willing to be responsible for—no matter what that voice says."

Even after I moved in, that voice continued to try me, logically and articulately presenting a case for why I shouldn't be living there, why I didn't deserve to, why I should let a large family live there instead. And I learned to just as powerfully and passionately present my retort, "No, this is mine and I want it. I want it, and that's reason enough. And I can go wherever I want to go, taking exotic trips up mountains and down canyons. I can speak, I can write, I can take care of myself, giving myself whatever I want." And after some time and convincing, that inner voice began to quiet through the certainty and consistency of my response.

Updating: Changing expectations so we change our results

In even the most successful peoples' lives, there are a handful of programs that have never been updated. We avoid these areas of success and satisfaction, sure we can't do them, having failed earlier in our lives and having decided we can never do that. We can never have that. So we've learned to live without it, accepting "our limits," no longer trying to enter these areas of our lives, telling ourselves it'll always be that way. Our teacher told us, our coach told us, our best friends told us, our ex-spouse told us, and we've told ourselves they were all right.

In our inner computer, when we enter a permanent program it runs—always, whenever, every time. It never ever misses. And every time we tell ourselves always/ever/never, we reinforce the lock, the way we lock the tabs on an audio cassette so we can't record over it accidentally.

Then over and over we replay these locked programs to ourselves and others. "Whenever I get involved with a man/woman, then... Whenever I get involved with a friend, then... Whenever I have a new boss... Whenever I trust anyone..." These programs become the stories of our lives, the ones we tell everyone in the first phase of getting to know us. And so we copy our old programs into their computers, programming them to play them out with us. "Don't hurt me like my mother did. Don't disappoint me like my dad did. Don't yell at me like my bosses have."

And the Positive Command Brain enters those instructions as positives, "Hurt me like my mother did. Disappoint me like my dad did. Yell at me like my old bosses did." And even if they try not to, even if they only do it one time, even if they're upset about something else altogether, we immediately notice it. We react to it and it validates our old program. "See, I was right. You're just like all the others." And then we distance ourselves emotionally or physically.

Events that disappointed us as children always disappoint us as adults. What always disappointed us about our parents is what always disappoints us about our teachers, our managers and governments. It's been our never-ending story, the program we've lived through over and over, the one that's locked somewhere deep inside us. The one that keeps attracting these circumstances. Our self-fulfilling prophecy, the program we're always struggling hopelessly to complete. The one no one can ever fulfill.

Our journey through The Three Kingdoms of Expectation

Before we have the wisdom to update our lives and memories, we need a broad perspective on life as a whole. For as long as we continue seeing things the same way, we can never ever change. And no one and nothing else can ever change either. To change reality, we have to first change our mind, looking much broader and wider and deeper and higher than ever before.

Wisdom was handed down in stories long before it was written down in books. Stories were told from generation to generation, stringing together wisdom and information so we could remember it. Audiences have told me over and over that they remember my stories better than anything else. Sometimes they even stop me on the street in a city I'm visiting, telling me how powerful the "black-plastic-flower-pot" story is, or "the barnacle" story or "the little-boy-in-the-bathroom."

Here is a mythic story you may want to hand down to your next generation. Wise stories usually begin with "Once upon a time." but this one begins... Our first expectation in life was necessarily a powerful one, after all we were helpless, born into a little immature body that couldn't take care of itself on its own. And so we immediately and optimistically assumed, "Everyone will be there for me, always and ever. No one will ever fail me."

So then venturing forth confidently into life, we began to suffer disappointments almost immediately. And since our very survival depended on being right about our Primal Expectation, we felt upset whenever someone wasn't there for us, whenever someone didn't give us exactly what we wanted.

Since we believed that other people were all Perfect, we started to wonder what was the matter with us. "I must not be good enough, good looking enough, smart enough. I must not be tall enough or short enough, skinny enough or fat enough. I must not be lovable enough, or else they would have done what I wanted." From now on I'll try to be more obedient. I'll try to do what they say to do exactly."

But after fruitless efforts with mothers and fathers, with sitters and teachers, we were forced to update our Primal Expectation, telling ourselves, "Some people are Perfect, but not this One." So, we immediately left that person physically or emotionally, and continued our search for The Perfect Person, the person who would always be there for us.

This was a life-and-death matter and record keeping was now essential. So we started two files which we kept safe in our minds. But one of those files was usually empty, the file for Perfect People. Whenever we met someone new, we put them on trial in that file. There was a distinct possibility that this new person was Perfect, because, up until now, this person had given us exactly what we wanted, been attentive and caring, never ignoring or forgetting exactly what we wanted.

In the second file, we put everyone else we'd ever known. That was the file for Imperfect People, people we knew who hadn't come through, who hadn't listened and responded perfectly every time. This file became very heavy and crowded.

After searching and searching, after trying and trying, and keeping everything that had ever happened clearly in mind, we went through a dark crisis, falling deep into disillusionment and finally deciding we had to update our Primal Expectation. "There is No One who is always there for me. No One who's always Perfect."

At this point we were faced with a vital choice. "Will I stay disappointed retreating into depression, feeling abandoned and mistreated for the rest of my life? Or will I update my approach and go on?" Moving on, we decided we knew what the problem was—we were too dependent on other people.

Our bodies had now grown and matured and we were learning to do a lot of things for ourselves. So since we couldn't count on anyone else, we decided we'd learn how to count on ourselves.

But now we needed to find The Perfect Method, the one method that would do everything all the time, never ever failing us. Then we'd always be able to take care of ourselves, without having to depend on anyone else. So we began to explore different methods. As soon as one didn't work, we searched for another, and another, becoming more and more independent, still wanting people around of course, but not needing any one of them to do everything all the time. Now we wanted people to teach us the skills they knew. We needed teachers and coaches to help us learn to be skillful.

We went to schools and universities, obtaining degrees and certifications, practicing our skills over and over. But The Perfect Method eluded us. And we kept going on to the next and the next, seeking teachers and masters, gurus and corporate heads, potentates and religious leaders. But we were always disappointed. Because none of their methods worked all of the time. Under all circumstances. No one of their methods was Perfect.

So we faced our second life crisis, our second earth-shaking disillusionment. Our Second Expectation hadn't worked either. What in the world is the matter? And at this crucial moment we had to make an even more profound choice. "Now that I've been deeply disillusioned a second time, will I stay disappointed and retreat into despair and depression, feeling abandoned and mistreated for the rest of my life, or will I update my approach and go on again?"

Creating a Third Expectation, we decided to take a more inclusive approach, putting everyone and everything together in one file, throwing away the other file, and labeling them all—Sometimes Perfect. So now we are discovering who knows what and where they are, asking questions of many people, realizing that if we know enough people, who know enough skills, Some One or Some Way will always be Perfect.

We are learning to enjoy Everyone and Everything on Earth, at the times when we need them, at the times that they work, and finally with this Third Expectation in mind, we are beginning to discover that Everyone and Everything is Perfect—Sometimes.

But how much of the Big Picture were we seeing when we decided they were Imperfect People?

We only saw one side of what was going on when we were children. Our side. We weren't aware of our parents' side—their needs, their skill levels, their emotions, their priorities. To update, we have to look at the other side of the picture, look at who we were always asking to do Everything. What was happening for them? Did they have the skill and expertise to do what we wanted? Did they have the time? Did they have the money and energy? What were their priorities? What balance were they seeking?

As children the people we had available were family and caretakers. They were our only experts. We didn't have the options we have as adults. We couldn't even tell our parents when our needs were unmet. We couldn't ask for what we wanted. We couldn't search for someone else, more skilled, more attuned and more available. We couldn't pay someone to assist us with what we wanted. We were in our crib, our playpen, our home, in our childhood.

The things we didn't know then

If our mother was pregnant and not feeling well, we might not have gotten picked up when we wanted to. Our diaper might have gone unchanged for hours and hours. We might not have been fed just when we were hungry. If our mother was in graduate school and she was preparing for an exam, she might not have been interested in playing our games, going for a walk, or listening to stories. If our father had a critical boss and his job was in jeopardy, he might have come home upset and irritable and we might have thought it was something we did, or we didn't do, that had made him upset. If our parents were yelling over money they needed and didn't have, we might have assumed they were yelling about us. We might have assumed we weren't wanted or loved.

We thought everything in life revolved around us. We took everything personally. But everything wasn't personal. There were other reasons they weren't there for us. They loved us and they couldn't always do what we wanted. That caused them pain too. Sometimes they got mad with themselves, and sometimes they got mad with us.

My mother told me the truth over tea

We need to let go of the way we've always seen our past, climbing up higher to super-vise our perspective. (From the Latin *visere*, to see, *super*, from above.) Seeing it from here and now. We need to discuss some basic understandings we didn't have as children. We need to think about the phases of relationships, crises people go through, and what it felt like to be our parents. Why they sometimes said no. And why some of our needs have continued to go unmet and will continue to be unmet until we update by ourselves or ask an expert to update us.

When I began updating my life at thirty-three, I was still struggling to get the attention I always wanted from my mother. She had not been there for me since four. And I wanted to know why, so I decided to ask her. I picked a comfortable spot at her kitchen table, putting out a pot of tea. And we sat down to talk after years of being polite but closed. There were two things I needed to know. Why did she drink? And what had happened to her when I was four? I waited. She hesitated. And I reassured her. I really wanted to know. I was an adult. She was an adult. I wanted to feel close again, to let go of old pain. And she looked deeper when she felt safer and her answer really shocked me.

Her favorite brother had committed suicide when she was eighteen. She was the one who found him shot to death in his room. The shock was overwhelming. He had been her best friend, the person she was closest to. And her parents were doubly wounded, losing their family business the same year. The Depression had changed everything and everyone in her life, and she didn't know how to handle it, and unable to pay attention in college any more, she dropped out.

Then she met my father. He adored her, spending all this time with her, making her feel special the way she felt with her brother, doing everything for her, giving her a stable feeling about family again. He had a good job with regular hours and they were happy fixing up a home and starting a family. But their expenses kept increasing. And when I was four,

157

with three little babies, he decided to buy another business, purchasing a large pharmaceutical firm, restructuring and reorganizing to turn it around. He began putting in longer and longer hours, and even when he was home he was down in the basement working at night. He didn't make time for her after that. Didn't tell her she was pretty. Didn't make her his highest priority. And she felt abandoned again, drinking the only way she knew how to soothe that deep ache.

I cried when she told me. I had never known about all this. "Why didn't you tell me?" But she reminded me that I was just a little girl when this happened and she didn't want to burden me.

But I had been burdened with her problems, problems I didn't know but I knew. I felt. I reacted, but hadn't known why. I had always wondered if it was me. Something I did. No, she said sobbing, "It absolutely wasn't you." She said I was a wonderful little girl, showing me the baby pictures she had put in my scrapbook, all the things she had written there. I heard every word for the very first time. And I cried as she read them to me.

"I'll never forget the first time the nurse brought little Susan into me to feed! I wanted her to open her eyes and look at me but she could only snuggle close. I was a little afraid that I would hurt her at first, she was so tiny and fragile then. Sometimes I had been awake for hours waiting for my baby. And then I remember so clearly the happiness and excitement of the coming Christmas—the tree near the nursery, poinsettias in every room. Then two days before Christmas, the nurses all gathered to help put on her "going home" dress, saying their farewells. Dr. Boyd, my sister and I sat waiting for her dad to return, happy as a lark. I remember that Susan made her exit from the hospital crying lustily as clerks in the lobby grinned. We had such a joyous ride home expecting Susan to cry but happy when she slept contentedly snuggled in many blankets. I would peep to see that she wasn't smothered, waiting to see her little hands move. It was beginning to snow and was very cold but it was a perfect day for us with our new little charge. The Connecticut countryside looked gorgeous to me. This was Susan's first Christmas."

And after savoring all that, I told her how it had been for me, how angry I had been with her for leaving me to care for the whole family, how it felt to always have to finish cooking every meal, to have to do all the dishes, shopping and errands. She had never known I felt all of that, too caught up in a blur she said to ever see things very clearly. And I told her I loved her, despite all of that.

We were close for the first time since I was four. I felt her love and her reality, and I finally understood that no matter what it had felt like to me, I was loved by my parents.

Updating our ideas about relationships

Relationships change. They don't stay the way they were in the beginning. If we expect that, then we'll always be disappointed. We need to understand the transitions, the development, the correctness of what happens along the way. We need to appreciate the perfection of the way relationships grow and change.

The first phase of a relationship: Falling in love and discovering likenesses

Primary relationships go through three phases. In the first phase we're discovering who each other is, communicating a lot, asking a million questions, wanting to do everything together and making time available. It's exciting. It's new. Full of possibilities. And we begin dreaming. Maybe this is the right person—then—noticing all the ways we're alike.

But other things in our lives get neglected. Our friends know we've begun a new relationship because we're never available. They call less. They ask less. The people we work with know too. We receive a lot more calls. We don't work as hard or stay as late. Preoccupied with our relationship, our performance may slip. We're busier with relating than with doing our job. And so the limits of the first stage are reached.

Our relationship is distracting and consuming us. We have to do something. We have to end it or commit to it so we can put our attention on the things we've been ignoring.

The second phase of a relationship: Living together and discovering the differences

Back to our jobs, back to paying bills, back to cleaning and spending time with our friends. We create a home together, owning our own pets. And our relationship becomes efficient, doing less together and more and more apart. Communicating faster and better but less frequently. Working toward the future, delaying gratification, focusing on increases, promotions and responsibilities, spending less time, listening less and less until we don't know each other any more, or what we are doing in our days or our daydreams. And the second crisis is reached. Why are we together? Do we both want the same things? Now we're so different. And we long for the way it used to be. Do you still love me? Do I love you? And if we affirm yes, then we move into the third phase.

The third phase of a relationship: Respecting and supporting each other

We create new agreements, prioritizing our time and energies again, vowing to bring specialness back into our relationship, integrating the best of both phases. We plan times with special people, parties and gatherings. We plan times alone—"dates" and trips, a magical night, an outrageous occasion—taking charge of each detail.

His wife hired a helicopter

One third-phase wife I know hired a helicopter, sending an engraved invitation to her busy husband's office, requesting the pleasure of his company at a specific time and place. She stated exactly how long he would be involved in this "pleasure" so he could schedule his time appropriately. And when the day arrived, she picked him up and blindfolded him immediately, driving him to a waiting helicopter and helping him in.

Once they were up over the ocean, she took off the blindfold. The sky was very clear. The sea below was turquoise. The ocean bottom lay contoured and wave-like as they flew to their island and were left there alone, to enjoy champagne and a gourmet buffet she'd brought in a basket. They had their own paradise for that moment in time.

In the third phase we make time for sharing dreams and fulfilling them. We are cooperative and creative, managing our time so we can do what matters most to us. And as busy as we are, our partners know they're number one—sometimes. At the times when it matters, at the times that are special. We are fulfilling our lives together and apart, knowing no matter what, we will work it through together. All parts of our lives are integrating and balancing. We're managing our own development, our children's and our society's. We love and value each other, respecting our differences as well as our likenesses.

Her thirtieth birthday

A doctor's young wife was an expert in making occasions special. Her food was always beautiful—the tastes, the colors, the abundant array. The result of creative shopping—buying yellow and purple peppers instead of green ones, radiccio instead of iceberg. She chose her husband's gifts lovingly, listening attentively for weeks to hints dropped in conversation. And the wrappings she chose made him eager to open them. Each occasion was designed to be memorable and unique. His last birthday had a gardening theme. Everyone brought a plant or a gardening tool—gerber daisies, blue daze and forget-me-nots, a shovel or a rake, clippers or gloves. There were flower pots on the table and drinks served in watering cans.

But this was her thirtieth birthday, and it was his turn this time. Nervous at first, he quickly called all the guests so he couldn't back out. He hadn't realized until now that he had been learning her special-occasion skills, recording her formula for when, how and what. He too had been listening for weeks to discover what she wanted, and now with mental list in hand, he drove to the places she loved to shop, getting knowing advice on which items she'd love. Thanking them and quite satisfied, he carried his big brown bag full of packages just across the street to be wrapped the way she would. And while waiting for them to finish tying all the ribbons, he stopped in her favorite card shop to find a card by her favorite artist, inscribing his own handwritten heartfelt message lovingly inside it.

He arranged for her sister to take her out shopping the afternoon of her birthday and once they had left, he went into gear with final preparations—

buying flowers and balloons, choosing bay shrimp, scallops and chicken to kabob on the grill, picking out a new marinade. Last he stopped to pick up the cake he had ordered specially decorated for her. The guests arrived and parked elsewhere so she wouldn't know they were there. "Surprise." And she was. He had done it. This birthday was indeed special, finally fulfilling her dreams.

But many times before he'd put business first. There had been lots of upsets that preceded this birthday, the upsets when he forgot to buy a gift, when he simply stopped anywhere on his way home to buy an inappropriate card, when he made no plans for dinner or anything else special. He told himself these things were her job, something she had to do.

Birthdays in his family hadn't been a big deal. Nothing much happened— a card, an expected gift, or maybe a dinner. But for the most part family birthdays were like any other days. But when he treated her the same way, she told herself he didn't care, he didn't really love her. These thoughts had haunted her, making her question their marriage or the wisdom of having children with him.

But her thirtieth birthday had started an update, re-opening the possibility that their marriage could turn around. Was this new behavior of his, this attention to specialness, a fluke or a trend? And she grew more hopeful as his interest continued, as he continued to follow through on agreements he had made with her. Christmas was coming. This would be the test. How would he choose to prioritize his time and energy? He was busy of course. And he could use that as an excuse, but he didn't. He made her Christmas special too.

He had taken care of her dreams, and now she believed he would take good care of a child's dreams too. She was ready to parent with him.

Crises and breakups

Most people experience disappointments as their relationships transition from one phase to the other. We liked being the most important person in the world, always talking and sharing, always doing things together. But that's not what we want in the second stage of relationships. We want our partners to be independent, successful on their own. First-phase behavior now appears abnormal and unhealthy, relabeled as jealousy, obsession or possessiveness. We don't want to be needed so much. We don't want to be worrying about or missing so much. We want to be able to be together or apart, doing what we said we'd do and trusting each other.

In the second phase the priorities in our separating lives aren't always the same. There are often disappointments—we're not always there for each other. Other people become the priority more and more—our children, our bosses, our friends. And old childhood hurts begin to get triggered, making us feel abandoned, not loved the way we were in the first stage of relationship.

Sometimes we break up just when we really should recommit—just when we need to create new agreements, just when we're ready to bring the specialness back. It feels easier to go back into the first phase of a new relationship than into the third phase of the relationship we're in. Like the first stage of a rocket, the first stage of a relationship is fiery and active, noisy and powerful, blasting us off into a new orbit in life. And we worship that first stage.

When the first stage burns out, we need to fire up our second stage rocket— more-better-faster. But then the second stage burns down too, and we have to fire up the third-stage engine—quieter still, more balanced, more stable, and designed to keep us in orbit all the way to completion of our mission.

No Mom, you don't need to come

Some dreams don't come true because we never ask for them. When others want to know what we want, we say we don't know or it doesn't really matter. But then when we get terribly disappointed, we realize we had wanted something specific. But we've been taught to be polite, coached to not ask, praised for accepting whatever we got—like it or not— with a smile and a thank you. Would you like more mashed potatoes? Do you want another cookie? And even when we did, when our stomachs were begging, we answered politely no.

I had just left on vacation, packed up and driven for hours to get there when I got a call. Cathy was in school and planned to join us on the weekend, but her throat had suddenly swollen shut and she couldn't breathe. She had admitted herself to the hospital and now her father was there with her. I asked if she wanted me to come home to be with her. I was perfectly willing to turn around without even unpacking. But she said she was fine. So looking after my own needs for rest, I decided we would stay.

But the next week when she joined us, she was quiet and distant. When I asked her what was wrong, she said it was nothing. So I asked if I could guess and she said that I could. I told her my guess was that she'd really wanted me to come, that she'd been frightened and scared, that being in the hospital without me had been very painful. And she started to cry, admitting she had told me to do the wrong thing, admitting that she had been mad with me ever since. But now she felt mad with herself, promising that from now on she would ask for what she wanted.

If one person can't give us what we want, ask another and another

I've done updates with many people who always wanted their mother or father to be interested in them, to understand their feelings. And when they never did, they felt unloved. Or worse, unlovable, figuring they weren't interesting enough, smart enough, pretty enough, funny enough, good enough for anyone to find interesting.

They had never seen that the reason their need was unfulfilled was that their parent didn't know how to communicate. Their parent didn't know how to be interested. Their parent hadn't been communicated with effectively growing up, and they couldn't give us what they didn't have themselves. Their mothers and fathers were frustrated with their own lives—angry with partners, bosses and children, whether they had one child or nine. Tied down with too much and too many, they didn't want any more, already out of balance and unhealthy.

But they hadn't learned to plan and choose about their lives. They hadn't stopped to think what another child would mean to them—the added care and responsibility, the added expense. They hadn't thought it through, hadn't dreamed it and chosen it. It wasn't that they didn't love us. They didn't want any child. They couldn't handle more, having no time for themselves—or for us.

In the third phase, we know that what we think is what we get—like it or not. So we learn to think about what we're wanting, choosing in advance to take on the fullness of what we choose, knowing that when we get what we dream, we get everything that comes with it—the joys, the frustrations, the certainties, the uncertainties, happy days and sleepless nights. We choose the whole thing, knowing we are willing to do whatever it takes. And we are able to say no, if we aren't willing or we're not ready.

Creating a new tradition—Parenting Vows

Until parents learn to choose in advance, until parents learn to manage their own lives, they will always disappoint their children, never able to make them feel loved and supported. Infant children need everything all the time. That's what dependent relationships are all about. They're dependent because they can't do things for themselves—can't feed themselves, can't get out of cribs, can't change wet diapers, walk or even talk.

And children's choices are limited. They can smile or cry, expecting us to figure out exactly what they need, to make the time and energy to meet those needs completely, replacing ourselves appropriately when we have other responsibilities to tend to.

The choice to have children is a profound choice, a choice that impacts the rest of our lives. It requires five years of being totally responsible. It requires sixteen more years of being very responsible, in sickness and in health, whether we feel like it or not. It requires $100,000 to $500,000 to pay for expenses. And it requires that we support and be interested in them forever.

We promise to love, honor and cherish when we marry. But there are no spoken vows when we create a new life. We need a new tradition—Parenting Vows—affirming our mutual willingness to be responsible for our children's lives, health, education and success—until death do us part. Let us vow to support their growth forever. Then if we part ways, our children will truly know that only the form of our relationship has changed, our love for them hasn't, married or not.

Updating what we mean by family

In the first phase of life, our family is either our genetic family, or those people who have chosen to take responsibility for raising us. The life skills we learn are the life skills they model. We learn to communicate at the level they can, we learn to communicate when and how they can, we learn to use the same words they use. We are loyal to them, their habits and beliefs.

But if our family doesn't meet those needs, sometimes we find someone else to be dependent on, substituting that person in place of our family. Then we need that person to do everything with us, to be always available, putting the same expectations on them we tried to put on our parents. If that person isn't always there for us, we get hurt again, scared or disappointed, angry or rebellious, finding ourselves becoming the "scared puppy" or "the alley cat." But those feelings aren't appropriate in our lives any more. There are other people in our lives—teachers and neighbors.

We need to find friends to share interests with—a friend to study with, a friend to play sports with, a friend to do music with, a friend to do art with, a friend to hang out with. We need to diversify our dependency so we become independent of any one person, discovering that we can find someone to share whatever we want, beginning to discover the value of every person, beginning to understand that no one is ever all.

In the second phase of family we've left home. We're advancing our education. Developing our career. Making our own money. Developing expertise, buying and trading it. Finding ways to get what we want the way we want it, moving beyond our original family, setting up second-phase family, living with a mate and children of our own, or living with a family of friends, learning to communicate our way and their way. Seeking new teachers and information, taking classes, doing trainings, finding new methods, not just doing things the way we did them at home.

We learn to manage our time in the second phase. Up until now, others have prioritized our time for us. But now we are learning to prioritize time for ourselves, deciding what we want and when we want it, taking into account the time it takes to get our bodies from one place to another, the time it takes to complete various tasks. We are beginning to understand why our parents couldn't always be there for us. Now we have the responsibilities they had when we were children. Now we have the schedules they had or even longer.

Walking in their shoes assists us in updating the past, letting go of limiting childhood perceptions at last, understanding our parents' pressures and frustrations. Their need to say "No," their need to manage time. And finally we understand that they didn't always know and they couldn't always do. We can feel what it was like for them in the second phase.

Updating freedom: He was farmed out

A thirty-year-old student was struggling to take charge of his life. He was resisting his own plans and commitments, unable to follow through.

He wasn't wanted as a baby. His father was a sailor, his mother was an aspiring actress. And he was farmed out, quite literally, to reluctant elderly grandparents who had raised enough children already. So they just did the basics, keeping him fed and clothed but leaving him on his own to do everything else. He was left to wander their very large farm, doing whatever he wanted whenever he wanted to do it, lying on the ground, damming up streams, running with the dogs.

When he had to go to school, his teachers struggled with him like a wild horse that had never been broken—unsaddled, unable to follow directions, bucking and baying, not used to having to do what anyone else wanted. He hated the confinement of the classroom asserting, "This teacher can't tell me what to do." Followed by an even more enduring decision, "No one will ever tell me what I have to do." And no one ever could. No one could teach him either. He got in trouble with teachers. He got in trouble with police. He got in trouble with drugs. He didn't learn what he needed to learn.

Now twenty years later, he was back in school, stuck in his old pattern, so busy arguing with himself and others, that he couldn't hear what was being taught in the classroom. When test time came and he had to play back what he'd recorded, he could remember his old arguments, but he couldn't remember the information. And when he failed tests, he became even more angry, blaming his teachers, and wanting his freedom more than his education.

Or did he? We talked about freedom in its three phases—the freedom to learn, the freedom to compete and the freedom to contribute. And we talked about permanent decisions—always, evers and nevers. Over the years he had become a creative person—an actor, a traveler and adventurer. His childhood had prepared him well for all that, but it had not prepared him for completing a professional training.

He wanted to learn now, but he lacked the basic skills. His grandparents had fed him and clothed him. But they hadn't paid attention to managing his education. They didn't require him to set aside time to do homework. So he didn't know how to set aside time to do homework. They didn't teach him to do what others wanted him to do. So he didn't know how to do what others wanted him to do. They didn't set limits for him. So he couldn't set limits for himself.

They had not explained to him that in the first phase of his life, his job was storing and recording basic information. His job was learning skills and being effective in school. Having completed this phase, he would have been prepared to handle more freedom, working more independently with a broader base of knowledge and skills at his command. But without these skills recorded inside him, he would be answering to others the rest of his life.

He needed to update that old childhood decision. "No one will ever tell me what to do." Now is not then. This time he really did want to learn, freely choosing to go to school, investing his own money, actually paying these instructors to teach him what to think and do. He wanted to complete his degree, gaining the freedom to practice the profession he had chosen.

We updated his old program. Sometimes he wanted people to tell him what to do. Sometimes he wanted people to teach him the skills and information he needed. Sometimes he wanted to be inside in a classroom.

He listened to his professors and whenever those old feelings came up—wanting to break free and run away—he repeated his new program. "Sometimes I want people to tell me what to do, to teach me how to do it." He reaffirmed the new freedom he wanted. "I want to be free to practice the profession I've chosen." And he calmed down inside. The arguments stopped. He could hear what was going on again recording the information he needed to learn. And when he played it back, they agreed. He knew it. He passed it. He completed it. Now he was free to practice his profession.

Will I walk my dog or will my dog walk me?

I had house guests staying over and was working with clients in my study when a neighbor knocked at the door. Excitedly she told my guests that she had found the large dog I was searching for. When my guests told her I was busy she was obviously upset. For several days she had noticed this dog wandering in a busy street in front of her office. Today was Friday and she was afraid he would get killed if she left him. He was a beautiful dog and she was sure I would want him. But what would she do with "my" dog overnight? She had a male dog herself so she couldn't take him home. My guests were in a quandary but they didn't want to interrupt me so they decided to let the dog stay overnight, asking her to come back in the morning.

Her story was true of course, but slightly out of date. I had told her fully six months before that I was looking for a dog, but after trying out several for a few days with disastrous results—like precious bird cages overturned, ceramics smashed and broken—I had definitely stopped looking. But somehow my request was still out on the streets.

So when I finished my meeting and walked into my living room, there was a strange dog there barking at me. Surprised and quickly letting him know that this was my house, I was slightly won over when he laid on the floor upside down and nervously wagged his tail. I was definitely disappointed they hadn't called me out to talk to her or simply told her no, but I went along with their overnight plan.

With six people in the house, somehow that dog sensed he should sleep quietly and obediently on the floor next to me. A very wise choice I acknowledged the next morning. Perhaps I'll let you stay one more day. And by Monday I was hooked and had made an appointment for the vet.

I was very aware of the necessity for intensive first-phase training. My dog, now called Mica, was sparkly and bright, running and playing, rolling up rugs and skidding to a stop. This was all very cute at thirty pounds, but soon he would weigh eighty or ninety. So I knew that if I didn't teach him to follow my rules now, while he still adored pleasing me, while I had "a size advantage," then later on he would be taking me out for walks, dragging me down the street at his mercy, the collar on my neck instead of his. And I wouldn't want to live with him.

I told Mica that I loved him and wanted him to live with me. We were in a committed relationship, and I explained that in order for us to enjoy each others' company, I would teach him what I wanted, and he could teach me, so then we'd be compatible and happy together. I was consistent as I trained him, doing the same things at the same time in the same way every day until he mastered the skill, until he did it before I even gave the command. But then I had to teach him how to wait, insisting he do it correctly and exactly, praising him and hugging him whenever he was successful.

I tailored my training to include what he wanted. He loved to lie in the sun by the pond, to go to the park and run circles until he was exhausted. I took him for two long walks every day and he seemed to have a clock ticking in his head, always knowing 6 in the morning and 5:30 in the evening. He'd get so excited that it took a few minutes to get himself enough under control to sit down. Then he waited until I got his leash, turned off lights and closed doors. He wouldn't move until I whispered quietly, "OK." Sometimes I didn't feel like following the program, but I kept thinking of him at 90 pounds not following the program, and that made it easy to do it.

At eighty-five pounds now we're very glad we trained each other. Our routines match perfectly. He knows what I want. I know what he wants. We're very happy together, knowing what it takes to be friends. And we stick to the rules, except on very cold nights when he slips in quietly under the covers beside me.

Now we are leaders steering our own lives

We need to look ahead to what we want, pulling up old anchors. Like starting a motor boat and setting off toward our destination with engines racing and roaring but unable to move until all the anchors are pulled up and stowed. Our old habits of expecting others to tell us what to do—like it or not—keep us stuck.

We're adults now, mature now, and moving through the three phases of life. First, we let others take charge. Second, we struggle to take over control. And third we assume responsibility for our lives and leading others.

Old thinking will hold us back until we update our past. And our old habits will get in the way of others now. We're leading in families and schools, in businesses and governments. Parenting, teaching, managing and governing are all parts of leading. As leaders we are responsible for cultivating the success of our children, students, employees and fellow citizens. We teach them how much they can change the world, by how much we change it.

As leaders we will often hold others back inadvertently, overpowering their desire to pursue their own direction, restricting their urge to create and contribute, demanding they do things our way. Like handing someone something, whether a pencil or a phone, but never letting go of it, we teach them to respect us, but then force them to wrench leadership away from us—or give up any hope of ever having it.

Or we hold them back in a much more powerful and subtle way, by the way we live our lives, using only first and second, and never shifting into third, never contributing and creating. Advertisers know that repetition programs in their messages, moving people to do things they don't know why they do, buying products they don't want, eating foods that don't nourish. But taking action just because their message was recorded holographically in their memory over and over and over. Advertisers understand quite well that, "What you think is what you get—like it or not."

Take careful note, if you don't know what you want, you'll probably get what someone else wants. And that someone could be a younger part of you, a parent inside you, a society or system you've never questioned until now.

Updating old failures: She couldn't sew a straight line

A young woman who was a manager at Kimberly-Clark told her failure story in a training I did. She had grown up in a small South Carolina town. When the girls of the town graduated from high school, they would all go to work at the sewing mill. So she and her friends followed suit and got jobs there. Her friends did very well, but she didn't. She couldn't sew a straight line. Her supervisor was constantly on her back. And she tried and tried, but she just couldn't do it. Finally she quit, feeling ashamed. She was the only one of all her friends who had failed.

Now years later as a successful corporate manager she relived those terrible invalidating feelings whenever her numbers were low, whenever her boss called her in. That failure had left a wound deep inside her, until we began to update her experience. We had gone through a number of versions of the story already. We kept climbing up higher and higher to look at it.

Finally she began crying and laughing, and this was the new Big Picture she saw. Because she hadn't been able to sew a straight line, she had left her small town. She had gone out in the world. She had traveled many places. And now she was a regional manager in an international corporation while her friends were still sewing perfectly straight lines, and wishing they could do what she'd done.

Only an inch of colon left

I was called in as a consultant by a surgeon who had a long-term patient in a major metropolitan hospital. The surgeon wanted to know why this teenage girl was in the hospital so much and why whenever she went home, she would quickly get worse and have to be readmitted. By now he had operated so many times that she had almost no colon left. The surgeries were needed but he was concerned she was creating that need.

As I entered her room, she looked like a fairy princess propped up in bed, with stuffed animals in-waiting all around the room. Several times as we talked, she rang for a nurse to get what she wanted She liked the food there and her favorite nurses filled her drawers with candy and gum. She had a remote control and was allowed to watch movies any time she wanted.

Then we talked about her life at home. She said she had to take care of nine younger brothers and sisters. And every time her alcoholic mother would got drunk she would beat her. Then we talked about her school and her tremendous fear of getting shot while coming and going. Then I asked her if she missed playing with her friends when she was in the hospital. No, she said, after eighteen months away she'd lost track of her peer group.

The surgeries were painful. And having no colon left meant she needed a colostomy, smelly, leaky and highly embarrassing for a teenager. But none of these things were as painful or scary as living at home. At least in the hospital her survival was assured.

The surgeon was sad as he listened to what I was saying, and he shook his head in agreement knowing it was true. "Regrettably," he said, "there is no better place I could send her."

For this beautiful teenage girl this was success. She couldn't find a better way. And her doctor couldn't either. Is this acceptable? Or do we need to update our society?

The keepers of the Gate to the Third Phase

Our parents, teachers, managers and government were the keepers of the gate to our third phase. If they blocked the gate, our progress was slowed.

When we tried new ways and failed and they insisted we had to go back to following the recipe—to using their old methods—then they blocked our way.

When we tried doing things faster and more efficiently, if they yelled or threatened us, taking away our allowance, our bonus or job, then they blocked our way to the gate.

When we made up our own recipe or created a new system, if they laughed at our efforts, if they didn't listen and assist us, then they blocked our way to the gate.

But fortunately we met a leader along the way who had the skills and the interest, who cheered us past effectiveness and efficiency all the way to our dreams. And we went past the gate creating the lives we want to be living. We are the gatekeepers now, able to show others the way to the third phase.

The Velcro of the mind

Our mind, like Velcro, hooks on to anything similar. So by doing a handful of updates, our inner computer automatically sorts through others that are similar. Each update we do updates all those other scenes as well. And a major clearing of our past begins to happen. Our enthusiasm comes back and we begin dreaming again, taking steps toward the future we want, assisting others in creating the futures they want, updating our children and students, updating our employees and teammates, allowing them to let go of old pain and disappointment. And their enthusiasm rises too. And we begin working on dreams together.

As we move toward what we want, we occasionally feel a pull backward. Our headway is slowed. The effort increases. And we know there are old anchors still stuck in our emotional waters. Then we know it's time to update again. And we use that resistance to find our way back to whatever old place still needs to be pulled loose. Having let go of yet another anchor, we move ahead even more easily.

Summarizing the updating skill

We update by rethinking our past experiences, giving them new meaning, examining them to see what valuable understandings we can gain, allowing ourselves to feel differently about exactly what happened, allowing ourselves to imagine how we would have wanted things to turn out, allowing ourselves to experience these successful possibilities—instead of getting stuck in the necessity of our old explanations. As the programmers of our lives we are responsible for all of our experiences—past, present and future—for the way we've filed and labeled them, re-filing them as needed, releasing their held energy.

Making a list of "most dreaded fears" is a very good way to find out where old childhood programs are still limiting our lives. Where we're still operating in the first and second phases only. To get into third we need to gain a new perspective, climbing up our highest mountain and looking down from up there, knowing as the leaders of our own lives we can set any course to get anywhere we want to go, if only we believe we can.

When we re-examine a fear, first we need to look to see if there really is danger. Could I get hurt? Could I get physically injured or damaged?

Yes, indeed gravity does work, cars improperly handled do kill, drugs improperly dispensed do damage and debilitate.

Or does it just feel like I'll get hurt—given the old "tapes" running through my mind, "This is just like…" "This always happens to me," "I know exactly how this will turn out." When in fact we don't know how it will turn out at all. Instead of saying "No" to ourselves like our parents, teachers or bosses did, we need to say "Yes."

We need to know we were loved and valued, even though they didn't do what we wanted. And we need to know that the whole process of life works out perfectly. We'll learn the lessons we needed to learn. We'll be wiser the next time. We will learn to use experts instead of being influenced by people who don't have the expertise we need.

Our limited view of what happened in our past, limits our dreams of what can happen in the future. As we move from first and second into third, we shift who we are from "Human Doings" to "Human Beings," creating the lives we want to be living, creating the world we want to be living in.

Now that you've updated your past, you will be stepping out there again interacting with others—with their thoughts, fears and expectations, with the details of their conflicting holograms. You will need to learn how to hold your own outcome even when you're tempted to substitute their dreads instead of your dreams.

By completing our past, we recover lost energy and power.

The Seventh Success Skill

HOLDING THE OUTCOME

As long as we hold onto our dream, we can pull ourselves up to it

Arriving to facilitate the second day of a seminar for the City of Miami, I heard people talking heatedly in the hallways, saw them standing in agitated small groups. Searching for the director I asked what was happening. She said one of our participants had died during the night. They wanted her to call off the seminar today so they could go to his funeral, but she said they had to attend.

My heart was pounding. This wasn't what I expected. I needed a minute to manage my mind and emotions. I could choose to upset myself further by continuing to detail out the disastrous day I had unconsciously begun to sketch. I could try to persuade the director to re-schedule the day. Or I could use this opportunity to produce the outcome I had come here to produce, using these circumstances to everyone's advantage.

What is an outcome?

Let's do a quick review. An outcome is an experience of a future success that is created by imagining ourselves already there, enjoying the satisfaction of completion or deletion. Pre-living a success—seeing it, hearing it and feeling it in great multi-sensory detail—programs that success into our Razz. The Razz then begins searching through incoming data, listening and feeling for opportunities to complete all the necessary steps—waking us in the night, alerting us in a store aisle, in the midst of a conversation, or while we're taking action. How about this? Did you do that?

Have you asked? Could you try? That is the Razz operating twenty-four hours a day to assist us in completing the outcomes we've programmed.

We steer our lives through attraction and repulsion. When we imagine future success and satisfaction we are attracted to that outcome. When we imagine future upset and failure, we are repelled by that outcome. Changing our thinking changes our direction. Many potentially powerful and successful people lurch aimlessly here and there, never stopping to recognize how what they are thinking affects their success and satisfaction.

Sometimes we switch back and forth between wanting and not wanting, like a spaceship firing rocket thrusters at the bow and the stern. Its forward movement is canceled by its equal movement back, so despite the burning of huge quantities of rocket fuel, that ship stands still. But if one thruster is a little stronger than the other, the ship slowly moves off in that direction. Sometimes we feel ambivalent because we are holding conflicting outcomes in our mind. We could do this, or we could do that, or even that. Then we're like a spaceship that has thrusters firing in several directions at once that ends up moving off in an altogether undesired direction, depending on the way the energy vectors interacted.

To move ahead consistently, we are challenged to hold the same outcome consistently—trusting in ourselves, in the perfection of the process, and seeing the obstacles we face as opportunities in disguise.

Honoring Enrique: Holding an outcome and finding a method

Before I began the seminar, I spent a few minutes backstage realigning on the outcome with the city director, finding out why she had decided to still hold the seminar, why she insisted they all come today. The outcome she had in mind was persistence. She wanted her employees to be able to get the job done no matter what, without excuses or the usual million reasons why not or why later. She said she was fine with whatever changes I would have to make in agenda and methods. And now though the situation had looked impossible initially, it was now looking perfect. I wouldn't just be teaching them how to hold an outcome, I would be modeling the skill as well.

Feeling prepared, I walked onto the stage of that large amphitheater and, looking out over a hundred unhappy faces, I began. "I was very sad to hear about Enrique's death during the night. I remember the things he shared with us yesterday and I know you're upset about having to be here instead of being allowed to attend his funeral. I was shocked and dismayed when I first heard what had happened, I wondered why the seminar hadn't been called off, but after talking with your director I understand why she wants so much to complete it. The success skill we had planned for today is how to deal with situations just like this one, situations that require us to hold an outcome despite unexpected problems and obstacles. The situations that cause most people to fail.

But now your director's outcome and your outcome seem to be in conflict. Let's look more closely to see if that's so. What is the outcome you would like to experience by attending Enrique's funeral? Many people voiced upset. "We're being ordered. We have no rights. Our feelings don't matter. We have to obey. This is rigid and unreasonable." And we noticed that these were the same complaints customers had about the city, the same feelings they experienced.

After the participants had expressed their feelings, the upset settled down, and finally someone began to answer the question I had asked. "The reason I want to go to Enrique's funeral is to honor him—his life, his service, his contributions as a man." How many other people want to honor Enrique? All hands went up simultaneously. Now we have an outcome we can begin working to complete.

Upsets come up immediately when we feel that our outcome is being blocked by someone or something. To move past those feelings we have to reaffirm our outcome—seeing it, hearing it, feeling it and savoring it. Realigning on why we should go through these unusual circumstances is what allows us to proceed.

We've been looking at outcomes, now let's look at methods? The outcome is what we want. The method is how we want to do it. If you needed to go to Chicago, how could you get there? They said flying was their first choice. But what if there's a strike or bad weather and flying isn't possible? Then we looked at other methods for getting to Chicago—

taking a train or a bus, driving, riding a bicycle or motorcycle, walking or running. These methods were slower and more work but still possible.

Going to Enrique's funeral is one way to honor him, but there may be other ways of producing the same result. What other ways come to mind? Someone suggested a moment of silence. I asked how many people would feel complete by observing a moment of silence. A few hands went up.

Then someone suggested we spend time talking about Enrique and his successes. "I'm new in this department, but I think I can understand how you are feeling. I remember the way I felt when my dad died last year. There were many things I had never made the time to say to him, many things I had never thanked him for doing and being." Other participants raised their hands to share stories of people they had seen every day but never gotten to know. They said this experience would support them in communicating and acknowledging people day by day, thanking them for their help and support or complimenting them on how nice a shirt looks or how much they enjoy their smile.

I asked those who had known Enrique to share some of his successes, and many people shared. We heard stories of a devoted son, husband and father, a man who had played an active role in a large and loving family. We heard about the services he had given to his community, coaching the Little League, active in his church. We learned how much he loved to take his grandchildren fishing and how much he adored going to the opera. For over an hour we heard about this man—his unique style, his quiet peaceful ways, his years of careful service. When no more hands were raised, I asked how many people now felt complete in honoring Enrique. And this time a large group of hands went up.

What other methods can you think of for honoring Enrique? One woman felt she would have to do something for his wife. She wanted to pay her respects to the family. Was this the day she needed to do that? No, she would do that later on, when the funeral was over and most people had stopped coming. Other participants planned to send cards and flowers.

Then once again I asked who still felt incomplete. This time only twelve hands out of a hundred were raised. I asked what method they wanted to use to honor Enrique. They honestly felt the funeral was the only method that would work for them. The director and I made an agreement with that group to leave at two o'clock which was the time they suggested, go to the funeral and come back and share their experience with us. And everyone agreed on that method.

When they returned from the funeral, we reviewed the difference between outcome and method, looking at the various methods their group had used to feel complete instead of incomplete, blocked and prevented. Then we looked at their customers' needs to feel complete. We talked about the variety of methods they could use to assist them in feeling satisfied and complete in the future.

The outcome is the experience we want to have, the feeling in this case of having honored a man, a friend and co-worker. The methods are the many ways we can go about achieving it—whether observing a moment of silence, eulogizing a man and his successes or going to his funeral.

Our internal generator

When we dream we create an energy, a power, a tension that gets us to move. Sometimes we tell ourselves wanting is irritating. Yes, wanting is irritating. Sometimes we feel wanting is uncomfortable. Yes, wanting is irritating and uncomfortable, it makes us get up and do things we don't feel like doing at that moment. Sometimes it makes us mad or disappointed. But in the long run, it would be far more uncomfortable, more irritating and disappointing to not want—not listening and not responding to that voice deep inside us that guides and compels us ahead on our mission.

Many people give up just when they're starting because they don't know how to hold onto an outcome, to work with the tension that creation creates. They let go of their dream, and then the power is released. Poof! They're comfortable, but then they don't get what they want. And soon new dreams begin to emerge, like sprouting seeds pushing through rocky ground reaching toward the warm sun they're seeking. We need to learn to allow our creative tension to grow, branching and leafing out into the experiences we want.

Confronting fears without letting go

We have all hologrammed mouth-watering dreams which—as much as we wanted them—never materialized. Excited and eager at first we took appropriate actions until we ran into obstacles and doubts. Then we began retouching our outcome, darkening the colors, eliminating the details, deepening the mood, and substituting failure and disappointment in place of the desired success. Repelled by that future, we substitute another outcome, heading back to where we were or moving off in another direction. Maybe other people didn't agree with us, or maybe it was more work than we anticipated, or maybe we were more attached to another outcome or a limit.

Holding an outcome—especially when we don't have the foggiest idea how to go about it—pushes us up against old familiar limits. (Remember, the word familiar comes from the word family.) As children we were brought up to always know how to do something before we started, so starting without knowing how we're going to do it will bring up old memories that will need to be updated, memories of times that we were punished for trying or we tried and failed miserably, getting scraped, cut or burned. Times we were laughed at by parents or peers for doing something our own way. Fears will overwhelm us from time to time making us doubt ourselves and our project, making the known and the familiar look better than our outcome.

To lead we have to be able to step into the unknown and unfamiliar. We may not know how, we may not know when, we may not know who, but the one thing we do know is that somehow we will achieve it. To succeed we have to be able to hold our hologram all the way to completion. If we let go too soon, then we fail. *Field of Dreams, Chariots of Fire, Flash Dance* and *Rudy* are all movies about people who held onto their dreams no matter what. Their stories inspire us, making us want to have our own dreams come true.

Updating our future as well as our past

To begin dreaming again, we need to take time to update, completing old scenes that are holding energy and preventing us from dreaming. As we begin taking action toward our outcome, we will also need to take time to update our future, noticing when we're changing our outcome from success and satisfaction to incompletion and pain, to frustration and misery, repelling us from what we really want. We are the programmers, the directors, the pilots of our spaceship. To be attracted all the way, we have to keep our outcome attractive, refocusing on what we want whenever we get negative, whenever we feel afraid or distracted. We are responsible for stepping back into our future success scene from time to time, recharging our batteries and moving us ahead again.

Think back to times when you were making a big purchase, like buying a home or a car, and you started to get negative, substituting high payments and additional stress in place of your desired outcome. Based on your substituted negative outcome you were sure you didn't want to make that purchase. Your motivation was gone until you took the time to revisit your desired outcome, walking back into your new home with a wonderful room for the baby, ample closets and storage, a fenced-in yard for your kids and your dog. Or you mentally drove that new car enjoying its safety and reliability, its greater efficiency and attractiveness. It was a treat to go places in, a source of pride and pleasure. And then you were able to confidently move ahead with that purchase.

We need to monitor the outcomes we are holding and notice if we are the ones who are the saboteurs, if we are the ones who talk ourselves out of the things that we want. If anyone else said the things we tell ourselves, we'd get fighting mad, accusing them of being negative and raining on our parade. But somehow when we hear ourselves saying them, we let ourselves believe what we're saying.

Architects and designers are skilled at creating beautiful images, but those images won't be realized unless the sound tracks they create also support their pictures. If they see they can, they tell themselves they can, then they feel they can and they can do whatever it takes. But if they tell themselves they can't build it—existing methods won't work, it'll cost much too much, then they'll never sell that design or they'll be able to find a contractor at the right price. If their inner conversations negate their inner pictures, they won't be able to go all the way to completion. Like going to the movies, the pictures we see, and the sound tracks we hear, create the feelings we feel and the actions we take. Any one of our senses can contradict the others. They must all work together. It takes two or more laser sources to create an attractive hologram. It takes two or more senses to create an attractive outcome.

When future outcomes become tainted, we have to do some inner redirecting, taking a few minutes to get back in touch with the scene that attracted us in the first place, getting in touch with the dream we'd experienced before the difficulties began, before the addition of payments and costs. Re-seeing that picture, re-hearing that conversation and allowing ourselves to become attracted and motivated again. Unless the information we've gathered makes us not really want it and we honestly decide that success, in this case, is deletion. But we have to be honest with ourselves, searching out our own truth. Do we still really want it but we're nervous or confused? Or have we really decided that this isn't the outcome we want?

The pan was too small

Outcomes and methods may get confused. Sometimes we find ourselves using the same methods over and over not knowing why, bogged down in rules and rituals and the way it's always been. Imagine that we're sitting around a large dining-room table, just having enjoyed a very delicious meal—the first meal ever cooked by a new bride. Her roast was crisp on the outside, but tender and juicy inside.

"Your roast was exceptional. I noticed you cut through the bone and bent it up against the main part of the roast. Is that what made your roast juicy and delicious?" She looked at me nervously, feeling hesitant and unsure.

"I don't really know. That was just the way my mother always made roast. It's an old family recipe handed down from generation to generation. Every holiday my mother used to send me down to the cellar to find my father's hacksaw. Then Mom would scrub the hacksaw well, and, with both hands holding onto the roast tightly, she'd saw through the slippery round bone. That was always the hardest part about cooking a roast."

And having said that, she was curious and leaning over to her mother she whispered, "Why did we have to cut through the bone and bend it back against the main part of the roast? Is that what made it so juicy and delicious?" Her mother sat quietly, scratching her head and looking perplexed. "I don't really know. That was just the way my mother always made roast. Ever since I was a child, I can remember the ritual sawing and mother wiping up grease off the floor when it fell."

Now her mother was curious too. So after dessert, they decided to call her grandmother in Cincinnati, asking her why she'd always cut through the bone and bent it up against the main part of the roast. But she started to laugh, "You must be kidding, my dears. You two still do that! I only cut through the bone because my pan was too small!"

But how many times in our lives and our businesses have we used pan's-too-small methods? How many complicated procedures have we followed exactly, not understanding that they had nothing to do with the result we were producing? How many times have we been told that's just the way we do it here. The way it's always done.

Addicted to our one-and-only method

Early on in learning a skill, we latch onto one method, the only one we know. And as long as that method produces the outcome, we keep using that method. But if that method stops working and we still keep on using it, then we're addicted, addicted to our one-and-only method.

We all have addictions, addictions to working or working out, to eating or not eating, to partners or people, to being nice or being tough, to cities or climates, to alcohol or drugs. Like barnacles on the light bulb we sometimes cement ourselves in place—until death or crisis do us part.

Wives leave husbands who are addicted to work and never come home to parent or partner. Husbands leave wives who become addicted to housekeeping, taking care of children, cleaning and shopping. Or they leave because of some kind of abuse—drug abuse, sexual abuse, child abuse, spouse abuse.

An addiction to a method is like an addiction to alcohol, even using more and more of it, we don't get what we want. The method isn't working, but we fail to refocus on the outcome we want, never asking ourselves, "Why am I doing this? What do I want?" And not stopping to look for other ways to get that.

And the people around us get worried. They try to tell us that our method isn't working. They keep on hoping they'll be able to get through to us. Subtle at first, they get angry when we won't hear them, when we keep on doing it and then accuse them of nagging.

If we don't change, then they have to change. Leaving us is hard. They don't want to lose us—only our method. But since we won't find a different method, they will have to. So our bosses fire us and hire someone else. Our mates leave us and go on alone or with someone else, unable to live with the method we're attached to.

Hopefully at some point we begin to feel our losses, and a decision point is reached. "What's really more important to me—my job, my family, everything I own—or this method?' But some people still choose the method. And the next decision point may not come until they land up in a hospital asking, "What's more important to me, my life or this method?" And some actually choose their addiction over life.

Then to rechoose our health, job and family, we have to be willing to do whatever it takes—joining support groups that will assist us in discovering our outcome and finding new methods—working out, taking up hobbies, creating supportive friendships and relationships, changing our life style, balancing ourselves by adding other methods.

My grandmother always told me, "There's no wind so evil that it doesn't blow some good." Addictions provide us with a profound opportunity to recognize the distinction between outcome and method. The outcome is what we want to experience. The methods are the ways we use to get it.

Becoming outcome-oriented instead of method-bound

We have to keep in mind that what we want changes as we shift through the three phases of success. In the first phase we want to please others, doing things right, being good and receiving praise. In the second phase what we want is to beat and win, coming out on top, looking good or better. Only in the third phase of success do we focus on outcomes and how we can complete them.

In the first phase, others provided our outcomes and our methods for us. They decided what we wanted and the method we should use. We tried to stay focused on what they wanted to happen, but sometimes we lost direction, focusing instead on what we they didn't want to happen—getting hurt, being wrong or bad. We constantly needed someone in the third phase to show us the Big Picture we couldn't see—why we were doing this and the whole complex of methods that were available for doing it. But to get us started, they only taught us one.

In the second phase of success, others still provided the outcome, what they wanted us to do. But they taught us more methods. And we tried to use their methods more and more efficiently, and use them better than others could. We were still method-bound, but feeling more flexible.

In the third phase, we become outcome-oriented ourselves, creating the Big Picture of where we are going, able to step into future successes by ourselves, confident about getting there and flexible about our ability to find the right methods, whether we suggest the method or someone else does. Outcome-oriented, we finally become cooperative.

The constant back pressure

In the first phase the recipe had to be followed exactly. We expected to do the same thing the same way every time. We expected to treat everyone the same way. Even Thomas Jefferson, the father of democracy, was concerned about that kind of equality, worried about educating different people the same way, saying there is nothing so unequal as treating unequals equally. But that was the phase of society we were in. That was what the citizenry wanted back then.

Fair used to mean the majority rules. A show of hands let us know what the majority wanted, and then everyone did that. One method was used for everyone everywhere. But we live in an age of minorities, not majorities. And now majority-rule produces more upsets than satisfactions, with so many of us finding ourselves in the minority—as women, as blacks, Hispanics, homosexuals, the disabled or any of the other vital minorities that make up the majority of our society today.

Becoming outcome-oriented will bring up old fears to be updated. First-phase feelings will come up from time to time—wanting to be right, needing to be safe—especially when we're upset, confused or uncertain.

Then we will unconsciously gear back emotionally, shifting into our old ways of behaving.

Without a method we feel a familiar internal pressure to quickly get method-bound. We get triggered by the first- and second-phase questions others are asking us. "How will you do it? Do you know how? Have you done this before?" They are feeling concerned because we're starting out with no method. It makes them not believe us. It makes them feel we're being irresponsible. It makes them mad. And they tell us how they feel, "If you don't know how to do it, you shouldn't be trying. You're just going to fail." And these responses further raise our old inner doubts and anxieties.

Up in The Ivory Tower

Upper-level management isolated themselves in The Ivory Tower to be safely away from the method-bound, from the doubters and nay sayers. Up "there" they could hold their outcome and nurture it among themselves, developing appropriate methods before the first- and second-phase employees even got wind of it. They could give it form first so the form-oriented would be satisfied, putting it in print so those who only believe what they read could believe it, systematizing the formula so the ones who need a systematized formula could follow it.

But now we need our leaders to come down from The Ivory Tower. We need them to guide us through the creation process instead of doing it secretly. We need them to teach everyone in the company how to create and hold outcomes, incorporating our input before the plan is ever finalized, letting us buy-in before they expect us to go into immediate undigested action. Management needs to model the third phase, sharing success skills so everyone in the company will be able to create solutions to the problems that come up every day, so everyone can solve the problems management doesn't have the time, experience or proximity to solve.

The challenge of the '90s is the creation of dreams, the detailing of holograms. Seeing, hearing and feeling the future now so that we can begin to create methods to get there. So we can begin to move in the directions we want to move, instead of being constantly pulled back by the past.

Using time but not run by it

In the second phase we were ruled by time. How long does it take? How many can we make? Who's going fastest? Who's going slowest? How many seconds did your call take? How many hours are you billing this month? We worked against the clock instead of working toward an outcome.

Second-phase, time-oriented people have trouble understanding the third-phase, outcome-oriented people. A graphic designer's boss felt she spent too much time looking out the window, wasting time that he was paying for. Every time he passed her desk he got madder and madder. He didn't realize she wasn't looking out the window at all. He didn't know that she was seeing his project in her mind, making necessary changes there instead of when she used his materials.

Sensing his upset, she started dreading going to work, knowing something was wrong, feeling pressured and watched. But he never said a word or asked a single question until one day he snapped. "I'm sick of your wasting time looking out the window. Get another job." And she did, taking her knowledge, expertise and experience along with her.

The second-phase double-bind: Shall I serve my boss or my customer?

All of us have had the experience of going into a retail store, restaurant or hotel and being ignored by employees—doing inventory, or unpacking or just talking among themselves. Irritated and ignored, we sometimes walk out in disgust, feeling like an intruder instead of a customer. These employees didn't understand that we were the very reason they were doing what they were doing. What was their outcome? What were they being paid to accomplish?

Customer-service personnel often need additional time with a customer, but then they get caught in the second-phase double-bind. They know what their customers want because they are sitting there with them, but they know that their evaluators' needs are quite different. And if they don't go on to the next customer right away, they will put their appraisal in jeopardy, and maybe their job. There is no congruence between customer needs and the needs of the system.

Many companies require customer-service reps to answer all calls within a specific number of seconds, pushing them to rush through necessary paper work or follow-up. Forcing them to go on to the next call even when they're off-balance from the call they've just had, from being yelled at or abused by an inappropriate customer, a customer who screamed and cursed, a customer who was raging. Customer surveys now confirm that they would rather wait a little longer to be taken care of completely.

After years of complaints and frustrations, after years of lip-service to quality above quantity, things are finally changing. Corporations are understanding that an incomplete customer is more expensive and more difficult to satisfy later on—requiring more of the rep's time and more time of highly paid supervisors and managers who are pulled away from supervising or managing their employees.

Customers can be satisfied more quickly, more easily and more efficiently by giving the customer-service rep permission to do whatever it takes to satisfy the customer the very first time, completing their outcome or assisting them in deleting it, giving customer-service reps the power that only supervisors have had up until now.

With the middle management ranks deeply cut, we are redistributing the management responsibilities, encouraging decision-making by the ones who know best—the ones who do the job.

Managing outcomes instead of time

There's not enough time to do what we have to do. Twenty-four hours a day—8 working, 2 driving, 8 sleeping, and 6 hours left over for everything else including overtime. In the second phase when we thought about time, we whipped out our schedule. "I have a meeting from 2 to 4. I have a conference call at 4:10. Yes, I've got time between 4 and 4:10." Everything was written down. Time planners came in every size, vinyl or leather, with or without zippers. We were focused on being at the agreed-upon location at the agreed-upon hour, forgetting to schedule time for moving our bodies from here to there. We drove too fast, ate too fast and exercised too little. Or too much too infrequently.

In the third phase we manage outcomes instead of time, stepping into the outcome before deciding which method we'll use—whether to call, write or meet. Then when we take action we know why we're doing what we're doing and we're able to change methods when they aren't producing the result. Each morning we take time to hologram our outcomes for the day, programming the Razz to assist us, knowing we could call the people we need to speak to or they could call us, we could go see them or bump into them in the hall. How is not as important as our outcome, even allowing the space for a little magic to be attracted in.

Inventors and innovators often report their new ideas came in the shower or while they were doing something completely different—something relaxing or something involving nature. Creative ideas seem to come when we aren't trying, when we're operating outside the 9 to 5 environment.

Creating and holding outcomes gives us a new sense of power. We choose everything we do, creating alignment with teammates on projects, asking to be sold on a hologram if we have resistance, asking others to share with us how they are holding a positive outcome, the specific details of the hologram that is making it attractive to them.

In the third phase we manage our whole lives, scheduling family events, fun events, health and relaxation with the same care and respect we give to business events, the outcomes we are paid to produce for others. We make time for maintaining our tools—our body, car, computer, vacuum cleaner and VCR. And each day we set aside a few minutes to success file, building our confidence, energy and enthusiasm. We either do our success filing alone or with family or team, celebrating our successes together. And we also take the time to see what's incomplete, rechoosing and rehologramming and replanning the next step.

Storing beach umbrellas

The maintenance workers of a well-known resort were called in for a meeting. Their workload was increasing, their hours were increasing, but their budget was decreasing, their profits were decreasing. They were asked to examine how they were spending their time each day and each week, to question the methods they were using, and to generate more cost-effective ways for producing the same outcomes.

The first item on the agenda was the storage of beach umbrellas. There were scores of huge bright-colored umbrellas positioned invitingly here and there in the center of town. Each morning they were pulled out of large PVC tubes where they were stored over night. Each afternoon they were taken down, carted to the storage area and carefully pushed back into the tubes. When the umbrellas were first purchased there were only a few, requiring a few minutes to put up and take down. But each year more were added until now it took four hours a day—from 9 to 11 when residents and guests wanted to sit under them enjoying a leisurely breakfast. And from 3 to 5—when people wanted to congregate in the shade of an umbrella in front of shops and restaurants.

The maintenance crew had never been asked to give input before. They were used to being told what to do and when to do it. And they felt shy at first, but after a few minutes and a few reassurances they began to make suggestions. Finally one team member said that the umbrellas were being damaged by their daily maintenance routine, the pushing and pulling in and out of the tubes was tearing and weakening them. Each of the umbrellas cost over a thousand dollars to replace. He felt that everyone would be better served by leaving them up, except in bad weather. Then the maintenance crew could spend that four hours each day doing other things. Because of that suggestion, the procedure was changed. And because of that change their attitudes changed too.

Later the team proposed hiring a waste management company to collect the town trash. It would be much less expensive and eliminate large capital expenditures that would be needed next year. This was unheard of. They had always collected the trash. It was the core of their job. Would there be layoffs if this happened?

We hologrammed what the crew would do with their time instead, questioning if the whole crew would be needed, and offering to support team members who wanted to start their own businesses in landscaping or cottage maintenance. They began to see new possibilities for their lives.

And according to their suggestion, trash pickup was eliminated and new businesses were spawned and are now thriving.

If you don't know what you want, you'll probably get what somebody else wants

Until we learn to be outcome-oriented ourselves, we are dependent on others to provide outcomes for us. Whenever we feel uncertain, we ask for an outcome. "What should I do now?" "What do you want next?" And then we feel better, knowing which way to turn, which project to start, which restaurant to go to. That method of choosing outcomes has gotten us where we are but not necessarily where we want to be. Until now we have preferred feeling certain to getting what we wanted. We have felt others knew and we had to find out from them.

But something else has been happening during this long process. We've been recording and accumulating information about what we like and we don't like, we have been imagining our own variations of what and how. We have accumulated in our memory millions of holographic pieces—pictures, sound tracks, feelings and methods we can begin to use to build our own outcomes now.

But hologramming is a lot of conscious work, requiring focus and clarity, requiring specificity and detail. And we're in the old habit of using others' focus and clarity, their specificity and detail. It's tempting to slip back into using other people, and then blaming them for manipulating us, or attempting to control us.

It's challenging to live with the tension of not knowing, or, the tension of knowing but not knowing how. Sometimes when we're feeling unsure of ourselves, we slip back into asking for others' outcomes. And having gotten what they wanted and not what we wanted, then we want to push them away, keep their certainty and clarity far away from us. We feel clearer and more certain when they're not around, and we choose to be alone or be with someone else who doesn't know either.

But others who know what they want will keep coming into our lives, and whenever we slip backward, we end up producing their outcomes. Until we finally realize that if we don't know what we want, we'll probably end up getting what somebody else wants. Therefore we'd better know what we want.

We are standing at the Gate to The Third Phase

The Gate to the Third Phase is creativity. We can open it or let it stay closed. To open it, we have to take the time to see, hear and feel what we want in our minds, moment-by-moment, constructing our own outcomes and living those realities in advance, using the opportunity we each have to invent something new, to contribute uniquely.

Then having created our outcome, we have to find the methods that work, methods of our own or the methods of others. In order to do that, we must share our hologram with others. Many others are available to share with. We can share our outcome with others in the first and second phases, others who need us to provide outcomes for them, who need our help in finding appropriate methods. Or we can choose to co-create holograms, adding the details, colors, shapes and textures others have created, amplifying our power to realize our outcome together.

The Gate opens when we assume our position as an equal, when we know what we want is valid, even though others may not always agree with us. And with our outcome in mind we can begin to find others with similar outcomes. We can decide to take action together. Or we can decide to take action apart. The Gate opens into a new world, a world where human beings create and cooperate, a world in which humanity learns to work as a team.

But to move through the Gate we must update old resentments, forgiving people who have told us what to do and when to do it, and acknowledging that, at the time, we needed them to tell us. We are all in the process of discovering what we want here on Earth.

For centuries we have turned to religions and governments to tell us what to do and what to want. The system worked that way for thousands of years. And our leaders became comfortable imposing their way. But all over the world we are starting to speak up. Walls are coming down. Individuals are saying, "No, don't decide for me. I know what I want, and I want you to listen now."

We need a new hologram for a world of minorities, a world of individuals. It is a hologram of participation, a hologram of speaking up and being heard and responded to. We need to use our technology, commerce and industry not just to tell and entertain but to listen and cooperate and lead.

We are still hesitant about speaking up. It still isn't comfortable. We aren't sure how yet. But as we move into the third phase we need to prepare ourselves to dream and communicate so others can dream with us. We need to prepare ourselves to lead to the future we want, teaching our children to know and speak up—learning it from our model. Our creative actions now will support them in living in a world where everyone creates, where everyone expresses, where everyone can find the methods needed to get the outcomes they want.

The 200 wants list

Let's review how to create. Now we have learned that success is completion and deletion. We know how to shift success phases appropriately. We are able to create holographic outcomes and communicate them to others who have the expertise to assist us. We know how to update our past and our future, having completed old limits and fears and recovered those energies. We know how to hold outcomes so we can pull ourselves up to them. We are now ready to begin creating the life we really want.

As children we could easily list 200 things we wanted but weren't allowed to do or to have. But can we now list 200 things we want to experience that we are allowed to do or to have, but we don't do?

Write down a list of 200 experiences you want. And as you are writing notice what your programmed-self thinks. I can't because there's no time or no money. I don't have the energy or I don't have the skills.

We've been trained to live in The Safe Zone of our lives, dreaming approved dreams, taking approved actions. But what about the dreams we came here to express, our own personal mission, our unique contribution? That new product or service or technology that lies latent inside us probably isn't in The Safe Zone of our lives. If it's new and it's different, then it probably won't be agreed with. It probably won't be approved of. It may be subtly or even blatantly discouraged.

Now in the third phase of our lives—as adults, parents, teachers, managers and the ones governing—we need to begin living up to our potential, innovating, discovering and contributing. We need to revitalize our dreams, letting them loose from the limits and restraints of the first and second phases. Climbing out of the playpen, stepping out of the rat race, venturing beyond the system already in place and out into The Potential Zone—that area of our lives where new things can happen, where dreams can come true for ourselves and our planet.

But stepping boldly into this creative new phase will require us to have additional success skills. The eighth success skill is the ability to shield our dreams in the midst of disagreement, in the face of dissent, in the confusion and uncertainty of not knowing how to do it, protecting our outcomes until they are strong enough to stand on their own. And the ninth success skill is the ability to switch ourselves and others back to positive when we slip into negative, when doubts beset us, when we are plagued with disappointments and obstacles. The tenth success skill is maintaining our health and balance.

Something new exists beyond the certain, the obvious, the usual. We are challenged now to move beyond the second phase, beyond effort, struggle and exhaustion. Beyond pleasing others, beyond the ways of our leaders. We are challenged to begin leading ourselves, contributing our accumulated knowledge and experience, our insights and hunches, our own unique ways of thinking and doing things.

As long as we hold onto our dream, we can pull ourselves up to it.

The Eighth Success Skill

SHIELDING YOUR DREAMS

Like infant children, infant dreams need our care and protection

W e're holding our dream, wanting it so badly we can taste it and smell it. Incubating inside, it wakes us up in the night making our hearts dance, our blood rush and surge imagining we're there. Now we're ready to share our outcome with others, but when we do, we run a risk. Suddenly the seedling we've been hot-housing is exposed, its fragile stems and leaves stand at the mercy of scorching suns, withering droughts and crushing winds. The weather our dream faces depends on who we reveal it to.

Think about the times you held an outcome for days or even years, finally verbalizing it to someone you trusted, bringing them into your confidence, having faith that they'd treat your dream with dignity and respect. But they didn't, rushing headlong into your inner reality erasing and redrawing your scene in ways you never imagined, and when the conversation was over, your inner reality had been changed. Your feelings were different. Having substituted their failure scene in place of your success scene, you were no longer attracted and excited, anticipating instead the failure they'd shown you. You stepped away from your now tainted dream, leaving it unfulfilled and incomplete.

What choices do we have in these situations? What skills do we need? The eighth success skill is shielding, learning to protect our seedling dreams after we've set them out. In this chapter we will build our own inner shields, discovering how and when to use them. We will examine our responsibility when approaching others' dreams too, learning to keep them safe from unwanted changes and alterations, from our unconscious editing, retouching and dubbing, learning to ask others whether they would like our input.

The people we share dreams with have power in our lives. They are our leaders now or were our leaders before—best friends, mates, parents, teachers, bosses or officials in charge of licenses and permits. When we confront disagreement, we may unconsciously do what we've done many times in the past, shifting back into first, giving over our power, telling ourselves, "They know better than I do. I must be wrong." Then the scared child within us is left standing there defenseless holding our infant dream.

Others will not experience our outcome exactly the way we do. Instead of becoming excited, they may sense our dream as a threat. Telling our mother we're going away on a scuba trip may immediately elicit a review, in gory holographic detail, of the article she just read about a diver killed in the very waters we're going to. Then our father chimes in about the regulator failures he's heard people discussing at work.

Over the years we may have learned to shield our outcomes from parents, not telling them what we're doing. And even if we do, telling ourselves not to listen to what they say: "They're worried about everything. They live in the past." And we lovingly respond to them, "Oh, get with it Mom. I know what I'm doing."

But a scuba trip is much easier to shield than an infant dream we're not completely sure about ourselves, something still so ephemeral that we can't get it to hold still and solid in our minds yet. Something we want to do but we're still afraid and uncomfortable about, like leaving a marriage or giving up a salaried job to manufacture a new product, or deliver a new service—leaving the known and familiar to begin creating the future.

Dreaming is essential for health, but completion is essential for happiness

Like gardeners, we must care for our tender seedlings, protecting them from those who would take it upon themselves to record in our minds all the reasons why not. They will be well-intentioned of course, wanting to spare us the pain of future disappointment and failure, but they won't fully realize the pain they will cause us if we follow their guidance and abandon our dreams.

Remember the patients without hopes and dreams who came in for minor procedures and died on the table? And the patients with desperate conditions who were inspired to stay alive by a passionate desire? Dreaming is essential for health. But the ability to complete dreams is essential for happiness. Dreaming dreams without completing them is the major cause of pain.

We're all closet-dreamers, constantly coming up with the new and improved. "This TV would work better if... This car would be more comfortable if... This shower would be more enjoyable if..." Then sometime later we read in the paper how someone else completed it, becoming rich and famous. Or we see it on TV, feeling a deep inner anguish. "That was my idea. I wonder what would have happened if I..." and we blame Lady Luck for being there with them instead of here with us.

The completion of dreams isn't a chance matter. A little luck helps, but even lucky people don't always complete things. Invention and production require the use of success skills. Even with the confidence to dream, our fears can prevent us. Even moving beyond our fears, our inability to hold a dream can block its completion. Even when we hold it, other people can still damage or destroy it unless we develop the ability to shield it.

Truth is a funny thing. It takes twelve people to decide. Despite trying their best, juries get hung up on what the truth is. We must honor our own truth, honoring as well the truth of other people, knowing our truths are not the same and allowing for the differences. The products we will need in the future will fail to be manufactured, the services we will need in the future will fail to be offered—unless their creators can shield their dreams as tiny seedlings.

The search for expertise

Holding onto our dream, we venture out for expertise, seeking the team that will assist us in completing it. Sometimes we're right about the people we choose to share it with. They understand our dream and they support us in completing it, offering ideas and agreement. And we soar even higher, strengthened and energized, having further detailed our dream, making it more real. Then there are two human beings holding and shielding that dream, two people searching for the others who will nurture it.

Dreams are like children. They need parents to protect them. A dream gains in power as people perceive its value, becoming more credible and gaining momentum. According to Victor Hugo, there is nothing so powerful as "an idea whose time has come." But until an idea's time has come, it is dependent and fragile. A parent is responsible for protecting a child, a leader is responsible for protecting an outcome.

But sometimes we guess wrong about who we choose to share our dream with, exposing our precious seedling to someone who sees not a rose but a baobab, a tree so dangerous that it can break apart a planet.[12] Someone who feels compelled to pluck it out by the roots, watching their face graying and tightening, sensing their body positioning and becoming rigid, preparing ourselves for the on-coming attack.

Creating your holographic shield

R2D2, the little robot in Star Wars, knew how to shield himself, high-tailing it out of there whenever he sensed danger. But sometimes running isn't our best option. Sometimes we must stand and present, selling our ideas rather than running away with them. Our purpose is to get the idea out there to those who can use it but may not know that yet.

How can we shield ourselves when we need to stand and present? Remember the holographic brain—seeing, hearing, feeling and creating in great detail, generating a powerful electromagnetic force field. We can create holographic shields to protect ourselves giving us the time and safety to sell and negotiate, the time to build a team. I have used my shield successfully when negotiating with angry parties, when presenting new ideas in meetings, when working one-on-one with warring couples, when mothering angry daughters. Try it out now before you venture forth using it.

Take a minute to imagine the kind of shield that will make you feel safe. It can be made of steel, or three-quarter-inch Plexiglas, stainless steel or stone or even white light. It's size and shape is your choice. You are its creator. It can go all around you or just in front of you. It can be round on the top or have no top at all. It can be rigid or flexible. Visible or invisible. It is essential that you sense it specifically, hearing the sound it makes as you move around in it, feeling what it's like to have it on your body, walking around protected within it, being in a hostile situation and feeling safe in it.

Learning how to muscle-test

Next ask someone you know and trust to "muscle-test" the power of your shield. Here's how to do it. Stand up in the middle of a room and hold out your right arm at a 90-degree angle to your side. Have your friend stand and face you and press down gently on your arm, just above the elbow, to assess your ability to resist being pushed down. Do it several times to get a baseline to use. Make sure your friend exerts a steady pressure. The purpose of muscle-testing is to assess strength or resistance, not to overpower you.

Next while you are standing there, imagine a past scene in which someone yelled at you, upsetting and embarrassing you, and destroying your dream. Imagine going back into that scene again in-gear—seeing out of those eyes, hearing out of those ears, experiencing those emotions and body sensations. Be in that younger you's body. And when you are there, nod so your friend can muscle-test your arm. Notice how those old feelings affect your current strength.

Next erase those thoughts and take a second to imagine putting on your shield. When it's in place and you're safe inside it, step into that scene again and have your friend muscle-test you again, noting the impact your shield has on your strength. Then switch parts and test your friend, following the same procedure.

Finally take a few minutes to hologram a project you want to complete—a trip you want to take, a home you want to buy, a degree you want to earn. Step into the pleasure of that completion, detailing it out fully, pre-living and pre-feeling it. Have your friend muscle-test you.

Now think of someone you're afraid of sharing that dream with. Someone who will disagree or try to dissuade you. Be specific about who that is and the scene in which it happens. Muscle-test your reaction. Then put on your shield and bring your infant dream in there with you, safe and protected from harm. Once you are feeling safe, step into that situation again and share your dream safely. Have your friend muscle-test you. Then switch parts and test your partner.

Having taken time to practice, you will be ready to use your shield when you get the first sense of attack, when you first notice someone erasing and reworking your dream without permission. I have done shielding thousands of times in corporations and schools, and what people have reported is that there is a significant increase in strength when their shield is in place. And that same increase in strength will allow them to feel stronger and perform better under difficult circumstances.

But if you find yourself unprotected, if you find your energy and enthusiasm damaged and lessened, if you've forgotten to put on your shield, here is an antidote. Take a few minutes to recall past successes you've had that other people doubted, ones that they later acknowledged, and ones they never ever came to appreciate. By adding these beyond disagreement successes to your file you can also build a shield for future dreams.

There's a time lag in the universe

There's a time lag in the universe between ideas and realities, whether a new technology, a new system, a new skill or book. It takes time to create the physical form necessary so that others can experience our idea through printing, manufacturing, marketing and distributing. New ideas take time to get used to. It takes time to update the reasons why not—why we shouldn't, why we can't, why it wouldn't work if we tried.

Unlike an electronic computer, our inner computer is linked to a body where data is recorded in each cell, where each thought is tied to a feeling, where each feeling is labeled as familiar or unfamiliar, safe or dangerous, usable or unusable. It takes time to change our feelings once we've changed our minds, requiring uneasy repetitions before our new idea or behavior begins to feel right, before it begins to feel "like mine."

Selling our outcomes not imposing them

It may take time to sell others on our outcome, especially if it flies in the face of the holograms they are holding. Pillsbury went through a challenging process to get production managers to open their shields to the new microwave technology. Production management felt the Dough Boy pressurized can was working just fine, they simply wanted to manufacture more of them.

Marketing managers had to hold their outcome of introducing microwave packaging for months. Then they had to shield it from the production forces that didn't want it, convincing them that microwave packaging was what the public would buy, proving that existing teams would be able to produce it, that it was in the best interests of the company to provide it before the competition did. They shielded and sold their dream successfully.

The creators of the VCR technology had to shield their dream for years before the VCR became a household item as necessary as TV. It took time to convince the movie industry that the public would prefer to stay home and watch videos when for decades they had been going out to see movies. People used to want to get out, but now that people are out all day they want to stay in.

Similarly CDs entered the marketplace slowly with a few creators holding and shielding what to most seemed like an unrealistic dream. No one had CD players, everyone had tape players. At first CDs were in a small section of the record shop. Now tapes are in a small section of the CD shops.

Ideas take time to become credible—time to get used to, time to learn to use, time to learn to need. ATMs were possible a number of years ago, but it took people time to get used to them, used to their convenience and their 24-hour service. ATMs felt awkward at first, but now they feel natural.

The media speeds up the time lag between ideas and realities, but emotional buy-in still takes time. The Berlin Wall is gone and Communism is no longer a threat, yet many Americans still hold their old feelings about the urgency of defense.

The emerging global marketplace is forcing us to update our resistance to cooperating. Interestingly enough, the wars which took our soldiers to other parts of the world were a prime force in tearing the walls down. Intermarriage of people and ideas allowed us to experience that we're all the same, dreaming the same dreams of being safe, loved and successful. Cultural programming may be different, developmental phases may shift, but our desire to control our lives is the same universally.

Letting go of our need for agreement

Leaders can operate in agreement but they don't have to. Needing agreement is a limit we have to learn to let go of. Agreement was required in the first phase when we succeeded by doing what other people wanted, the way they wanted it. Disagreement was wrong. Disagreement was punished. Disagreement caused chaos. First-phase societies shunned members who disagreed, driving them out, treating them as though they were invisible. Or killing them.

But in the second phase of success disagreement is encouraged. Find better ways. Be more efficient. Change things if you have to, as long as you produce. Second-phase leaders reward the most productive, even though first-phase individuals make fun of them, calling them names like teacher's pet, boss's favorite, obsessive and cutthroat.

We have to decide. Are we loyal to our bosses or are we loyal to our group? If belonging is our highest priority, then we may even slow production down to get along with the group. If competition is our highest priority, then first-phase group pressure will force us to learn how to operate in disagreement, pushing us toward management where the agreement is increased production, or pushing us into business for ourselves, creating our own agreement.

Chinese boxes: Understanding the process is your best shield

We feel angry and resentful if we fail to understand the process of success. Recognizing the three phases is essential for dealing with the emotional pressures we'll feel. These pushings are painful. The-way-it-used-to-be dies as we're birthed to the next phase.

Like a series of Chinese boxes, one inside the other, we begin in the center, growing and learning. Then the box gets too tight. We can't breathe, and it's painful, forcing us to break through to the next box. At first it's unknown and unfamiliar and we want to go back. But we can't. Accepting where we are, it begins to feel right, growing and expanding until that box becomes tight too, pressed against the edges until we break through to the next. And the next and the next in a constant birthing process. We may pull back from change momentarily, but life presses us forward—even against our will. Ease comes when we choose to go the way life is going.

Understanding the growth process is a shield, a shield against confusion, against feeling wrong and out of sync. Understanding the process of life assists us in going with the flow instead of fighting to stay back. We need to learn how to agree with possibility instead of impossibility. In the first and second phases, the new and creative is impossible and undesirable. Something to be shunned. Something we'll be punished for. Something we'd punish others for. Understanding the phase others are in allows us to sell our ideas while shielding them appropriately.

Selecting the proper environment for our seedlings

Young seedlings can't grow well when they're overcrowded, competing with hundreds of nearby seedlings for sun, food and water. Gardeners set each one in a pot in the greenhouse, monitoring their light, watering as needed allowing them to grow and strengthen. Then at the right moment they select a spot to set them out, making sure the light is right, the soil is appropriate, tilling and loosening it.

As individuals we must learn to shield our own dreams from competition and overcrowding. We must tend and till them with great care.

As parents we are responsible for shielding our children's dreams— their art work, their inventions, their new methods and improvements— creating a supportive environment for their seedlings to live in, treating their early ideas with the sanctity that they will use to shield their own ideas later on. They are learning how to shield by example. If we don't shield for them, then we won't learn how to shield for themselves. We must be a shield rather than a hot sun of disagreement or a withering, parching wind.

Teachers must also act as shields, protecting their students' dreams and assisting them in learning how to protect dreams themselves, modeling creating safety each day with each student, protecting ideas from other students' jealousy or misunderstanding, from discouragement and doubt, whether that dream is a drawing, a term paper or song. Each idea is a seed, a sacred beginning, the start of a harvest that will feed the hungry, the beginning of a product or service that people need and want. The shielding a teacher models for a student's second grade science project may enable that same student to bring a new technology into existence later on in life.

Managers must be shields for emerging third-phase employees, assisting them in being recognized for their improvements and inventions, creating an agreement system that includes them instead of excluding and isolating them. Managers are responsible for building a greenhouse for more efficient future systems and methods.

Governments as well must shield their creative citizens instead of putting all their energy into first-phase citizens, the ones who can't and aren't able, the abused and downtrodden. Laws and rules must be made adjustable according to the phase of the citizen. Once effectiveness is achieved, more freedom must be given—more latitude and permission. Once efficiency is achieved, more freedom must be given the seedling leader—more opportunities for exploration, leadership and funding. We must learn to meet the unique needs of each citizen. In the views of Thomas Jefferson, we must treat unequals unequally in order to be fair.

Parents must shield themselves

To raise future leaders, parents must learn how to shield their own confidence and self-esteem. Their children will not like being told "No," not like being taught and protected. Even though that "No" prevents injury and death, it simultaneously prevents self-control and exploration. If parents look for acknowledgment from their children they will find their children's anger and defiance painful and invalidating. Self-acknowledgment and acknowledgment by the other parent are the shields that we need to move through their normal resistant reactions.

As our children go from first phase into second, we need a "they-love-us" shield or we'll begin to believe that they hate us, that we really are stupid, insensitive and backward. They are learning to disagree with us, thinking the methods we've taught them were wrong, not as good as their ways, the ways their peers use. We must learn to shield our pride so we can allow space for their growth. We must hold that they love us even when they act like they don't, when they leave home, breaking all communication and contact. We must remember our own self-assertion, our own defiance and superiority, and we must protect them from the destructive heat of our unleashed resentment and pain. They are striving to be independent, finding their own unique methods and dreams, they are moving toward creativity and inventiveness, toward leading us in the future.

When they're out alone, we can hologram them within their own shields. When they don't come home on time we can imagine them safe instead of hologramming them hurt or in an accident. We must manage ourselves and take positive actions, recalling the consequences of the mother who told her son not to play with matches instead of telling him to be safe.

As we teach, we must shield our own confidence and self-respect from students who are frolicking and delighting in defiance. Shielded and safe, we are able to observe them battling toward inventiveness, tackling and scrimmaging, kicking and passing. We can stand safely on the sidelines as a cheerleader, instead of running out on the playing field as a competitor to be vanquished. We can facilitate their growth instead of becoming an obstacle to it.

As managers we have to learn to shield our self-respect when second-phase employees begin to overtake our skill levels, making us feel we have to control or compete with them, protecting our own feelings of competence as they surge on ahead of us, protecting our self-esteem as they improve on the systems we've created. Seeing their improvements as an acknowledgment of our leadership rather than something to stop. We need to be able to update our systems to include their ideas, shielding the part of us that feels hurt and superseded. As leaders we're successful when the next generation stands above us, not just at our level.

We need to shield our leaders as well, protecting them from our doubts and uncertainties as we break through the box of how it's always been and move past a world of war between nations and economies. We can shield our leaders' holograms instead of shooting them down and proclaiming them impossible. We can hold their outcome even though we don't know how to accomplish it yet, knowing that as we shield and nurture tomorrow's solutions we are creating workability for our children and grandchildren.

Following a Mack truck

Anyone can lead. Anyone can shield. I remember following a Mack truck one dark rainy night driving home alone from North Carolina to Virginia. For four hours I followed only able to see taillights. Winds buffeted my car, rain showered my windshield making it impossible for me to continue unless I stayed in his wake. Finally almost home he signaled that he was pulling off at the next exit. I leaned over to look carefully as I passed, wanting to see the face of the someone who had shielded me, someone who had allowed me to move ahead when I couldn't on my own.

Loving isn't liking and it takes liking to live together

Love becomes painful when day to day what we like is not what they like, what we do is not what they do, when our comfortable ways are uncomfortable to them. In relationships there are always differences, after all, we came from different parents, different trainings and experiences. But to live together there needs to be a commonalty of likes.

I gave this advice to my daughters when they selected their mates. When you're in love, find out if you're in like. Would you make good roommates? Would you make good business partners? These areas of likeness determine whether loving together can become living together. Or whether loving is something we share living apart.

A client of mine had been trying to live lovingly with her husband for years. She had changed. He had changed. But no matter how much they each had changed, they weren't comfortable together. They had to shield from each other to stay together. They had created a beautiful home, a wonderful environment with huge trees and wandering pathways, but

207

living in their paradise was bittersweet at best. They loved each other but they didn't like each other. And when they let down their shields, when they really told the truth, they needed to be apart.

We can shield when we have to, but shielding all the time takes too much energy. We need a support system we can resonate with—people who like the way we are, who enjoy the same things, and who respect our unique differences, appreciating the richness and texture they add. Constantly shielding ourselves is a signal to change. We need to find some-place where we can put our shields down.

Look at our planet. We each need our own space, living in separate houses and rooms, working in separate companies, separate buildings and departments. Living in separate communities and countries with their own rules. We each need our own space until we can come to know all the things we don't know, until we can own all the feelings we haven't owned. But we need to grow at a comfortable pace, integrating our parts little by little, and staying away from what we can't yet include peacefully. Constant confrontation may create an irritation that can't heal.

From our safe places we can go out to learn, using our shields whenever we feel threatened. These journeys beyond our Safe Zone are challenging and confrontive, requiring time to rebalance ourselves when we return home. Let us each choose a home, a relationship, a job, a community where we have the necessary ease and support to continue venturing out and including more and more. Finally seeing that each one of us is a cell in the body of man.

Like infant children, infant dreams need care and protection.

The Ninth Success Skill

SWITCHING WHEN YOU'RE STUCK

Once impossible
dreams may be possible now

When my girls were young I was a realtor. For several months I had shown a young couple homes, but we just couldn't find one like the one that got away. Two years before, they were ready to sign a contract when the owner of that house suddenly took it off the market. As we drove slowly past "their house" I could feel the disappointment. That house had become their reference point. Whenever they walked through anything else, I could hear the comparisons— "It's not quite as big as... I liked that floor plan better. The lot's not as large as..." Nothing measured up.

One evening they called me to say they had stopped by an open house, forgetting to tell the other realtor they were working with me. They had made an appointment to buy that house from her tomorrow afternoon. Is it the house you really want? Is it equal to or better than your dream? Does it make you both happy? "No, but time has run out and we just have to buy."

After all the hours we'd put in, it didn't seem possible they could buy something they didn't want—and buy it from another realtor. They seemed committed, but something inside me just couldn't let go. I was still holding their dream—seeing it, hearing it, feeling it and wanting to complete it.

So despite these discouraging circumstances, I switched back to believing that finding a house they would love was still possible, and I called back to tell them how important it is to hold a dream all the way to completion. I asked them to go look at houses with me one last time in the morning.

"I still believe it's possible—possible tomorrow." And out of loyalty they said yes.

The next morning I was out early jogging as usual. Block after block, up curbs and down them, I kept seeing myself finding exactly what they wanted. The house they had lost was nearby so I decided to run by it. As I approached I saw a man hammering a sale sign in the lawn. Now I really ran. Out of breath, I called my clients telling them to meet me at "their house" at 9 a.m. "What?" "Yes, your house on Rodman Avenue. It's back on the market."

As they walked into that house they were ecstatic, their faces lit up. It was exactly what they wanted. After the contract was completed and they knew "their house" was really theirs, they hugged and kissed me, thanking me for keeping their dream safe even when they'd abandoned it.

Switching them back to possible had prevented a disaster. They would have signed an agreement on a house they didn't want, just at the moment when the one they did want had become available.

Off course more than on course

Navigational equipment guides an airplane to its destination, but while it's in flight it's probably off course. Off more than on, it still arrives on schedule. Off course. On course. Off course. On course. The designers of its guidance system expect it to zigzag.

Human beings have an inner guidance system that works the same way. First we decide on a destination—an experience we want to have—and we hologram that experience so we create the energy to get there. Then we begin taking appropriate actions, monitoring the feedback coming through our senses. Does this look right? Sound right? Feel right? Am I on course? Or off course?

But unlike a pilot in a cockpit who is paid to fly a plane full of passengers to an agreed-upon destination, we human pilots frequently change our destination mid-flight. Thinking we're off course, we downshift from third phase where everything looked possible into second where everything seems much harder. Re-examining our methods, we review details and strategies, making course corrections. But if obstacles continue to beset us, then we gear back into first phase again—that familiar black-and-white reality of right/wrong, good/bad, should/shouldn't, can/can't. And we shift our thinking from possible to impossible, giving up on our outcome so we can feel safe and certain again.

Having switched to impossible, everything looks different, joy and excitement are squeezed out by difficulty and effort. The things we saw as attractive and doable now look difficult and unattractive. Not sensible. Not worth it. And we're even embarrassed to admit we ever thought we could do it, focused instead on all the reasons why not—our lack of skill, our lack of time, our lack of money and knowledge. Then caught in a polarity response, we convince ourselves we can't and we shouldn't—we give up.

Why do we so often fail to reach our desired destination? Often it's because we were scared and negative from the start. Over the years I've been amazed at how many times sincere, committed people in my seminars tried to tell me what they wanted by telling me what they didn't want. "I don't want to get hurt. I don't want to get divorced. I don't want to get sick. I don't want to get fired. I don't want my child to feel disappointed." They were accidentally putting fears and doubts in as outcomes, failing to understand the Positive Command Brain. So the destination they thought they were setting out to reach was negated from the start. They were headed for what they didn't want instead of what they did want.

Some people think they fear success, but it isn't success they fear. It's the sensations they've experienced as they headed to success before and then decided to turn back, the tearing ache of disappointment and embarrassment that giving up created. That is the painful destination they hoped to avoid by switching to impossible. By never ever trying. Most people head out in a blaze of glory, but they get bogged down along the way and talk themselves out of it. Or let themselves be talked out of it by well-meaning others.

To navigate successfully, first we need to have a well-constructed destination in mind—one we can see, hear and feel up ahead. Next we have to devise appropriate methods for getting there, and then we have to develop the skills needed to keep ourselves moving all the way to completion. It also helps to have a "plane load" of people on board also committed to reaching the same destination.

Once we set out, we need to notice when something we don't want suddenly looms up ahead. When seated at our control panel, we immediately and unconsciously flip our polarity switch to impossible, losing sight of our destination and heading away from it. Now instead of approaching what we want we're avoiding it.

The switching questions are: "What do I want?" and "What do you want?"

In order to reset our emotional switch into positive, we may have to update something from our past that's resurfacing—an old failure or disappointment, a beginner's rule that we learned when we were children or just starting something. Then having updated old fears and limits, we can realign our course by asking ourselves the switching question, "What do I want?" Answering that question replots our course. Each time there's an obstacle we re-ask and re-answer. And by the time we close in on our destination, we may have pursued thousands of different course settings along the way. We can assist others in correcting their course by asking them the same question, "What do you want?" Asking this question is a powerful support. Having someone there to switch us is a good reason to share dreams, a good reason to relate. Two or more people holding the same hologram not only amplify that dream's power, but when doubts overtake them, any one of those dreamers can throw the switch back to possible by asking the switching question. Helping us switch supports us in surviving unforeseen circumstances, unexpected obstacles, doubt and exhaustion. The real power of switching is the real power of a team.

Success filing the times you switched yourself or others switched you

As we engage in conversations, we also engage in switching—whether we like it or not. Whenever someone says they can't, we either agree or we can challenge—saying "Yes, I think you're right." Or "No, I think you're wrong. You can still do it. How about this way?" We need to give those we love permission to ask us switching questions whenever they notice we're abandoning our dreams. And we need to ask them to hold onto our dreams for us until we switch back. Or we decide to delete.

Take a minute to open up your failure file, sorting for times that people you trusted agreed with your doubts, and so you gave up. Then recall times when you agreed with someone else's doubts, advising them to settle for something other than their dream. Was that person your child? Your student or employee? Was that person a citizen you were responsible for governing? And did they continue all the way to success or did they use your agreement to give themselves permission to quit—permission to fail?

Then recall times when you switched despite someone's doubts. When you heard them say it was impossible and that made you keep trying. Or times when someone heard your doubts and convinced you it was possible.

There's a great cosmic match going on all the time between possibility and impossibility. Which side are you cheering for? Safety and security—or dreams, satisfaction and fulfillment?

What's possible changes as we move through the three phases of success. What's possible at first is doing what we're told to do, the way we're told to do it. What's possible next is competing and winning at what we're told to do. Finally in the third phase what's possible is what we want. We begin to create and implement our dreams. And people operating in third are scary to first- and second-phase people. First-phase people have a habit of switching into negative. Feeling afraid and uncertain themselves, they want to protect the others they care about, regardless of which phase they are in. Success for them is safety, and they chronically give up their outcomes to be sure or secure.

Sometimes we argue over possibility, "Yes, you can. No, I can't. Yes, you can." Sometimes we use our leadership power to prevent what others want. "Yes I can. No you can't. I forbid you." Or we threaten them with the loss of love, satisfaction or freedom. "If you do that, I'll be mad. And I won't give you your allowance." "If you don't pass this test, then you will fail. And have to go to summer school." "If you don't do what you're supposed to do, you'll be fired from your job. We'll fine you or jail you."

Sometimes what we use our power to prevent would be harmful and injurious. But sometimes what we use our power to prevent is creative

213

and innovative. But it's something we're not comfortable with, we don't agree is possible. Hopefully in the future we'll learn to agree with possibility more and more. Switching is a vital team skill, whether our team is our family, class, business or nation. We have to work together to stay on course, switching whenever we get stuck, switching discouraged teammates or allowing teammates to switch us, putting our confidence in them until we can rebuild our own confidence. We need to choose our teams wisely knowing our teammates will influence our success or failure.

Quitting is reasonable, but to succeed we sometimes have to be unreasonable, switching to positive even when we see the reasons why not, even when the feedback looks absolutely hopeless, even when we feel, "There's absolutely no way." We have to be able to turn on our internal light whenever it looks dark, whenever our energy drops, whenever our internal pictures gray and fade, and enthusiasm slips away. The truly powerful leader can even be going backwards and still know he's on his way.

Stuck in what we don't want

It's easier to know what you don't want than what you do want, easier to be a critic than a performer or creator. In the first phase of learning we learn to do what others want. In the second part of learning any skill we do what others' want but we do more and more of it. It's only in the third phase that we choose what we want for ourselves.

Often the first step in choosing is discovering what we don't want. We can't imagine what we do want, and when we're asked we just stand there with a blank look in our eyes, scratching our heads—whether we're a father yelling at his son about wet towels. Or a teacher scolding our students for coming late to class again. Or a boss orienting new employees by telling them the things we don't want them to do, creating fear of failure and causing them to begin doing exactly what we don't want.

Switching allows us to imagine a positive future amidst a negative present—when the child still alive inside us feels that we shouldn't, we can't, it's impossible. When circumstances indicate the road there is blocked, switching allows us to focus on success, satisfaction and fulfillment getting ourselves back in balance, reducing the tension and disease that would be created by continuing to dread and avoid.

We switch by asking ourselves, "What do I want instead? By answering this switching question we refocus on our outcome, allowing the Razz to guide us to our destination, instead of heading toward what we don't want instead.

A four-way switch

1. **Monitoring continuously:** We have to monitor our thinking moment to moment, paying careful attention to what we're seeing, saying and feeling. Is it what we want? Monitoring as well what other people are thinking. What they're doing and not doing. What they feel is possible and impossible. Knowing their thinking impacts our thinking, making us try harder or allowing us to quit.

2. **Hearing the negatives:** We need to notice negative phrases that are embedded in our conversations: "I don't want, I don't like, I can't, there's not enough, there's no support or no agreement for. You won't, you can't, you shouldn't, you'll fail if..." These internal and external negatives indicate that there's been a switch. Red lights are going off on our inner-control panel. Alert messages are appearing. Attention programmer, are you changing your hologram? Or is someone else trying to?

3. **Shielding our hologram:** To switch back to positive, we need to review what we wanted at the start, re-experiencing our original unadulterated hologram, feeling its reality again, re-establishing our destination and setting a new course, switching from "I wanted to but..." into "I still want to and I will." And then shielding the dream from opponents, putting our holographically constructed shield in place until the environment is supportive again.

4. **Searching for positives:** We need to begin asking questions that will lead us to positives: What do I (you, we) want instead of the negatives I'm experiencing? What else would work? Who else has expertise? What have we learned? What step can we take? Asking these questions initiates a search for possibilities, a search for a new method to get us there.

Straight-line thinking blocks our progress

As children we learned to think in a straight line, doing what others told us to do step-by-step. I want that so I need to do this, then that and the other, following the recipe that has been handed down, and following it exactly. But as leaders we can no longer use old recipes to get to new territories. Facing the unknown and unexpected, we must be willing to perform the unknown and unexpected—doing whatever it takes, including all the negatives along the way, understanding that "what I didn't expect," "what I didn't want to have happen" is merely a step along the way and learning to include it all in the process of success. Even though we are riding on the horns of a dilemma, we can still get there.

Being the boss and not bossed

In our homes if we reset a breaker and our power keeps switching off, then we need to look further than the breaker for the problem. If in our minds and bodies, we keep on switching to negative, then we need to look deeper for the cause. If we continue crashing up against obstacles, if the course seems to be constantly fraught with difficulty, if the obstacles presented are more than we can deal with, then we need to reassess our outcome. Is the outcome out of alignment with the larger forces that be? Is what I want of other people what they really want?

A man who'd worked in construction for years bought himself a factory. Now he was the boss instead of the bossed, and he felt proud going to his plant every day, managing and administrating. But he wasn't making any money. His expenses were coming right out of his pocket.

This had been going on for two years with no sign of improvement and many signs that it was continuing to get worse. By now he had used up his savings and was substantially in debt. It took several hours of examining his outcome with him before he could see the situation more clearly. He thought his outcome was to be a boss, but now he understood that his outcome was to serve his customers.

But his customers didn't want what he had. The factory he bought had been successful in the past. The old man who sold it had given correct numbers. The business had indeed made that man very wealthy, but his product had been supplanted by a brand-new technology, a better way of doing the same thing more cheaply. So no matter how much money he put into that business, no matter how much time and effort he gave, it just wouldn't work. He needed to switch to another way of serving customers, so satisfying their needs would satisfy his—and make money.

"It's okay to quit"

As we were growing up, our parents were responsible for switching us. How much effort should we put in? How much is enough? How far is far enough? When should we quit? We learned to switch from the way they switched us. "Come on, you can do it." "Do it once more." Or "You've tried hard enough. It's time to go in." Parents sometimes switch us to failure.

A woman in my seminar had been a talented young pianist performing her first recital in the auditorium of her grade school. All the teachers were there. And all of the students. Midway through her performance, she couldn't remember what came next and so she stopped. Her mother who was standing in the wings walked out onto the stage, telling her she'd done enough. "It's OK to quit." So incomplete, she left the stage avoiding the momentary pain and confusion of beginning again only to face the enduring embarrassment of knowing she had quit. Her mother switching her to negative halfway through her performance set a pattern in place that was still running her life forty years later. If on the other hand, her mother had understood how important it would have been to switch her child back to positive, telling her to look up at her music there in front of her, directing her to start over again, moving her beyond the temptation to quit. But after the woman had updated this childhood scene, she was able to break through her old pattern of incompletions and become much more successful.

Our parents and caretakers had the opportunity to switch us whenever we fell off a swing, or crashed on our bike, or didn't make the team, or had an accident driving, or lost a job. They were responsible for holding the hologram of our success and well-being, no matter what. Then following their lead, we learned to do the same.

Unless they didn't know how to switch us. Then, unable to include what we'd just done in the process of success, they switched our entire future to negative—telling us we'd never amount to anything. We'd never turn out. And they reminded us of that future every time we failed, forcing us to constantly struggle against that being true. But sometimes even when they had lost faith in our future, a powerful voice boomed deep inside us. "No, you're wrong about me. You wait and see." Negative parents either produce negative children who believe what they were told or children who learned how to switch by themselves.

Many parents can't switch us because they can't switch themselves, feeling it's far safer to stop than push forward. Safety and survival are their most important outcome. That's what they were taught and what they are trying to teach us, honestly believing it's in our best interests to do what they told us. Turning back seems normal to them, after all most people give up their outcomes when they face the unexpected—unexpected events, unexpected expense, unexpected opportunity.

It was different when our parents grew up. It was a more stable time when people kept the same job their whole lives working toward a gold watch or an acknowledgment dinner. Loyalty and obedience were enough then, but not now. With the current rate of change we have to begin shifting our loyalty from leaders and methods onto outcomes.

Flexibility is essential. The rigid tree breaks against a raging wind. A flexible tree stands long after that wind has past.

Teachers are responsible for switching us too

Entering school, our teachers took over the responsibility for switching us. Without their skills, we could never have gotten past our last failure.

To be successful now, we have to stay on course to the places we haven't been, places that threaten the very survival of our old values. We must learn to discriminate for ourselves between real threat to survival—something that will hurt us or kill us—and threat to our survival mechanism, the old recipes we learned as beginners. "Is there danger present? Is the danger fire, accident, cuts, burns, pain, or shock?" Or is the danger here that we might do something new—we might get one step closer to what we really want?

As parents we are responsible for teaching our children how to use these ten success skills. The most powerful way we can teach them is to use them ourselves, knowing what we want and staying on course, living a satisfying successful life. Our children may get to their destinations without us, but they will get there far easier with us modeling and leading. They may be effective without us, but they will move ahead more easily toward creativity and leadership when we know how to lead them, when we not only teach these ten skills but we use them ourselves.

Some parents tell their children to do things they won't do for themselves. Eat the right foods. Rest and relax. Follow your dreams. Yes, telling them is good, but our example speaks much louder than our words. Our children learn more from what they see, hear and feel than from our words alone. Ninety-three percent of what we learn is learned by example.

Switching to positive moves us ahead to leadership instead of backward toward follow-ship. Our children learn how to deal with the unexpected from us. If we yell and blame and abandon our goals, then they will do the same. We are their model. For years and years they recorded those pictures, sound tracks and feelings. Those recordings became the data base they automatically access whenever they need to switch. Unconsciously those recordings give us a hunch about what to do next.

Urging them on is good but modeling them forward when obstacles occur is the greatest gift we can give them. "Do as I say and not as I do." We've all heard that saying. Let's update that old saying to "They will do as you do, not as you say."

The first phase of skill development is a very scary time. An uncertain time. A time with few reference points. A time when big mistakes can be made. A time when interest and enthusiasm are the main things a leader looks for. Get them excited, get them going. Then switch them back on course whenever they get off, whenever they slip back into can't and impossible.

What an awful choir

An elementary-school music teacher had a new choir that he thought from the start was honestly awful. Over and over he told them how bad they were, how they weren't learning a thing. And then it got worse. They got more and more angry and discouraged. A standoff all year—they hated him as much as he hated them.

The next year he had the same group, but this time he decided to switch his approach. Being negative hadn't worked so he decided to be positive. He success filed each day at the end of the class, telling them all the improvements he noticed, complimenting their specific performances, switching them whenever they got down on themselves, pointing out their progress from a week ago or a month ago.

And they switched when he switched. Following his lead, interested and involved, inspired and committed, they won the state championship.

Don't write any more until . . .

A perky young mother began college. To do that she had to juggle two kids, a part-time job, a husband and a home. A poor student in high school, she had ended up running away from home to become a prostitute in New Orleans.

Her writing was excellent, and with the encouragement of a professor she began a book of short stories about her life. Her work was so good that she was nominated for honors and awarded a full scholarship.

She was buoyed up and dedicated until she got her first story back cut to shreds. Her professor suggested she read other writers to learn about their styles. He suggested she change the ending of the story—her very favorite part. What she heard him say was that her style was all wrong. She thought he meant, "Don't write any more until you can learn to write like these other authors." Devastated she switched into negative, reliving the old experiences she still had in her high school failure file, replaying what her teachers had said when she was really failing. She was unable to sleep at night, afraid to even try any more.

Her professor didn't know what she was experiencing. Confident and flexible in the third phase of writing, he was used to correction. But he was unaware of the impact his correction had on her, and he wasn't there to switch her. Her attitude about writing changed, her participation dropped off.

His critique had been valid but inappropriate. He hadn't stopped to wonder if her love for writing would survive. In the first phase, feedback needs to be positive. The most important task of the first-phase leader is to build confidence and momentum. As students practice, they get better. But if they quit, their skills never develop. Practice makes perfect.

By understanding these ten leadership skills, the professor would have given his feedback with the first phase in mind, telling her she was good, so good in fact that he had spent extra time sketching out a long range plan for career development. How we give feedback is vital.

First, feedback needs to begin with success filing. Let them know something good about their performance—past or present.

Second, update failures. If they have done less than their previous performance, reinforce how well they did before, pointing out the specific aspect of those performances that were better.

Third, create a hologram of how this feedback will assist them in performing even better. Begin filing future successes. Tell them how well they'll be doing in one year or ten years. Create future success in their mind.

Managers take over where parents and teachers leave off

Next, bosses and managers step up to lead, taking over the responsibility for switching. If the child resisted the parent, if the student resisted the teacher, the employee will resist the manager. Attitudes toward authority are passed down from home to school to work. If we didn't learn to success file at home or at school, we will need the manager to build up our confidence. If we learned to quit trying when things got tough, if our confidence is low, we will need the manager to switch us, to allow us to keep going all the way to completion. If we haven't updated our failures, then the manager will need to be able to update past failures with us. As with the parent and teacher, the manager is also responsible for modeling these success skills.

If parents have taught their children these skills, if teachers have continued their practice and development, then managers will recognize this competence and be able to develop skills more efficiently. The manager receives a great gift from preceding leaders.

221

Governments can switch us too

Government can contribute to their citizens in ways that go beyond mere laws, codes and red lights. Government can begin to acknowledge their citizens' effectiveness, efficiency and creativity, holding up their successes as models for others, publicizing the wonderful things their people are doing rather than focusing on debt, drugs and crime. Government has an opportunity to update our past failures, providing direction for what would work better in the future. Government leaders can switch us when we get discouraged, when we feel there's no way to handle health care, pollution or inflation. Our leaders can inspire us, talking us through our confusion and uncertainty. When negative situations seem insurmountable, our leaders can show us ways out.

As individuals in government agencies and departments, we can ask people switching questions to assist them in expressing what they really want. "If that's not what you want, what do you want instead?" As we lead them we may continue to hear them state what they don't want instead of what they do want.

Affirmations haven't worked for many people until now because they were affirming what they didn't want instead of what they did— "I don't want to get hurt. I don't want to fail that exam again. I don't want to feel disappointed this time." But since what we think is what we get—like it or not—they ended up getting exactly what they didn't want. Then they told themselves affirmations don't work. Affirmations do work, but they don't work the way they worked them. We must affirm the positive, taking one last powerful step—the step of the leader, pressing forward beyond what we don't want to what we do want instead—seeing it, feeling it, doing it as well as saying it.

As we listen to our conversations, we will hear our own doubts, switching them to keep ourselves outcome-oriented. "I don't want it to rain. What do I want instead? I want clear sunny weather." "I don't want to get hurt. I want to be safe." "I don't want to feel scared. I want to be secure." "I don't want to get sick. I want to be healthy."

The challenge in the third phase, the phase of creating and leading, is to be clear about the programs we create and run. Clear about the programs other people around us run as well, seeing their pictures or asking for more detail. Clear about their sound tracks or asking them to tell us more. We need to feel their feelings inside us, asking when we feel confused or uncertain and continuing to ask questions until we can switch to a positive outcome, until we can take positive action. We need to be able to update ourselves and others as needed.

We model getting what we want, and we're interested in what our children want. We are meeting our own needs and we're interested in our students' needs, their questions and doubts. We are feeling satisfied ourselves and want our employees to be satisfied so they will be able to satisfy our customers. We want all those we lead to succeed. Their success is our success too.

Customer service is teaching us to serve ourselves, asking what we want and finding out ways to get it. Transformation is occurring in the marketplace. Customer service is making us outcome-oriented, not just nice, not just effective and efficient, but creative, imaginative and inventive, getting the job done no matter what. We are learning to communicate at much higher levels, learning to cooperate and use experts to do what we can't do, or we don't want to do. We are learning to update our own upsets and the upsets of our customers, learning to shield ourselves when they are yelling and negative, holding the outcome of success and satisfaction even when they're threatening to never use our product or service again.

We all make mistakes, but mistakes can be forgiven if we know how to correct them, searching for positives and re-directing their focus. "What do you want instead?" is a "mental hand" reaching out to assist another person, the leader question of a leader, moving us beyond competitive success all the way to fulfillment.

Once impossible
dreams may be possible now.

The Tenth Success Skill

MAINTAINING HEALTH AND BALANCE

When health is handled, we can create the world we want

I was shocked to hear that my friend Randy had a heart attack at thirty-nine. The owner of a health food restaurant, a faithful exerciser, holistic and appearing healthy, he was suddenly struck down. The many of us who knew him felt our own mortality shaken. If it could happen to Randy it could happen to anyone.

Randy and I had dinner together four weeks after his angioplasty. I was interested in knowing about the pressures he'd been experiencing and the signals he had missed. We chatted about his business—the hiring and firing, the tensions of cash flow. But as we continued to talk a more important factor emerged.

His heart wasn't in it

He and his wife dreamed of serving customers healthy delicious food in a comfortable relaxed setting. They planned to franchise their format across the country. But the way they expected to feel about the business wasn't the way it felt. The long enjoyable early days of setting up and trying out had accelerated into more second-phase work than they wanted to do. And they couldn't find others who wanted to do it either. Compounding demands broke apart their relationship.

For the last year they had lived separate lives with separate people in separate cities, tied together only because they owned the same business.

Unable to find partners or buyers, he couldn't let go. But "his heart wasn't in it."

But this Randy sitting here in front of me was a far wiser man. Holding on too long had almost cost him his life. The strain of heartless work had put a strain on his heart. And his heart had struck back, demanding full attention. Now he was asking the ultimate health question, "What do I want?" He was reprioritizing his life.

After hearing his story I felt compelled to tell him about a throbbing sensation I had been having in my chest. He urged me to get a physical, and he sat there beside me as I called for an appointment. After my doctor had proclaimed me fit and healthy, I continued to search out the reason for that throbbing. My body was sending me some sort of message. Was I working too hard? Or doing the wrong exercise? Were there incompletions in my work or relationships?

We're prewired for healthy lives

If we write a word down on paper, how do we know whether it's spelled correctly or not? Unconsciously we compare that spelling with the one stored in memory and we monitor the sensation that comes up in our chest. That sensation is called a mid-line response. If there is tension there, discomfort or throbbing, we know something is wrong. Either the word is spelled incorrectly or we don't have a correct spelling recorded in memory. Then we turn to an expert—a good dictionary or a good speller.

We must pay close attention to the signals our body sends—the aches and pains, digestions and indigestions, increased energies and exhaustions. Our body sends us signals about the correct "spelling" of our lives. These sensations are the sum of complex inner computations that we must learn to interpret.

Heaven now

Our planet is a potential paradise filled with myriad plants and animals, diverse terrains and climates, varying cycles and seasons. A planet of abundant resources, inhabited by people with skills of all kinds. We are each here to complete a unique mission. But first we must discover what that mission is.

As children and young adults we succeeded by pleasing others. But entering the third phase we succeed by pleasing ourselves. By pursuing natural preferences and following special interests, we start to identify what that mission is. As adults, we can choose to take over as the programmer of our lives at any moment—updating old needs and limits leaders have programmed into us, sensing our own course and choosing our own team. Whenever we meet someone new, we sketch out our holograms, sharing specific details with them to discover alignment. Having chosen teams and partners, we are challenged to keep our holographic conversations going—adding more detail, more color and texture while simultaneously noticing "details of disagreement" spotlighted as we take independent action. By using the feedback that is pouring in through our senses, we continue to choose what to complete or delete, recognizing the impact our choices have on health and happiness. "I wanted to do that, but now that I've lived it, that's not what I want any more. What I want now is…"

In the third phase we are responsible for maintaining our balance—deciding right and wrong, what we should and shouldn't do, what we want and we don't want. In the third phase we know we are the only ones who know "right" for us. By saying yes to what works and no to what doesn't, we finally begin to create the lives that we want.

But what happens when we ignore, misinterpret or cover up the signals coming in? When we comply, making others' preferences more important than our own? We get sick. We get tired. We lose energy and enthusiasm, becoming stressed and depressed, disinterested and dispassionate, shutting down our emotions to keep doing what we don't want to do. Then we become more and more upset with the people who disappoint us—after all we've been doing the things they wanted, but they are not doing the things we want. When they won't take care of us and we won't take care of ourselves, then we feel abandoned and child-like. But we've abandoned ourselves, failing to take care of our own wants and needs. And we will continue to feel pain and frustration until we shift into third and take control of our lives.

Is that all there is?

When we drive, what happens if we fail to shift gears appropriately? If only one gear is working? Or two instead of three?

What happens if we fail to shift success phases appropriately, if we get stuck in one or two instead of using all three? If we get stuck in the first phase, we get rigidly obedient—preoccupied with right and wrong, doing what we're told to do the way we're told to do it, and failing to question who is telling us or why. But what happens if we get stuck using only the first and second phases? This is the dilemma we so often face today, the reason why so many people are asking, "Is that all there is?"

The Baby Boom Generation has grown up in a first- and-second-phase mass-production America. Our grandparents were focused on manufacturing basics—trucks, planes and cars, homes and appliances, telephones, radios and TVs. Then our parents began to produce second-phase products, products that did more-better-faster, that were bigger and smaller— microwaves and computers, Walkmans and Talkmans, VCRs and large-screen TVs. Products with fewer calories, more taste and higher fiber.

But now we are discovering what came along with it—air pollution and ozone loss, deficit spending and huge credit card balances, and abuses of all kinds—lies and deceptions, rampant bribes and pay-offs. We are experiencing the effects the second phase of success has on a society, on our families and health. Stressed and exhausted, our lives have become a series of breakdowns and illnesses, outbursts and resentments.

Endlessly wanting more and more, second-phase leaders can never be satisfied. They weren't acknowledged by their leaders so they can't acknowledge us. Their parents thought praise slowed people down, making them soft or too big for their breeches. So they spent their lives acknowledging failures instead, pointing out what we didn't do whenever we didn't do it.

Feeling unacknowledged, we were forced to find other ways of feeling successful—so we cemented ourselves onto the only other method we could think of—using our leaders' measures to acknowledge ourselves. So instead of success meaning someone said we were good and right,

227

success came to mean getting better grades, improving our scores, climbing on charts and graphs, receiving better appraisals.

But competitive success is a harsh and demanding master, forcing us to do more and more, driving prices down, pushing costs up. In order to stay competitive executives keep cutting their staffing levels lower and lower, consolidating and reorganizing. Lean and mean is what we call it euphemistically, but understaffed is what we call it when we're having a rough day.

Manipulation, bossiness and lying are all overlooked as long as we produce. Short cuts and secrets, misrepresentations and deceptions become acceptable and expected. We do whatever it takes to get a score, grade or promotion. The rights and wrongs, the goods and bads, the shoulds and shouldn'ts—the morality of the first phase has been left far behind. The pressure keeps increasing. Mortgages and payments force us to say, "Yes sir, I will." Instead of, "Hell no, I can't. No, I can't do any more, any better, any faster!"

Without acknowledgment from parents, teachers and bosses, and with no place to communicate our frustrations and pressures, the tension keeps building. This is the logical—or illogical—extreme of a second-phase society, covering up the pain with alcohol, marijuana and cocaine. Eating fast foods faster and faster, gaining weight but never gaining satisfaction. Trying to fill up the emptiness we feel in our lives.

Leader Navigation: We need to know two points

Two points are needed to navigate our lives— we need to know where we are, and where we want to be. Then we need the skills to get from here to there. Without these skills we'll get somewhere but not where we want to be. We've focused so much on getting ahead that we haven't paid attention to being here now. We're like kids in a car asking, "Are we there yet?" Or their parents who answer, "No, it's a lot farther."

We couldn't stand the tension and dissonance of simultaneously knowing where we were and where we wanted to be, so we stopped noticing where we were. Many things went unnoticed, unspoken and undiscovered, put in separate files, separate fences, separate houses, separate corporations and countries. But those containers are breaking open now, the volume and pressure of everything we didn't notice is pushing its way out.

Finally we are talking about everything that's happened and how we felt about it all, no longer hiding anything from anyone, no longer protecting leaders—parents, teachers, managers and governments—from the consequences of their actions. And we are discovering atrocities we can hardly believe. Atrocities in families. Atrocities in business. Atrocities in cities. Atrocities in countries. Atrocities in rain forests. In rivers and oceans. In the ozone and health.

This is a different time. The pace goes much faster. The demands are more intense. We do a whole lot. We're constantly learning how to do more with less and less, only making time to do things that matter. Sometimes we look back to the good old days—the pace, the family life, the way we imagined it would turn out for us. But that time is past.

Confronting what we didn't want

In the second phase we didn't notice that we were destroying ourselves as well as our planet. Shocked by the consequences, we want to look away but we can't. We have to stay conscious—like it or not. Ready or not.

This is the Information Age, but the information we're processing isn't the cold-hard-factual-information we expected to deal with. It's warm-soft-human information that requires us to understand and feel. Information that pushes us back into the parts of our lives we put aside squeamishly, the parts that were apparently long since forgotten. The walls and baffles, the barriers and partitions are breaking open everywhere at once, for each and all of us.

We've already tried numbing. But now we know the price of numbing. We have friends who killed their pain and altered their moods and whose lives were destroyed. We have friends who died because they weren't paying attention—inhaling something they worked with, something they sprayed, ate or touched. They didn't know they needed to pay attention, but they did.

We have to be more and more conscious as the pace continues to accelerate. Systems no longer last a generation any more. They may not last a day, updated worldwide by changes at one terminal. This is a generation where what we eat matters, what we breathe matters, what we drink matters. How we exercise matters, who we have sex with matters. How we communicate matters. How we raise children matters. We have to be concerned about it all. We are each responsible.

Outcome management: A priority system
Outcome 1: Maintenance of our health, safety and survival
Outcome 2: Maintenance of our support system
Outcome 3: Work and money production
Outcome 4: Maintenance of money and credit
Outcome 5: Re-creation and enjoyment
Outcome 6: _____
Outcome 7: _____
Note: Other programs can continue to be added as long as the higher priority programs are complete

---

Priority outcome one: Health and safety come first

Throughout our lives safety and survival are vital. If we can't survive, we can't continue to play our part. If we die, we forfeit the opportunity to use our accumulated skills to serve ourselves and others here on our planet.

Our parents were preoccupied with our survival as we started our lives, and our survival will continue to preoccupy them throughout our lives. They were responsible for us as infants. Our survival depended on the quality of their care. They taught us what to eat and how to eat it. They told us when we were sick and what to do to get well. They helped us know when to change our diet. When we were tired, they made us take a nap. When we ate too much, they taught us how to heal our stomach ache. When we were feverish, they tended and fussed over us. No matter what happened, they were responsible.

We only learned as much about health as they modeled. If they had a poor diet, they taught us to eat the same way. If they relaxed with TV, watching TV became our way of relaxing. Their behavior was our reference point. Their behaviors were comfortable and familiar to us. What they did was what we did—until we got too sick, too tired, too much in pain. Until we found more skillful teachers to update our knowledge. Or until we devised methods of our own.

In the third phase of any skill, we don't have to think about what to do. We know that we know. We cook without thinking, our attention is on our kids. We drive without thinking, our attention is on our meeting. We maintain our health without thinking, directing our attention to doing our job. Our accumulated health and safety skills have become a part of our inner program.

We have to stay conscious while we're learning a skill, but once we can perform that skill safely and correctly, the program we've recorded runs the skill automatically. Then we become subconsciously competent, relying on our Razz to let us know when we need to pay attention. Our second-phase goal is to be subconsciously competent in all skill areas, able to perform effectively and efficiently and creatively without devoting all of our attention. Subconscious competence frees us to focus our attention on other priorities. But then we have to become consciously competent again to teach that skill to others, leading them to the same level of competency—or greater.

Moment by moment we unconsciously monitor for anything unusual, relying on our Razz to alert us. "You are not feeling right. When did you eat? What did you eat? When did you exercise? What kind of exercise? Do you feel stressed? What specifically is stressing you?" Our inner computer monitors our system levels—blood pressure, heart rate, pulse, temperature, color and thirst—alerting us to unusual highs and lows. Once alerted we can begin to ask the questions we need to answer, paying close attention and taking corrective action until we feel better. Then when we're balanced again, we can shift our attention back to higher priorities. But if we don't handle our health, then we will constantly be held back from what we want to do and feel, limited by our failure to handle our number-one priority.

Priority outcome two: Maintaining our support system—family, friends and co-workers

As we move into the second phase of any skill, we shift our attention from safety to efficiency. With our pre-programmed Razz monitoring safety, we can let go of survival consciousness to explore our skill further.

Already effective, we're becoming efficient, improving and experimenting with methods and procedures. Some changes we try work. But some changes don't. We learn to correct and decide for ourselves. We were used to having someone there to supervise us all the time. Sometimes we still want their input, methodologies and acknowledgments, but now they are off helping new learners. So we begin to rely on ourselves and our peers.

In the first phase of life, our families made us feel safe and cared for. But in the second phase, our support system expands to also include friends, neighbors, co-workers, spouses and children. This new support system feels like family, making us feel that we matter, giving us a sense of belonging. Our support system still has a high priority. We need to keep in touch with the people we care for, with the people who care for us.

Supportive relationships contain some implicit agreements. We will be there for each other. We will make time and energy. We will take care of ourselves so we have something to give each other—we can only give what we have, not what we don't have.

Saving some seed corn

Farmers who raise corn have three top priorities. They want some corn to eat. They want some corn to sell. And they want some corn for seed. If they eat it all, if they sell it all, then they have no seed left to plant. If we eat up our health, burning our candle at both ends, if we eat up our support system, constantly taking but not giving, then we will have nothing left to plant. The wise farmer feeds his family a portion of his corn, sells a portion to feed others, and saves a portion to seed the next harvest.

We enjoy healthy relationships when we use our success skills to support each other—sharing our holograms, holding specific outcomes, sharing methods and updating them together, switching each other back to positive when we slip into negative, cheering each other on, alerting to dangers that threaten health and balance, and celebrating our ability to get what we want. Together we keep our success files full, savoring the satisfaction and fulfillment of life.

Priority outcome three: Work and money production

With our pre-programmed Razz now monitoring our safety and support systems, our attention can be directed ahead to what we want next—to learning new skills, to further school and training. Our parents spend their money to pay for our educational programming. And we spend our competence to earn scholarships or loans.

This investment in skill development will allow us to earn more money later on. A toll-taker works eight hours at $5 per hour for a total of $40 a day. An executive works eight hours at $200 dollars an hour for a total of $1600 a day. Our technical and people skills allow us to make more in an hour so we can establish security for now and for later.

We accumulate money for the expected—our children's care and education, a new home, recreation and retirement. Today's adults can expect to live twenty years in retirement. But the money for that twenty years must be made in the prime years of their careers and set aside in a pension or privately invested assets. Social security will not be enough to meet our retirement needs now that we're living longer. It will take conscious planning to live well our whole lives.

We are also accumulating money for the unexpected. Saving money now will make it available when we need it. Buying insurance now allows us to budget for the unexpected—times we're hospitalized, periods when we're disabled, for hurricanes and earthquakes, insuring that money will be there when it's needed. We can pass wealth to our children by saving early in our lives. These investments become an asset we can borrow against if needed.

Like a pan of water sloshing

Our relationship to the universe changes as we shift through the three phases. First we're religious, concerned about right and wrong, loyal and

233

devoted. Then we're industrious, worshipping production, rebellious and independent, worried and stressed by money and time. But as we shift into the third phase our world becomes holographic. We recognize ourselves as wholes not just parts. We know by changing ourselves we can change our whole world. We see the Earth as an organism, needing each cell to be healthy and happy. We trust more than what we've learned, we trust our creativity, our connection to a Higher Force. We focus on spiritual truths— who we are and why we're here, what we came to contribute, the special gifts we each bring. Transcending the leaders who have guided us so far, we connect with our God, however we define that. A higher power. A world order. A perfection beyond correction.

In the third phase there is ease and a new appreciation for order—for what it means to be a child, student, employee or citizen. What it means to be a parent, teacher, manager, or someone in government. And what it means to lead others. In the third phase it all fits, like the life cycle of a plant.

A rotary system

Large organizations use a multiple-line rotary system. Their incoming calls are answered according to priority—the first one answered first, the second one second, or urgent calls answered more quickly.

We also use a rotary system for organizing our lives. When health is handled, that line is available to take the next call. When the support system is handled, that line is open to take the next call. As long as higher priorities are complete, our energy flows on to whatever is next, unless our Razz interrupts the process with an urgent higher priority. "Health alert. You're not well." Then our energy is called back to our highest priority.

When we have surgery, we may take books and magazines with us to the hospital, expecting to read them during the long days in bed. But our recovery becomes our highest priority. Our energy becomes preoccupied with cell repair and restoration, leaving little for anything else. Even a phone call is taxing. A visit, all we can muster. Walking, sitting and bathing become exhausting labors. Our energy is being used up by our highest priority—health and survival.

Then healthy again we work to catch up, pushing to complete our project, leaving little time and energy for anything else. Focused for months, when we're almost complete, when the pressure eases off, we notice we've had blinders on while we were working like horses. We've ignored our support system. Our mate is complaining. Our children hardly know us, no longer waiting up for us. And we've said no to our friends so often they've stopped calling.

We haven't taken care of the people who support us. Without them, when our project is done, when the awards are handed out, when the congratulations are spoken, there will be no one there to cheer us. And success without them feels empty and disappointing.

Priority outcome four: Maintaining money and credit

Avoiding bills and checkbooks, worrying and dreading, filling up our heads with "not able to" holograms—money pressures make us sick. When we overspend, when we charge more and more, when the interest on our credit cards becomes a chronic drain, we need to look over our money picture with an expert. We need to set up a budget and learn how to use it. But when our spending matches our budget again, then we're in balance. If we need more money, we make more money, but not just spend more on credit. The '80s were a highly inflationary period when if we wanted it, we charged it, and the bill was an unanticipated consequence that showed up to haunt us.

The credit crunch of the late '80s taught credit card companies valuable lessons. They had programmed the public to "just put it on the card." They had programmed the public to buy whatever they wanted, on time, on their money. So when the economy tightened, when people lost their jobs, credit card companies got a lot of expensive feedback about how far to extend credit. Their collection departments struggled to collect even a small part. Hopefully they have learned that lesson, putting out more responsible messages to those who use their cards. Charge what you need and what you can afford, not necessarily whatever you want. And remember "When you charge it, you are also in charge of the bill."

Leasing ourselves out so we can complete others' outcomes

In business we sell our skills and abilities and charge others for using them. We lease ourselves out long term or short term. We produce results for others, and for that we are paid. The money we receive becomes available to spend on whatever we want.

If we spend more time on our needs than on others' needs, then our cash flow is negative. If we charge too little, we give our work away, then they receive more than we do when the job is complete. If we charge them too much, it doesn't feel right and our customers stop calling us. We are all looking for balance.

If we meet others' needs more than our own needs, our cash flow may be positive. We have the money we need but we may not have the health. Or the time to enjoy it. Our cash flow may be positive, but our lives are out of balance.

Our Razz and the rotary system can assist us in balancing. When we notice an error we've made, we correct it, communicating to others the correction we've made, and coming into supportive alignment again. Errors happen on both sides. We make them. They make them. Correction is the key to balance. Why do we keep on losing our balance? Earth is a correctional institution. Remember?

All work and no play makes a dull boy or girl

Our balance is affected by how efficiently we use time and skills. If our holograms are detailed, if we update when we're stuck, if we take advantage of our rotary system, then we spend our time doing what matters most. Then we make time for the other things we want—for re-creation and enjoyment. My grandmother always said, "All work and no play makes Johnny a dull boy."

Play is essential for the child still alive inside us. Re-creation gives us time to create ourselves newly. Recreation is essential for creation. Inventors know that well. "Light bulbs" start to flash when they're walking in the woods or enjoying a hot shower. Wham, there it is, the idea we've been looking for coming out of the blue. Out of re-creation.

New programs can be added to our lives as long as our higher priority programs are complete. Completion is an on-going process. We're incomplete in the morning as we make out our lists—wanting to do, wanting to get. Then we take the actions we can today, delegating to others, finishing and acknowledging—complete for today. Then again tomorrow we take the actions we can take, delegating to others, finishing and acknowledging and completing tomorrow.

The Razz is operating twenty-four hours a day, waking us if we're incomplete, waking us if we ignore a higher priority, urging us back to balance. But if we cover up the signals, if we take sleeping pills when we need to wake up to the thoughts that keep rousing us, we fail to use the powerful management tool we've been given. If we use painkillers to cover the pain we need to feel, we will fail to pay attention to what's jeopardizing our health. If we ignore what our friends and supporters tell us we're blind to, we are not using the corrective input we're receiving. We must learn to take "the urgent calls" that come in.

The old lady and the oil light

An elderly lady was quite meticulous about her car. She had it serviced regularly. She took it to be cleaned. She loved her car. It got her out and about to the places she wanted to go. One day as she was leaving the parking lot of her condo, she noticed that her oil light was on. She had just taken it to her mechanic who said it was fine. Believing her mechanic, she decided to drive it, but that red light kept bothering her. So she took matters in her own hands, heading upstairs to get a roll of masking tape and a small pair of scissors. Returning to her car, she measured the light carefully, cutting a piece of tape precisely that size, she put it in place. That light wouldn't bother her and she felt better for a while, until one day her car caught fire on the highway. And she cursed that damn Detroit. "They don't make cars like they used to."

But that story cuts a little too close to the truth. Maybe it's not masking tape we use. Maybe it's aspirin, food, alcohol or activity. All too often we cover up the warning lights in our system. Then our Razz can't get through to us.

Pain, a visitor with a vital message

We need to learn to welcome pain, not as a permanent boarder but as an occasional wise guest—one bringing a vital message we urgently need to hear, one with information about our number-one priority. One bringing information about how to balance our lives. One committed to our health and happiness.

By developing the skill of maintaining health and balance, we can live more full and satisfying lives. The energy we used to spend in periodic crises can now be redirected to taking successful actions.

When our health is handled, we can use our energy to create the world we want.

Part Three

LEADERSHIP

Our success multiplies each time
we lead someone else to success

The Gate to Fulfillment

BEYOND PERSONAL SUCCESS

By leading we experience
not just satisfaction but fulfillment

Exhausted from a fourteen hour day, I had been asleep for fifteen minutes when a call from my daughter Cathy suddenly woke me up. "Mom, I think my water broke."

Those words took me back to thirty-one years before. I had been baking cookies with one eye on late news, when a sudden gush of warm water rearranged our evenings plans. Grabbing prepacked bags, Don and I headed for the hospital immediately, and in less than two hours I was holding Cathy in my arms.

With that memory prodding me, I packed quickly and drove the hour and a half north to West Palm Beach, praying I would arrive there before the baby did, and rehearsing what I'd say if I was stopped.

But what happened to me didn't happen to Cathy. After two hours, Dad-to-be Alan and I were still tossing and turning on lumpy cots in her room. At sunrise we took pictures of her sitting up in bed, ready and beautiful. But she wasn't in labor. The birth was thirty-four days early, so the doctors ran tests to determine her baby's maturity. Twelve hours later, the results were all positive. They would induce labor the next morning at six.

After twenty minutes on Pitocin, a printout of high spikes and low valleys confirmed Cathy was in labor. Alan stood to her left, breathing through the pains with her. Her sister Margaret and I took turns on the right.

The pain increased and she needed anesthesia, but the anesthesia failed to work for this anesthesiologist's wife, despite three painful attempts at inserting the needle correctly in her spine. My doctor-daughter Margaret and I winced as we watched Alan stand helplessly by observing a procedure that he had done successfully two hundred times go wrong on his wife. Having instantaneously assessed that jumping over the bed and jerking the needle out of that doctor's hand was illegal and inappropriate, he remained as calm as those circumstances allowed.

And Cathy rose to the occasion. Focusing on her breathing, she managed herself masterfully for twelve grueling hours with only a minute between pains. Then as the head crowned, the obstetrician shouted, "Keep your eyes open." And on the next push, he helped Cathy reach down and deliver her own baby. At 5:47 p.m. Dylan Ford Rosenberg's cone-shaped head and slippery supple body finally emerged, and Cathy pulled him lovingly up to her chest, gasping and sobbing as she glimpsed their new son the first time. We all stood awed by the miracle of birth.

His waxy face looked exactly like Cathy's had—the same tiny nose, the same peachy complexion. But this baby was my daughter's, not mine. Our babies looked alike, but our deliveries were quite different. I had been taken off to labor alone, comforted only by a call-button and overwhelming anesthesia. My husband paced the halls, while my mother, recovering from shock therapy, sat limply by in the waiting room, knowing I was her daughter but not remembering my name.

As Cathy began to nurse, I reflected on the profound changes in the generation between these births, changes in my life and in my society. Today I can ask for what I want, and, even when I'm told no, I still hold my outcome. And I've long since learned how to avoid individuals who are trying to manipulate and control me—attempting to get their way by blocking mine.

But I hadn't known how to ask for what I wanted when I was Cathy's age, and even if I had, the hospital staff would have told me no. What I wanted didn't matter to them, bound by procedures, right ways and wrong ways, have tos and musts. So confined in the first phase, I simply did what I was told.

This was a three-phase birth. First and foremost, Cathy and Alan focused on their baby's safety and health. Second, they expected their staff to perform effectively and efficiently. Third, and most satisfying, Cathy and Alan had made choices. Dylan's birth was their creation. They had been preparing for months—visiting local hospitals to discover the one they wanted, interviewing obstetricians, pediatricians and delivery nurses to ensure that personalities would be compatible.

Cathy had chosen a room with a sunrise view of the water. It had never occurred to me to look at rooms when I delivered, to find which ones I liked and which ones I didn't. So when Cathy asked me to walk through the halls to check out rooms with her, I was constrained by a certain residual compliance. I had taught her to shift into the third phase of success, and she was quite comfortable there—even more comfortable than I was at times.

Cathy and Alan chose to leave the phone turned on during labor so their friends could check progress. Nurses came as needed, doctors did too. There was no secrecy, no separation or aloneness. Anyone could hold her hand. Anyone could brush her hair, not just genetic family but family of heart. The entire birthing process took place in her room. Alan and I slept there the whole time. And Dylan stayed too, his tiny rolling glass-sided bed always within eye-shot of his mother. We bonded as a family in those precious first days.

The grandparent level

I have reached a new level—the grandparent level. My leadership responsibilities have expanded again. My children are now asking me how to raise their child—how and when to feed him, how and when to bathe and pick him up. I am no longer just parenting, I am teaching them to parent.

Cathy and Alan—though in the third phase of many things—are in the first phase of parenting, needing to learn my goods and bads, my rights and wrongs, always and nevers. They are temporarily dependent, not knowing how to handle their own screaming child in the night. Not knowing what to do when a fever spikes suddenly, or a rash erupts painfully.

Their phone calls have increased, their visits increased too. And my perceived value has increased as well. Oh how I wish I had known about this stage as we were going through the teenage years—the rebellious and unappreciative years. The years when I was viewed as "stupid and out of touch." The years when my only value seemed to be paying their way.

Soon we will be teaching Dylan to use language, helping him to learn how to sort and file his experiences—the ones that are safe for him and the ones that are dangerous, the things he can reach for and the things he should draw back from. What's possible and impossible for him—if only temporarily. We are installing his basic program for life. And we will be responsible for updating it appropriately.

But by the second week, I began noticing Cathy's resistance to my input. Her self-confidence was building, she was beginning to feel competent. And I was already backing off, shifting to the second phase of leadership, remaining nearby in case she needed me to shift back into first again. Even when there was nothing specific for me to do, I was busy holding the vision of Cathy and Alan as successful parents, looking forward to Dylan's creations and inventions, to what he will teach us, to what he will contribute.

The ten responsibilities of a leader

The ten skills for succeeding are not only essential for our own success, but for the success of our children, and the children of our children. How far our children go depends on us. Will they simply succeed by obeying and conforming? Will they get stuck in stress and competition? Or will they—because of our leadership—succeed all the way to cooperation and teamwork, to a planet that works for each one of its citizens.

First, we are responsible for being trustworthy leaders, letting those who follow us put their confidence in us until we can help them develop self-confidence. We are responsible for their safety and education until they can take over that responsibility for themselves.

Second, we need to sense when those who follow us need more freedom, when they are ready for independence. We must know when to shift from acknowledging their compliance to rules, to acknowledging their winning, to acknowledging their changes and creations, remembering the crucial need we will all have for their creativity and leadership in the future.

Third, we need to assist our children in dreaming their dreams—pre-experiencing desired outcomes with them and assisting them in finding appropriate methods for completing them.

Fourth, we need to communicate skillfully, making it safe for them to share their likes and dislikes, choices and preferences—handling their infant dreams like tiny precious butterflies. By respecting their wishes now, we are encouraging them to respect other peoples' wishes in the future. We are leading them to cooperate.

Fifth, we must provide all the expertise they will need until we can find other experts to assist them or until they learn to select experts on their own.

Sixth, we are responsible for updating their fears and disappointments, for developing these skills ourselves or finding experts to assist them. We need to continue to update old rules and limits, helping them expand their Safe Zone while contracting their Danger Zone. We need to open their way into The Potential Zone, the zone where they will create the future.

Seventh, we need to hold onto their outcomes with them, especially when they don't have the foggiest idea what to do, especially when they get discouraged or fall into impossibility. We need to cheer them all the way to completion.

Eighth, we are responsible for shielding their dreams from the cold drafts and scorching heat of other peoples' disagreement. We need to say to them the things they will need to say to themselves, "Yes you can. Let's find another method." Or, "Let's hold onto this dream ourselves until we can find others who will nurture it too."

Ninth, we are responsible for switching their negative thoughts back to positive. "I know you feel you can't, but you can." "What do you really want?" "How will you feel when you've done it?" "What difference will it make in your life or the lives of others?" And, even when they are disappointed in us, we need to encourage them to keep asking for what they want, from us or from others.

Tenth, as leaders, we are responsible for maintaining their health and balance—monitoring their food and exercise and the effect it is having, noticing their moods and emotions, offering diversity and distraction when they become preoccupied with something they want—or they don't want.

Marriage vows and parenting vows

Marrying is the first step we take toward parenting. But in a generation when more than half of couples end up divorcing, new vows are needed—parenting vows.

Before that precious moment of choosing to parent, let us take a solemn vow together that no matter what—no matter how much money we have or we don't have, no matter how much time we have or we don't have, no matter what happens in our lives or what doesn't happen—we will make certain that our children are supervised, safe and secure in the first phase. That our children will have the independence and support they need in the second phase. And that—no matter what—we will lead them on to create and lead in their generation. Let us vow to manage our lives and our relationships so that we meet the needs and wants of our children—whether we are living together or apart.

Buying a mother-of-the-bride dress

Challenges to leading will occur along the way. Our children expect us to know how to move past our own incompletions, our own struggles with parents, to move past our own needs to compete and to win.

I remember times when my past pain almost overwhelmed me, like the day Cathy and I were getting ready for her wedding, out together buying a mother-of-the-bride dress. Suddenly as we sorted through racks of elaborate lacy gowns, something old and powerful in me ran from the store. I was out the door before I could grab myself inside and choose once again— "to be a mother who is there for her child, supportive and interested, nurturing my child's dreams, not just my own."

I battled in that moment with a part of me that didn't want to give Cathy the things I hadn't been given. A part that remembered the day my mother stayed home from Dad's funeral because she didn't feel like going. She was unable to see that we needed her to lead us, that the funeral was our opportunity to stand up as a family and acknowledge Elwood Ford. I remembered when my father, disapproving of my marriage, refused to give me away—until after I decided to ask someone else. I still recall the flood of disappointment I felt as I pulled my long embroidered train into the limousine. This wasn't the way I had wanted my wedding to feel.

When old pain rushed in, I didn't want to buy the dress Cathy wanted. I didn't want to give her the wedding I didn't have. But all the work I had done on succeeding and leading allowed me to refocus. This was her wedding, and she didn't have to pay for what had gone wrong with mine.

Often as a leader, I have had to give what I never got. And each time, I had to battle with past pains and disappointments, times my realities were much less than my dreams, times I was left feeling incomplete. I've experienced the same challenges in business as well. Busy when someone asked me to explain something to them, I remembered the times people hadn't stopped to help me. And I was tempted to let my past upsets make upsetting them right, but my intention to be a leader let me put aside my work, or set a better time to help later.

I have felt these same pressures in the classroom as well. Needing to control the class to please the administration, even when that much control didn't work for my students, I was able to remind myself of the real outcome I wanted—for my students to succeed, now and in the future. I was their leader, the one who could be flexible.

The Rite of a Leader

It was time for a promotion, and early one morning I was called into my manager's office. She smiled warmly as she congratulated me. "You have been successful in your work, and now we're going to promote you to leadership."

247

Then she quickly pulled a rope from her pocket, tying my arms securely together in front of me. "Your arms will be tied for one week, tied to remind you that you can no longer do the job yourself. Your responsibility has changed. Until now, you have relied on your doing, but now you must learn to rely on the doing of others.

If they don't know what to do, you are responsible for explaining to them what to do or finding others who can. If they do not have the skills they will need, you are responsible for developing those skills. Whatever your people want, it is your job to provide it. Because from now on, your success is their success. Their results are your results. And their creativity is your creativity too.

That first day was difficult, but now the rope was making sense. Oh how I wanted to take that rope off, so I could do the job right or more quickly. I did not have leadership skills, I only had doing skills. It was frustrating not being able to explain what I wanted. I knew how to do it, but I didn't know how to teach it. And it took time to figure out.

We must each choose to "tie" ourselves to leadership, understanding that it doesn't matter now that we can do it "all by ourselves." Our challenge is to assist others in doing what we have learned to do. We are transitioning "from every man for himself" to a team of human beings living here on Earth, caring for the planet, its plants and its animals, and caring for our bodies—physical, mental and spiritual.

Opening the Gate to Fulfillment

We are standing right here at the Gate to Fulfillment. We can choose to move past personal satisfaction and the successes that depend exclusively on our individual efforts. We can begin experiencing something much more—opening ourselves up to fulfillment.

Then our success files will begin to fill up much more quickly. Our efforts will be multiplied by the efforts of all those we lead. Their successes will become our successes. Their creations will be our creations. Their solutions, our solutions as well.

In our rapidly changing world, we can cooperate to solve problems that individuals have never confronted, much less solved. We can begin to handle the first-phase needs of everyone on Earth, feeding and nurturing the child in each one of us. We can teach everyone here on Earth the basic skills they will need to dream and communicate—so others can help them.

We are living in the Age of Creativity and Leadership, a time in which "how to" has been replaced by "what do we want?" Earth is becoming a planet where we are each empowered to wish and dream, to ask and be responded to, a planet where "dreamer's hooks" are planted all over.

This is no longer just wishful thinking. This is a reality we are now capable of creating. Yes, our children are watching. What will be our choice?

My parents led me as a child.
My children lead me as an adult.

My love and my thanks to my grandmother, Minnie B. Ford,
my parents Elizabeth and Elwood Ford,
my daughters Cathy and Margaret,
my son-in-laws Alan Rosenberg and Steven Chaneles,
my grandson Dylan and all the grandchildren
who will come to join us in the future.

249

An invitation to leaders

If you are
an individual who would like to host a seminar in your community,
please let me know.

•

If you are
a teacher or principal who wants to set up training
for parents or teachers,
please give me a call.

•

If you are
a leader of a corporation or organization and
you would like to hold seminars in your company or organization,
call me to plan them.

•

If you head
a corporation or school district or university and
you would like to sponsor community service trainings,
please be in touch with me.

•

If you are in charge
of a government agency, House or Congress,
please let me know in what way I can assist you.

For information and scheduling please call:
Our Children Are Watching
305-892-2702

We are all leaders, whether we realize it or not.
Now is the time for us to become conscious of our leadership and
actively move ahead in creating the world we want.

My love and best wishes
Susan Collins

Glossary

Addiction—A condition created by using one and only one method, even if that method ends up costing us our aliveness or our life.

Automatic transmission—The mechanism of a car that shifts gears appropriately. The shifting mechanism of good leaders that lets them shift the way they are leading—from controlling, to offering independence and feedback, to aligning with the creativity and leadership of a teammate.

Acknowledgment—Another way of saying "That's good" or "That's great." Another word for praise, thank you or "Attaboy."

Baby Boomers—Individuals born between 1946 and 1964 who belong to the largest generation in history. The oldest members of this generation will turn 65 in 2011.

Barnacle—A small crustacean that free-floats as a larva but then attaches itself permanently to ship bottoms and rocks in its adult stage. You have probably seen clusters of white barnacles on wharves at the ocean or had them cut your feet as you walked on large rocks.

Bananas—Plants that have taken over my yard. The banana plants I found as discards are now twenty feet tall with bunches of fruit so large that a few days ago a whole tree was pulled over crashing into a nearby palm and snapping it off. These bananas are meatier than the ones in the grocery.

Beginner's rules—The good/bads, right/wrongs, should/shouldn'ts, have tos and musts we learn when we start.

Book or manual—A leader in print.

Brain preference—Most people prefer one sensory system, either thinking primarily in pictures, or talking things over inside their heads, or getting a feel for things.

Competitors—Individuals who have learned the basics and are striving to improve their skills so they can be better than or best. Individuals in the second phase of success.

Confidence—Having faith in. We can have faith in ourselves. Or we can have faith in a leader who helps build our self-confidence.

Conveyor-belt-of-life—Life keeps presenting us with opportunities. We get to choose which ones we take. But like a man in an airport waiting for his suitcase, it doesn't make sense to take one that isn't ours.

Co-programmers—Two or more people who are creating the same result, communicating until the details match, clarifying differences and filling in the missing pieces. What co-programmers have in mind is succeeding together.

Creative leaders—Individuals who have already proven to themselves and others that they can do it all by themselves. Individuals who no longer need to do more-better-faster. Individuals who know what they want and are willing to do whatever it takes to move past the past into the future.

Cross-training—An opportunity for people in different areas of a company to learn each others' jobs so they can make those jobs easier. So they can begin to co-program and cooperate. So they can become teammates.

Crotons and heliconias—The azaleas and boxwoods of the tropics. Croton leaves have many colors on one plant—greens, reds, golds and fuscias. Heliconias have large sprays of exotic red-and-yellow bird-like flowers. I collect large bunches of them whenever I'm expecting guests.

Danger Zone—The parts of our lives that feel scary and risky. The parts we instinctively try to avoid. The parts we anticipate getting hurt in again.

Decision—Like an incision, a decision literally cuts away possibilities. I will do this but not that.

Dependent—Needing constant input and supervision, asking a million questions and expecting immediate answers, eager to please but anxious and fearful, not knowing right from wrong. These are our qualities when we're in the first phase of success.

Down shifting—Gearing back from third into second into first in order to respond appropriately to current driving conditions. Gearing back from creativity to competition to obeying in order to respond appropriately to current success conditions. Gearing back from support to supervision to control in order to respond appropriately to the current leadership conditions.

Dream—A desired outcome, the very thing we want, the very way we want it. A pre-experienced future event that will attract us to take all the necessary steps. A reason to be alive.

Electro-magnetic force field—The attractive force field that is generated by a multi-sensory thought, a thought we see, hear and feel in great detail. Today scientists can measure the power of a thought.

Escher—An artist known for his drawings of lizards which seem to pop out from two dimensions into three.

Eye signals—The eye movements that tell us how a person is thinking. When their eyes go up, they are seeing what they're thinking. When eyes go ear-to-ear, they are hearing what they're thinking. When eyes go down toward their body, they feel what they're thinking.

Expert—Anyone who can do what we want to do. An expert might be a pair of extra hands or a highly skilled individual who can take over our whole project. We are responsible for choosing appropriate experts, experts who are willing to co-program, to align on the details that matter to us.

Failure—Failure is incompletion. We fail when we are not willing or able to do something completely ourselves. Or we fail to ask experts to assist us.

Followers—Individuals who depend on a leader to tell them what to do and how to do it. Individuals who are successful for doing what's right and good. Individuals who are trying to do what they're told to do. Individuals who, at that moment, are in the first phase of success.

Gears—The parts of a car's transmission that allow the car to operate differently at different times—when starting, when accelerating, when cruising along the highway. Success gears are the parts of our inner success mechanism that let us shift our approach—from following, to competing, to creating and leading. We drive well when we shift gears appropriately. We live well when we shift success phases appropriately.

Gourmet—Someone who can cook up something wonderful out of any ingredients. Someone who can make something wonderful out of any circumstances.

Holding an outcome—The ability to keep the details of a desired hologram in mind even when conflicting data is pouring in, even when we are confronted with difficulties and obstacles, even when it's starting to look like it's impossible. The ability to hold an outcome is a prime quality of a leader.

Hologramming—We begin to create what we want by living it in advance, in living sound and color. When we've done that, then we have programmed it into the part of our brain that will alert us to opportunities.

Herculean—An adjective to describe something as difficult and challenging as what Hercules did—hold the Earth up by himself.

In denial—Not facing up to the need to make changes.

Independent—Wanting the freedom to try things on our own, confident and full of other ways of doing things. Not wanting to be told what to do. Eager to compare our results with the results of others. These are our qualities when we're succeeding in the second phase.

In gear—We're in gear when we are seeing, feeling and participating in an event, when we're there. In-gear thinking is essential for generating the energy to get going, but it can be detrimental when we continually step back in gear into old pain and disappointment.

Inner computer—The intricate electro-chemical information system we usually call our mind and body.

Integrity—From *integer*, achieving a oneness between what we say and what we do.

Interdependent—Willing to share knowledge and information, willing and able to share dreams and methods for getting there. A quality of a person in the third phase of success.

256

Interest—To be within a person's thoughts and feelings, to want to see what they see, hear what they hear, feel what they feel, do what they want. To cooperate with others we have to be interested.

Koi—Fish of the carp family, raised by the Emperors of Japan for hundreds of years. Koi are collected for their beautiful designs—usually red, white, black or gold.

Leader navigation—The ability of a leader to know two points: the point where she or he is and the point where she or he wants to be.

Licenses and certificates—Papers issued to acknowledge that we have successfully completed the first phase of learning a new skill. Drivers' licenses, diplomas and professional certificates allow us to move on to practicing independently.

Little Prince—The main character in my very favorite book by the same name. The author Antoine Saint-Exupery had just crash-landed in the desert a thousand miles from anywhere only to wake up to The Little Prince standing over him saying "If you please, draw me a sheep." Of all the other books in existence on this planet, *The Little Prince* is the one I most recommend to parents, friends and lovers.

Lop-eared bunny—A rabbit with ears that hang down instead of standing up. Their ears fold over beside their eyes, making them look a little hapless but sweet.

Mac—A Macintosh computer. My dear friend and writing companion, friendly as computers go but still awfully stubborn if you don't know how to tell it exactly what you want.

Mack—A large truck, elegant and shiny, with polished chrome details and grills. The bulldog is the symbol of a Mack truck.

Mantra—A word or series of words or tones which are repeated meditatively.

Matthew Fontaine Maury—My childhood hero whose statue is on Monument Avenue in Richmond, VA. Maury, a commander in the Confederate Navy, issued *Explanatory Sailing Instructions For Mariners* in 1848. Using his charts of the winds and currents of the oceans mariners were able to reduce their sailing times by 10-15 days, just as he predicted.

Method—The way we get to a desired outcome.

Method-bound—Preoccupied with how to do it instead of why we want to do it in the first place.

Mission—What each of us, deep down inside, knows is the very reason we came here to Earth.

More-better-faster—The mantra of the second phase. Every day in every way I have to do even more, even better even faster than myself or anyone else.

Mouray eel—A serpent-like fish that, like a jack-in-the-box, springs out from behind rocks as divers swim by.

Outcome—The experience we want, the destination we have in mind. To be powerful and attractive, outcomes must be hologrammed in great detail.

Outcome-oriented—The mind-set of a person operating in the third phase, the attitude of going for it, the ability to stay focused on a desired result no matter what.

Out-of-gear thinking—An essential part of the updating process. By going out of gear we can disconnect from painful feelings long enough to heal them. By going out of gear we can gain the same perspective on our own lives we have when giving advice to others. Going out of gear to do an update can make us well, but living out of gear can make us sick. We live out of gear when we disconnect from our feelings, when we shut off our energy and enthusiasm for life.

Papaya—A delicious tropical fruit containing powerful digestive enzymes. Papayas develop on trees that grow very quickly here in South Florida. They can get to be ten feet tall in one year. If I were to describe the way a papaya tastes, I'd say it's a cross between a honeydew melon and a peach.

Playing back—Feeding back the communications we receive, not just the words they say, but the parts of the message we receive through their voices and bodies as well.

Positive Command Brain—To understand a negative command we must first understand it as a positive command. The command, "Don't think about pink elephants," first requires us to think about pink elephants. To the brain, "Don't think" equals "Do think"—at least until we switch by asking what we do want instead.

Potential Zone—The parts of our lives we used to dread and avoid that have now become the very parts we want to explore, the very things that might give us the quality of life we want.

Razz (Reticular Activating System)—A network of nerve fibers connected to the eye. The part of the brain that alert us to what's incomplete, to what we might want to do, to opportunities at hand. It's our inner computer's search-and-find command.

Re—A prefix commonly used to indicate an update in thinking or doing— remaking, reorganizing, reselling, revamping, relocating, remarrying.

Recipe—A step-by-step methodology for how to do something new.

Rockfish—A fish in the waters off Miami that settles against a wall invisibly like a rock.

Safe Zone—The parts of our lives and experience that feel safe and secure to us, the things we're sure we can do already.

Satisfaction—When we've finished something, when we've acknowledged that we've done it and we've acknowledged others who did it with us, then we feel complete and satisfaction sets in.

Save—A computer command to store data permanently. A human-computer command to store internal data permanently, especially the successes we need to remember to feel successful and confident about our future.

Scores, charts and graphs—Measures of second-phase work. The most important part to a competitor.

Seeing The Big Picture—Getting an overall view of success and leader-ship—the three phases of success and the corresponding three phases of leadership.

Sensory fill-in—The tendency of the human mind to fill in whatever details are unspecified. Sensory fill-in is the mechanism that produces upsets, disappointments and unfulfilled expectations. But I thought you meant...

Shield—A protective inner device we can learn to construct that allows us to move safely into new or difficult situations. Something which gets "too heavy" if we use it all the time.

Shifting—The process of moving from one success phase to the next. Having learned to do things right, we go on to do better. Having done better, we then learn to create.

Sorting, filing and labeling—Terms we usually use in an office when we're arranging papers in files or storing information in a computer. But as the operators of our own inner-computers, we must also sort, file and label our experiences in order to gain wisdom.

Success—Success is completion and deletion. We succeed when we do things we said we would do. We also succeed by eliminating from our lives the things that don't work.

Success filing—The day-to-day process of acknowledging things we have completed. And the day-to-day process of acknowledging things other people have completed too. Success filing is the first skill of a leader.

Switching—By asking ourselves or others "What do you want instead?" we can realign our course in the direction we want to go.

Ten skills for succeeding and leading—Skills successful people use consistently whether they know it or not. By using these skills ourselves, we can not only get what we want in life, but we can assist others in getting what they want too.

The Technology of Success—Two- or three-day seminars in which I teach the ten skills for succeeding and leading. These seminars can be tailored for any and all leaders—parents, teachers, managers and those in government. Experiential and emotional like this book, these trainings produce powerful positive changes in people's lives.

Three phases of leadership—In the beginning we need a leader to take charge, always be there and in control. In the second phase we need a leader to back off, giving us room to explore and improve. In the third phase we need a leader to be a teammate.

Three phases of success—What we mean by success changes. What we mean by success in the first phase is following and obeying. What we mean by success in the second phase is improving and competing. What we mean by success in the third phase is creating and leading.

Three brain languages—We use different words to communicate what we're thinking—to show them what we're seeing, to tell them what we are telling ourselves, to give them a feel for where we are. Speaking the same brain language creates alignment. But speaking different brain languages produces the same difficulties we face when communicating with someone speaking a foreign language.

Throwing a dreamer's hook—By creating a powerful, detailed hologram of something we really want, we hook ourselves onto that reality so we can pull ourselves up to it. So our reticular activating system can assist us in grabbing hold of opportunities to get there.

Updating—A process of completing old hurts and disappointments that are blocking us unconsciously from getting what we want. By completing our past, we can release trapped energy, making it available to use now. By completing our past, we rekindle confidence and enthusiasm.

War stories—Tales people in business tell about the horrors of corporate policies and layoffs.

Word signals—Specific words we use, consciously or unconsciously, that signal whether we're seeing, hearing, feeling or doing things in our minds. Word signals for visual processing are: see, picture, show. Word signals for audio processing are: hear, listen, talk. Word signals for feeling or doing are: sense, feel and grasp. Using word signals wisely lets us be more successful more easily.

Notes

[1] Albert Mehrabian, *Non-Verbal Communication* (Chicago: Aldine-Atherton, 1972) 108.

[2] Antoine Saint-Exupery, *The Little Prince*, (New York: Harbrace Paperbound Library, Harcourt, Brace and World, Inc. 1971), 78-90.

[3] Michael Talbot, *The Holographic Universe*, (New York: Harper Collins, 1992) 13-24.

[4] Karl H. Pribram, *Brain and Perception: Holonomy and Structure in Figural Processing*, (Hillsdale, NJ: Laurence Erlbaum Associates, 1991).

[5] Karl H. Pribram, *Languages of the Brain: Experimental Paradoxes and Principles in Neuro-Psychology* (Monterey, CA: Brooks-Coles, 1971).

[6] Denis Waitley, *Seeds of Greatness* (Old Tappan, NJ: Fleming H. Revell Co., 1983) 106-109.

[7] Susan Collins, *The Technology of Success* (Miami, FL: Susan Collins, seminars, tapes and manuals, 1980).

[8] Leslie Cameron-Bandler, *They Lived Happily Ever After* (Cupertino, CA: Meta Publications, 1978) 39-48.

[9] Cheryl Russell, *100 Predictions for the Baby Boom: The Next 50 Years* (New York, NY: Plenum Press, 1987).

[10] A. Haeworth Robertson, *Social Security: What Every Taxpayer Should Know* (Washington, DC: Retirement Policy Institute, 1992).

[11] Susan Collins, *The Me Book: An Illustrated Manual For Being Human* (Santa Monica, CA: Roundtable Publishing, 1983).

[12] Antoine Saint-Exupery, *The Little Prince* (New York, NY: Harbrace Paperbound Library, Harcourt, Brace and World, Inc., 1971) 19-24.

Index of stories